W9-AGE-910

How to Fight for
What's Right

This is the property of
the Greater Vancouver Association of the Deaf

How to Fight for What's Right

THE CITIZEN'S GUIDE TO PUBLIC INTEREST LAW

John Swaigen

with
Richard E. Woods
and
Alan D. Levy

James Lorimer & Company, Publishers
Toronto, 1981

Copyright© 1981 by James Lorimer & Company

All rights reserved. No part of this book may be reproduced or trans-
mitted in any form or by any means, electronic or mechanical, including
photocopying, or by any information storage or retrieval system, without permission in writing from the publisher.

ISBN   0-88862-423-9 cloth
       0-88862-422-0 paper

Canadian Cataloguing in Publication Data
Swaigen, John, 1944 —
     How to fight for what's right

Includes index
ISBN 0-88862-423-9 bd.   ISBN 0-88862-422-0 pa.
1. Courts—Canada—Popular works.
2. Procedure (Law)—Canada—Popular works. I. Title.
KE 8212.Z82S92   347.71'05   C81-094327-1

James Lorimer & Company, Publishers
Egerton Ryerson Memorial Building
35 Britain Street
Toronto M5A 1R7, Ontario

Printed and bound in Canada.
6 5 4 3 2 1   81 82 83 84 85 86

DEDICATION

To Joyce Young, this book's inspiration and mine.

How to Fight for What's Right is the second in a series of books published by James Lorimer & Company in association with the Canadian Environmental Law Research Foundation (CELRF). *Poisons in Public*, published in 1980, was the first title in the series. CELRF and its associate legal clinic, the Canadian Environmental Law Association, were founded in 1970 by a concerned group of lawyers, scientists and conservationists. CELRF's aim is to use the law to halt environmental degradation and promote sound environmental planning.

In seeking to improve the quality of the environment through legal reforms, CELRF requires the support of concerned individuals and corporations. Tax-deductible donations to support long-range environmental law research and reform are essential to CELRF's continuing work. The foundation's registered charitable receipt number is 0380584-53-13.

Canadian Environmental Law Research Foundation
5th Floor South
8 York Street
Toronto, Ontario M5J 1R2
(416) 366-9717

CONTENTS

Part II: Before the Courts and Tribunals

4. Who Pays?   35

5. What to Do and Say and What to Avoid   46

6. Legal Traps and Tactics: Maintenance and Champerty   62

Part III: Keeping Out of Court and Out of Trouble

ACKNOWLEDGEMENTS

This book was made possible by grants from the Donner Canadian Foundation and the Canadian Human Rights Foundation. It is a project of the Canadian Environmental Law Research Foundation.

Two people deserve special thanks: Michael Perley, Executive Director of CELRF, shepherded the book through all its stages with his usual quiet efficiency. Joyce Young edited the book and imbued it with her own experience and insights into the problems and possibilities of public interest activity.

I would also like to express my appreciation to the members of CELRF's editorial committee for their support and suggestions—Ron Mann, Rene Sorell and Alan Levy; to Bill Law, who guided the project through the press, and to several people who commented on drafts of individual chapters—Paul Copeland, Brian Iler, Mary Jane Mossman and Clayton Ruby.

J.S.

PREFACE

In 1974, a real estate developer sued a citizens' group for $500,000 for conspiracy to interfere with its business when the group asked its Municipal Council to prevent development of ravine lots along the Credit River. When the case came to trial four years later, the developer's lawyers abandoned the suit against them. Had the case against the citizens' group been successful, their homes and life savings would have been at stake. The right of citizens to voice concerns to their elected representatives could have been endangered. Even though the case was dropped and costs were awarded individually to the citizens, they were under a cloud for four years. The suit effectively hobbled their work as a group over that period. Rather than submitting briefs to various public agencies on matters of environmental concern, the group was forced to spend most of its energies trying to raise funds for the legal costs of its defence.

In 1975, a community legal clinic funded in part by a federal government grant, a grant from the City of Toronto and a grant from York University, provided legal services to members of the public who would not necessarily have been reached by the Ontario Legal Aid Plan. The clinic developed a trust fund into which tenants paid rents rather than pay them to their landlord because the landlord failed to keep the premises in good repair. In court, the landlord was successful in an application to evict the tenants. The court also ruled that the trust fund was not authorized by the Ontario Landlord and Tenant Act. The landlord's lawyer asked the judge to award costs against the tenant's lawyer who was one of the staff of the clinic. The judge refused to order the lawyer to pay the court costs personally, but only after considerable discussion. He admitted that the clinic was trying to fill a social need, but felt that there were dangers inherent in an organization undertaking and sponsoring litigation without the need to have regard to legal costs.

Environmental groups, civil rights organizations, consumer groups, the poor and their lawyers face special problems seldom encountered by the average litigant or his lawyer. Many of the lawyers practising in community clinics or specializing in public interest law are young and inexperienced. It is difficult for them to advise their clients about problems that might arise or to protect their clients and themselves from sophisticated forms of harassment designed to reduce their effectiveness. Very little has been written on the subject of some of these forms of harassment, as they have not been a serious problem until recently when public interest litigation became a more important part of the legal system.

The staff of the Canadian Environmental Law Association and the Canadian Environmental Law Research Foundation have had eight years of experience in the practice of public interest law and have been called upon frequently to deal with such questions as what can I say to the press while my case is in progress? What is my liability if I lose my case? Can I legally join a demonstration or picket line? Is it ethical to set up a test case? *How to Fight for What's Right: The Citizen's Guide to Public Interest Law* is a book that was written to answer these and other questions and give citizens and their lawyers a fighting chance against big, wealthy, aggressive and occasionally unscrupulous opponents.

Michael Perley
Executive Director
Canadian Environmental Law Research Foundation

INTRODUCTION

The past two decades have witnessed a tremendous growth in efforts to implement social change and redress social injustices. The Sixties were a time of rebellion, demonstrations and activism. Such dormant issues as the civil liberties of minorities, pollution and women's liberation were raised. It was a time of exploring new values, seeking new lifestyles and trying to create a new and more humane society. This social revolution left its mark on the Seventies. Existing public interest organizations that had been established to promote better race relations or protect consumers broadened the scope of their interests and added an advocacy wing. They turned to more aggressive tactics than they had used in the past. When existing groups failed to do this, new "activist" groups sprang up to fill the void. New laws were passed creating public rights — rights that required enforcement to be effective.

Lawyers were also caught up in the process. New areas of legal practice began to emerge in the Sixties, focusing on poverty law, civil rights, public rights and the representation of public interest groups. In the Seventies, public interest law grew to include efforts to improve the administration of justice and the accountability of government agencies.

Some young lawyers in private practice began to build their clientele largely from a new class of legal clients: penitentiary prisoners, immigrants, minority groups, the poor, the elderly, community groups and other public interest groups. The changes in society were reflected in an increased amount of *pro bono* work undertaken by large private law firms. This often required reorganization of the law firm's internal structure and created a tension between the requirements of public interest law and the requirements of serving private clients such as government and large corporations.

Within a few years new "models" of legal practice emerged. In situations where legal services could not be financed by clients because the issues affected everyone (for example, protection of the environment), or because the potential clients were too poor, new types of law offices were set up. Often referred to as "storefront" offices, they were financed by such charitable foundations as the Ford Foundation in the United States, by local Bar Associations and by new government funding programs aimed at increasing accessibility of legal services to the public.

Finding new and more effective strategies to speed social change or redress grievances has proved a major challenge for both public action groups and the legal profession. Today public interest groups are taking to the streets, the backrooms of Legislatures, the boardrooms of corporations and the courts with increasing frequency and sophistication. But in meeting these challenges, new problems arise. Such institutions as the charitable association and the private law firm, originally designed to fulfill one function, are being remoulded to meet contemporary needs. The courts, too, are increasingly being asked to change their focus from resolving private disputes to upholding public rights.

More and more, the attempt to redefine roles is bringing public interest groups and their lawyers into conflict with the powerful interests in society. Because the emerging roles and rules are unclear, there is also a risk that groups and lawyers may come into conflict with present laws and, in the case of lawyers, with traditional interpretation of legal ethics. For both, the challenge is to develop effective strategies without running afoul of the law. With that goes the challenge to anticipate and surmount the countertactics and strategies rapidly being developed by their opponents to intimidate and silence them. As one U.S. writer, Gordon Harrison, has said:

> Along with the normal risks of bruises from hard-fought lawsuits, public interest law firms are vulnerable to political attacks. Adversaries in law, as every litigator knows, will now and then resort to tactics in and out of the courtroom to weaken and discredit an opponent. Lawyers who defend unpopular clients often find themselves harassed. The NAACP Legal Defense Fund and California Rural Legal Assistance have suffered political attacks. Some powerful opponents who feel themselves badly and perhaps unfairly injured may not only fight the issues, but impugn the competence and motivation of opposing counsel.

Ambiguities in traditional codes of professional ethics for lawyers, coupled with confusion about how they would apply to public interest cases, make public interest lawyers particularly susceptible to this kind of attack. We generally expect lawyers to be professionals who won't make value judgments: whose services are simply available for hire. The lawyer will take cases regardless of whether he agrees with the viewpoints of his clients. He will take these cases because he has to pay his bills and make a profit to continue practising law, and because he has been taught that *everyone* has a right to his day in court and to a lawyer. How long and hard he will fight for his client depends upon the strength of his client's case, what his client hopes to gain for himself and the ability of his client to pay his fees.

In public interest cases, however, there are other considerations, and the rules of the game change. The lawyer may represent only certain classes of clients or take only cases that further a particular set of goals. The lawyer and the client may both agree that even if the private benefit sought by the client is achieved, the case will be continued in an attempt to establish the principle for which the client is fighting or to protect some broader interest. Perhaps no money will change hands. And a case may be fought even though everyone knows it is unlikely to succeed, because even a lost case may lead to social and legal reforms.

Opponents sometimes try to seize upon these differences between "private" law and "public interest" law and magnify them. They try to show that professional ethics, developed primarily in the context of defending private property and financial interests, are being violated by the public interest lawyer. They may argue to the court or tribunal that the case is an expensive undertaking for their client, while it costs the public interest client nothing or is paid for out of the public purse. They may insinuate or state boldly that this is an abuse of the court's or tribunal's process. They may imply or state that the lawyer does not really represent the client but some external, sinister force.

Sometimes opponents go so far as to suggest that the client's case is not the true reason for the lawyer's appearance, and that he has ulterior motives — to change or even overthrow the present system. They may seize upon ambiguities in the present status of public interest legal clinics and the changing role of public interest lawyers and report them to the Law Society for so-called unethical practices, such as "advertising," "soliciting," "touting" and practising law without a licence. They may try to convince government agencies to stop funding a legal clinic or public interest association, or lobby the government to revoke a group's charitable status.

Usually these efforts are fruitless. Many government agencies and even some members of provincial Law Societies are aware of the widespread support for public interest activities and public interest law. They recognize the need to remould the law and the legal system to deliver legal services to people for whom the law was not previously accessible. Professional codes of ethics usually make some provision for lawyers to take unpopular cases and represent poor and unpopular clients. Only experience will show whether it is necessary to develop new codes of ethics for public interest cases, or whether traditional ethics can be interpreted to include the kinds of problems discussed on the following pages.

This guide will be useful to environmental groups, civil rights organizations, consumer groups, the poor, to the lawyers and other staff members of community legal clinics and storefront law offices, and to lawyers in private practice taking public interest cases. You face special problems seldom encountered by the average litigant or his lawyer. You are expected to anticipate and deal with problems that are rarely experienced by lawyers in private practice — problems like maintenance and champerty, revocation of charitable status, interventions and constitutional references, and standing. You are trying to adapt private laws and remedies to public problems, and often that is like fitting a round peg into a square hole. You are addressing new social and legal issues, and you don't know where you stand because the questions have never before arisen in this context.

There are handbooks on how to lobby effectively, how to organize a community group, how to raise funds, how to get publicity, and many other aspects of organizing a successful public interest campaign. To my knowledge, this is the first book in Canada on many of the legal issues that arise in public interest advocacy. Throughout, I have tried to describe only the law relating to various public interest advocacy strategies and tactics, without commenting on their propriety or effectiveness. My interest here is the legal implications of tactics rather that their morality.

I hope public interest groups will use this book to develop new ways of using the law and the courts to attain their ends, and that lawyers will be better able to anticipate their clients' needs and respond more quickly to requests for legal advice on public interest matters. The guide is not intended to provide legal advice in any specific case, and it is not a substitute for a lawyer. This book will give groups a better understanding of how to keep out of legal entanglements and a feeling for when to seek a lawyer's advice. If you are a lawyer, it is no substitute for thorough research or consultation with other lawyers who are more familiar with the specific issues raised here.

I hope this book will encourage individuals, groups and lawyers to engage in public interest advocacy and will help make their efforts more successful and freer from harassment. I particularly hope that readers will be encouraged to use the legal system to promote social change. Effective public interest advocacy is central to effective government and to attaining the ideals of democracy. No public agency alone can represent the public interest. The "public interest" is made up of many separate public and private interests, and public interest advocates can ensure representation of those interests that would not be protected through traditional political or legal procedures. The legal system can no longer be the exclusive preserve of private property and financial interests.

In seven years of practising public interest law, I found I had to deal with many issues and problems that seldom arise in traditional charitable activity or in the traditional practice of law. There were many questions and worries. What can I say to the press while my case is in progress? Will my group lose its charitable status if it takes a case to court? What is our liability if we lose? Can we legally join a demonstration or picket line? Is it ethical to set up a test case situation? How can we raise important issues in the courts or enforce the law without first being adversely affected by the very injustice we want to challenge?

Solutions to these practical, day-to-day problems are not easy to find. Many of them are new problems that have only begun to sprout as the Canadian public interest movement gained its current momentum and sophistication. There has been little time to investigate the legal problems and opportunities that spring from public interest advocacy.

This book covers three important aspects of public interest law: how to get into court to further your cause; how to anticipate and deal with some of the problems that arise during public interest cases before courts and tribunals; and how to keep out of trouble and keep out of court.

It is intended to be of use primarily to people who have no legal training, but it is also written for lawyers who represent public interest groups, legal workers in community legal clinics and "storefront" lawyers. I have assumed that readers will know some common legal terms, but many other legal terms are explained in a glossary at the conclusion of the book.

I have not attempted to describe the different kinds of law, the different levels of court or the various court systems. The basics of the legal system have been described in other books. Nor have I described the rules of evidence and the rules of procedure that apply to prosecutions for criminal offences, prosecutions for offences that may result in fines or imprisonment, or lawsuits for compensation or injunctions. Regulatory boards, royal commissions and tribunals all have different rules, and finding your way through that maze may require another book!

What I have done is to describe the issues, problems and situations — the questions of ethics and the dilemmas — that are peculiar to public interest advocacy.

The guide is divided into three parts. The first part details various ways of getting public interest cases into the courts. In the past, citizens' groups have run into severe legal roadblocks in their efforts to use the courts.

Part II covers many of the problems that might arise when you are in court or intervening before boards and tribunals. The purpose of Part II is to forewarn you and to help you handle these problems if and when they arise.

But going to court is only one form of advocacy. Organizing demonstrations, writing briefs, books and articles, lobbying politicians, issuing press releases and many other activities make up the spectrum of public interest advocacy. As a result of these activities you may inadvertently break the law and find yourself in a courtroom as a defendant. Part III deals with how to keep out of court and out of trouble. It points out some of the activities and mistakes that may leave you open to charges or lawsuits by others.

You may have the impression that working in public interest advocacy is like walking through a minefield. It isn't. The problems raised are the exception rather than the rule. The purpose of the guide is to help you *avoid* these problems in the first place, and to help you deal with them if they do arise. The chances of encountering the kinds of harassment described are still very small in Canada, particularly if you attack the issue rather than the person and recognize when you need legal advice.

This book is intended to encourage more public interest activity. As a spokesperson for the Canadian Environmental Law Association (CELA), my job frequently involved speaking out against actions by government agencies and corporations on behalf of both CELA and individual clients. I represented groups in courts and before boards and tribunals, and gave hundreds of interviews on radio, television and in the press. During that time, I was never subjected to any serious harassment, nor were any of my clients. This was not due to any particular brilliance on my part, but merely to the fact that most opponents play fair most of the time.

Knowing something about the legal system and the laws affecting public interest advocates will enable you to use the law to further your goals and speak out on today's pressing issues without fear of running afoul of the law.

Part I:
Getting into Court

1.

The Special Interest Requirement: Standing

This section proposes some innovative ways of getting your issues before the courts — methods that are particularly relevant to public interest lawsuits. People with a private financial or property interest in the outcome of a case have an automatic right to take legal action or be heard by boards and tribunals; public interest groups do not.

WHAT IS THE STANDING BARRIER?

The standing barrier has been imposed by the courts to prevent people from meddling in the affairs of others. It requires that to take legal action a person must have an interest in the subject matter of the legal proceedings that is greater than and different from that of the general public. While the courts feel the standing requirement reduces frivolous suits and prevents the courts from becoming overloaded, it has also proved to be one of the most serious barriers to public interest lawsuits. Before deciding to take legal action the public interest litigant and his lawyer should be familiar with standing.

Before you decide to launch a lawsuit or make an appearance before a board, a tribunal, a commission of inquiry or some other administrative agency that is holding public hearings, you should ask yourself whether you have "standing." If there is any doubt, come prepared to explain why you think you do.

WHAT ARE THE REQUIREMENTS FOR STANDING?

There are different requirements for standing, depending on the kind of legal action you intend to take. Generally, there are few restrictions on the right to prosecute an offence under our federal or provincial statutes, but standing in civil suits may depend on showing that you have a private interest to protect or have suffered some personal harm from the violation of the law. Not everyone has the right to sue or to appear before boards and tribunals. Only those who have a "special interest" have this right unless the court or board grants the privilege of participating.

This right of access is called standing or *locus standi*. The courts started to place restrictions on standing late in the last century for a variety of reasons: among them, to prevent people from meddling in matters that were none of their business, to avoid the courts becoming overloaded and to assist the government in carrying out its responsibilities without too much interference. These restrictions have turned out to be one of the main barriers to public interest litigation, and potentially a bar to representation of the public interest before administrative agencies that hold public hearings.

In this chapter, we will briefly describe the different standing rules governing various kinds of legal proceedings and public hearings to help you determine whether you will automatically have standing, and if not, the kind of interest you will need to establish to obtain standing. Because the "special interest" test was developed in civil suits, and this is where standing restrictions are most prevalent, we will start with a description of the kind of interest required for standing in civil actions.

HOW CAN STANDING BE SECURED?

Civil actions and standing

If you are suing to vindicate some harm done to you personally, or to protect a financial or property interest, standing is not usually a problem. However, if you are seeking to vindicate or protect a public interest like environmental protection, you may not have standing to use the courts. If you are asking the court to review the legality of some action by a government department or agency (judicial review) or suing to stop some public nuisance (harm to the public in general or to public property), you may not have standing.

Traditionally, the courts have said that no one may launch a lawsuit to vindicate a public interest (as opposed to a property or economic interest), unless:

(i)   he can show that a statute is intended to give him a special protection or benefit that has been invaded; or

(ii)   the interference with the public right is also an interference with his private rights; or

(iii)   although no private right is affected, he can show some special damage or interest beyond that of the general public.[1]

Otherwise, only the Attorney General can sue. In theory, the Attorney General has a special interest in enforcing the law for the benefit of the general public, since he is the government's chief legal officer. Therefore, when you see the law being broken by a government department or agency, but you have no financial or property interest to protect or suffer no harm greater than the rest of the community, the proper procedure is to ask the Attorney General to sue. This process assumes that the Attorney General is above politics. However, the Attorney General is a member of the Cabinet, and may not be willing to sue a department or agency of his own government. He might be equally unwilling to sue the kinds of large, powerful corporations whose unlawful activities are so widespread that they affect the general public. For example, if the corporation gives a great deal of financial support to the political party that forms the government or if a successful lawsuit for pollution would cause a company to shut down one of its factories and put many of its employees out of work, the Attorney General might be very reluctant to enforce the law. In fact, experience has borne this out. When a cement company owned by a prominent supporter of the Progressive Conservative Party was destroying unique sand dunes on the edge of a provincial park, it was two private citizens, not the Ontario government, who launched the 1973 lawsuits that put an end to this practice. The provincial Attorneys General have rarely filed suit against major industrial polluters or against public agencies that appear to be breaking the law.

In cases where the Attorney General has refused to sue, judges have ruled that you cannot challenge this decision. You may, however, ask the Attorney General to allow you to sue on his behalf. This is called a "relator" action, and any person can sue, despite a lack of standing, if the Attorney General gives permission to do so. In this case, you launch the action in the Attorney General's name, although he is a party in name only. For example, a lawsuit launched by George Brown against the Widget Company of Canada Limited would be filed as "Her Majesty the Queen on the relation of George Brown v. Widget." You are responsible for all aspects of the action, and for paying the costs of your opponent if you lose (see chapter 4 on costs). Occasionally, an Attorney General has agreed to lend his name to a relator action; for example, when a citizens' group devoted to preserving parkland attacked the approval of a Vancouver housing subdivision in 1964.[2]

This standing barrier has been eroded in recent years, since the Supreme Court of Canada made two exceptions to the rule in 1974 and 1975. As a result, it is no longer clear that the Attorney General is the only person who can sue to redress a public wrong, or that you must ask the Attorney General to sue and be refused before the court grants you standing. For many years, there had been an exception for municipal ratepayers seeking a court ruling that municipal bylaws are invalid or that expenditures by municipal councils are illegal.

In 1974 and 1975, the Supreme Court of Canada created further exceptions. It recognized the standing of a taxpayer to challenge the constitutionality of the federal government's official languages legislation,[3] and it gave a citizen of Nova Scotia standing to challenge the constitutionality of provincial censorship legislation.[4] Whether these two cases merely created yet another narrow exception (i.e., challenges to the constitutionality of legislation) or whether they declared that the court has discretion to grant standing in all types of public interest cases is not yet clear.

In most provinces, the courts have taken the view that they now have discretion to grant or deny standing in any case, even if the plaintiff lacks a "special interest." However, in 1976, the Ontario Court of Appeal appeared to say that its discretion was limited to constitutional cases.[5] In 1978, on the other hand, the Ontario Divisional Court interpreted that ruling to mean that the discretion of Ontario courts is broader than constitutional cases, but narrower than will allow the court to grant standing in all public interest cases. In this case, one of the judges stated that the Ontario courts have discretion to grant standing in any case in which the validity of a statute is questioned, while another judge stated, "I believe that it is in the discretion of the court to consider whether status should be given in any particular case."[6]

Even though it is still uncertain whether a private citizen or public interest group will be granted standing to launch a public interest lawsuit, it is now clear that once you reach the courtroom the court will likely rule on the merits of the case (that is, decide whether there has been a breach of the law) whether or not it grants standing. This is a result of a suggestion by the Supreme Court of Canada. By suggesting that the courts should hear the merits of the case at the same time as they consider whether the plaintiff or applicant has standing, the Supreme Court has reduced the negative effects of the standing rule.

This approach may not make much sense logically, since if a person does not have standing he should not be in the court to begin with, but it seems to ensure that for practical purposes the courts will make a ruling in most cases on whether the law has been broken. That way, the court will rule on the legality or illegality of an activity that is challenged regardless of the plaintiff's standing. This is helpful to public interest groups, but it does not make standing irrelevant. Arguments about standing may still greatly increase the cost and lead to delays in hearing the merits of an action.

Private prosecutions and standing

Standing is not usually a barrier to a private prosecution. (Normally, the police and other law enforcement officers enforce the law, but occasionally private individuals will decide to enforce statutes themselves. These are known as "private prosecutions.") Generally, any member of the public may prosecute offences under provincial statutes designed to protect public health and welfare (for example, highway traffic, public health and consumer protection statutes) and may prosecute many criminal offences, without showing that he or she has any private interest to protect or has suffered any personal harm from the breach of the statute. That is, there is usually no restriction on standing. For example, any member of the public can prosecute politicians for improper electioneering or for breaching conflict of interest legislation by voting on matters in which they have a financial interest. Corporations can be prosecuted under statutes prohibiting pollution or misleading advertising. Tenants can prosecute their landlords for ignoring their statutory duty to keep premises in good repair.

There are some exceptions. For example, some provincial statutes state that prosecutions may not be initiated without the consent of the Cabinet minister who administers the legislation. In any case, provincial Crown Attorneys have the right to take over the prosecution from a private complainant (you) and proceed with it themselves or halt it. However, unless a provincial statute specifically states that a private prosecution is not allowed, any member of the public may lay charges and prosecute on his own or with the help of a lawyer, and the Crown Attorneys will seldom interfere.

This right of private prosecution is an important safeguard against the refusal of government officials to enforce their own legislation, as the private citizen can always take legal action if the police or other government agencies won't.

Standing before government agencies

Many important decisions affecting the public interest and private interests are made by special government agencies or by politicians or civil servants on the basis of recommendations from these agencies. Often these decisions or recommendations are made after the agency holds public hearings. Agencies that hold public hearings take many different forms and fulfill many different functions. For the sake of simplicity, we will generally refer to them throughout this book as "boards" or "tribunals." Sometimes, these boards and tribunals enforce the laws. If a used car dealer rolls back the mileage on a car, a pesticide sprayer who is supposed to be dusting crops sprays a provincial police picnic by mistake, or a collection agency unduly harasses someone, they may be brought before a board or tribunal with authority to decide whether their licences should be suspended or revoked. Other boards and tribunals decide whether to issue licences and if so whether to impose conditions on the licence (for example, a requirement that a travel agency carry insurance to reimburse customers who have paid for tours that are cancelled or accommodation that isn't available).

The law is usually vague about who may be a party at public hearings held by boards and tribunals. Usually, the legislation that establishes the board or tribunal specifies that certain people who are directly affected by its hearings have the right to be a party, and gives the board or tribunal the discretion to grant standing to anyone else. For example, the statutes establishing licensing and regulatory boards usually give automatic standing to the business applying for a licence or whose licence is under review and authorize the board to give standing to anyone else it wants to hear from. In Canada, standing before such boards has rarely been a problem. They are usually very liberal and allow almost anyone to appear before them.

This has also been true of most kinds of tribunals and special inquiries. But there have been occasional problems. For example, at a coroner's inquest into the suicide of a prison inmate in solitary confinement, the coroner refused to allow a lawyer to appear before him representing other inmates. The inmates had knowledge of the circumstances of the suicide and wanted to show that the harsh conditions of solitary confinement had driven the prisoner to suicide.[7]

In another case, two community groups were excluded from a judicial inquiry into the propriety of a $35,000 political donation from a garbage disposal company to the Ontario Progressive Conservative

Party, which formed the provincial government. The donation was given in 1974 while the firm was trying to win approval for garbage disposal permits at Maple and Stouffville from the same provincial government. Two of the three permits were issued to the company a few months after the political contribution was made. The company's application for a third permit was before the Environmental Assessment Board when the donation was brought to light. An internal company memorandum was made public that stated that the $35,000 donation was to be "part of the program to ensure the viability" of the Maple waste disposal site application. The Ontario government responded by setting up a Royal Commission to determine whether the donation involved any corruption.

Residents of Stouffville and Maple had hired lawyers to argue against the first two waste disposal permits at earlier hearings before the Environmental Hearing Board back in 1973 and 1974, and also before the Environmental Assessment Board (the successor of the EHB). When the judicial inquiry was announced, the Stouffville and Maple community groups sent their lawyer to appear at the judicial inquiry. Mr. Justice Samuel Hughes, the judge in charge of the inquiry, denied both groups standing.

The Maple group decided not to challenge the denial of standing, but the Stouffville residents challenged it in the Ontario Divisional Court. The court ruled that if there was any possibility that wrongdoing was involved in the permits being issued, concerned citizens should be given standing. The court noted that people who had participated in the original applications before the Environmental Hearing Board, and who had previously made allegations of impropriety in connection with these applications before they had even heard about the $35,000 donation, had a substantial and direct interest in the matter. The court ordered Justice Hughes to let the Stouffville group take part in his Royal Commission.[8]

In the rare cases where boards and tribunals have denied groups or individuals standing, the courts have usually overruled this decision. Whether the courts will force a board, tribunal or commission of inquiry to grant standing to groups or members of the public may depend upon a variety of factors, including: the precise wording of the statute establishing the board and setting out standing requirements; the purpose of the statute and of the public hearings; whether the parties are knowledgeable about the facts to be investigated at the public hearings; whether, in the court's opinion, the parties have a contribution to make to the hearing; and whether their interests will be directly affected by the outcome.

Judicial review of and appeals from decisions of boards and tribunals

The legislation that establishes boards and tribunals frequently provides for appeals from their decisions. In addition, unless the legislation prohibits it, the courts have an inherent right to review whether the boards and tribunals treated all the parties before them fairly and in accordance with certain minimum rules of "natural justice." Even when legislation prohibits this kind of review, the courts usually have the right to review whether a board has acted within its jurisdiction.

If it is unclear who may be a party to public hearings before such boards and tribunals, it is even less certain who may have standing to challenge the actions or decisions of boards and tribunals. Statutes seldom spell this out clearly. Lawyers and community groups might assume that since they have standing at public hearings, they are automatically entitled to standing in subsequent appeals or judicial review proceedings. This is far from certain, especially when the original grant of standing may have been discretionary and may not have been subjected to any objections or discussions during the hearings.

There are very few instances where the standing of someone who has taken part in public hearings and wishes to take part in subsequent proceedings has been challenged. Recent cases treat standing at subsequent proceedings as a matter to be considered in the circumstances and on the merits of each case. In deciding, the court might consider such factors as : the individual's or group's previous history of involvement in such proceedings; their previous activities and interests in relation to the issues dealt with in such proceedings; the contribution they made to the hearings from which the appeal is being taken; and, of course, the intent of the statute and the precise wording of the statutory provisions governing the particular board or governing the proceedings arising out of the board's hearings.[9] Even if participation in earlier hearings doesn't give an absolute right to participate in subsequent proceedings, it could be argued that a grant of standing at public hearings creates at least a *prima facie* right or a rebuttable presumption of standing at subsequent proceedings. Or it could be argued that this participation shifts the onus to the person challenging the intervenor's *locus standi*.

CONCLUSION

The liberal view of standing taken today by boards and tribunals, and the liberal approach of the courts in granting standing to parties in appeals from the decisions of boards and tribunals, are not cause for complacency. Regulatory boards and tribunals or commissions of inquiry are increasingly making decisions or recommendations on matters of broad public interest. The fact that most boards have taken a liberal approach in recent years may lull some lawyers and community groups into a false sense of security.

You should be aware that the businessmen trying to convince tribunals to issue them a licence or confer some other special benefit or privilege are developing a tendency to argue against grants of standing at the outset of hearings. Both the boards and the applicants for licences or privileges know that community groups and concerned citizens who are granted standing at public hearings may use this status to claim further entitlement to standing in subsequent political, administrative and court proceedings. For instance, developers seeking a re-zoning will seek to prevent ratepayers from appearing before the zoning tribunal because if the developer wins and there is an appeal — for instance, to the provincial cabinet — the ratepayers may take advantage of it. These agencies, therefore, are under pressure from applicants to deny standing. In the absence of any legislative guarantee of standing or policy pronouncements by Parliament and provincial Legislatures, there is a risk that these agencies, for expediency, may become more restrictive in recognizing parties.

Generally, you either have standing or you do not. One suggestion to maximize your chances of getting standing in civil suits is to ask the Attorney General to take action, even though it is no longer clear that it is necessary to do so, or to ask his permission for a relator action, before you launch your own lawsuit. It's advisable to do so anyway, just in case the court rules that these steps are still prerequisites to getting standing. In the case of hearings before various boards and tribunals, the best advice is to find out what kinds of interests are likely to be recognized, and to establish your interest in the matter and your concern with it as early as possible in the decision-making process, preferably long before public hearings are even announced.

If all your efforts to get standing fail, don't lose hope. The next chapter suggests some ways to get your day in court that may not be affected by the standing barrier.

2.

INTERVENTION IN COURT PROCEEDINGS

If your standing is in doubt, you can possibly get into court by intervening in someone else's case. In many instances citizens are not directly affected by a case but recognize that an important issue is at stake and needs to be fought through the courts. If the issues raised in a private lawsuit might affect larger classes of people, you may ask the court to permit you to appear as a "friend of the court." Or you may ask to intervene because your group's interests may be affected by the outcome of the case. This chapter discusses two kinds of intervention: the *amicus curiae* (friend of the court) and the reference.

WHAT IS THE *AMICUS CURIAE*?

A procedure, developed in England, permits a stranger to an action, known as an *amicus curiae*, or "friend of the court," to be represented before the court. The *amicus curiae* is not present to aid one of the parties to the litigation, but rather to assist the court. Historically the assistance was volunteered to correct the court in errors of law. It has been expanded considerably in the United States, and there the current practice is quite different from the historical role of the friend of the court.[1]

The *amicus curiae* in the U.S. is usually a group that is interested in a particular aspect of the case. The determination of one or more issues in the case will have some impact on the group or the community it represents. Therefore, it intervenes in the action to file a brief and, occasionally, to make oral argument. Most often the group will intervene at the appellate stage, when the case has been taken to a higher court that can overturn the decision of a trial judge.

The large civil rights groups in the U.S. have taken full advantage of the procedure and made the *amicus* brief a well-known and respected institution. On numerous occasions the American Civil Liberties Union, the National Association for the Advancement of Colored People (NAACP) and the Commission on Law and Social Action of the American Jewish Congress have filed *amicus* briefs in the appellate courts and the United States Supreme Court, often with considerable success.

For example, when the U.S. government was arresting and deporting large numbers of Chinese immigrants in the early 1900s, the Chinese Benevolent Association of New York hired a lawyer to appear in court whenever such indigent travellers, who had no one to help them, were charged. Later, other public interest groups appeared in cases involving the legality of child labor, school segregation and capital punishment.

HOW DOES THE *AMICUS CURIAE* ARGUE A POSITION?

The written brief is the working tool of the *amicus*. By extensive presentation of social data, scientific reports and scholarly opinions, the brief documents the impact of the issues with which the court is (or should be) concerned. The persuasive quality of the brief stems from its purpose, which is to deal with some concern larger than the self-interest of a particular litigant, and from its approach, which tends to emphasize and encourage social, moral and philosophical considerations, rather than strict interpretation and enforcement of law. The brief invites the court to step back from its usual task of settling an argument between two parties and consider the profound consequences that its decision will have directly or indirectly on other segments of the community. The courts in the United States have been more willing to do this than Canadian courts. While there is provision for oral argument, the trend in the appellate courts in the United States is to restrict the *amicus curiae* participation to the filing of a written brief. The parties receive the brief in both their written and oral arguments.

Frequently, the *amicus* procedure is the only way open to a public action group to raise important issues in the courts. Because of the restrictive approach of common law toward the issue of "standing," a group may not be permitted to act as an actual party litigant to a civil action. An illustration of how the *amicus curiae* brief acts as an end-run around the standing blockade is seen in the comments of a United States Court of Appeal when Dr. Benjamin Spock and others appealed from conviction for counselling violation of draft laws:

The brief of the Unitarian Universalist Association, *amicus* is the only one which envisages that, although the defendants may have committed illegal acts, their conviction might impermissibly affect First Amendment rights of third parties. In considering this matter we are not troubled by questions of standing.[2]

HOW DOES THE *AMICUS CURIAE* WORK IN COURTS IN CANADA?

In Canada, there are no formal rules recognizing the *amicus* or regulating *amicus* procedure. Nevertheless, lawyers have occasionally been recognized by the courts as *amici curiae*. Almost always, people have asked the court's permission to enter the proceedings, but there are rare occasions when the court has sought help from an *amicus* on its own initiative.[3] All of the reported Canadian cases have involved counsel appearing to make oral representations. Some of these cases have involved procedural matters[4] but the courts have also permitted *amicus* interventions in substantive matters. Whether to allow an *amicus* presentation during a hearing is strictly within the court's discretion. In fact, to interrupt proceedings by insisting on addressing the court as *amicus curiae* without the court's permission is contempt of court, as a spectator in a courtroom in England found out several years ago. He insisted on addressing the judge during a trial in which he was not called as a witness. When told to sit down, he said he was addressing the court "as *amicus curiae*." The judge cited him for contempt.[5]

Although the *amici* have played a limited role in Canadian courts, there are instances where judges have permitted such intervention. A judge of the Supreme Court of Ontario permitted the Canadian Jewish Congress to appear as *amicus curiae* when a landowner whose deed contained a clause prohibiting him from selling his property to "Jews or persons of objectionable nationality" applied to have the clause declared invalid. The court agreed with the owner and the CJC that such clauses are improper and declared them to be illegal.[6]

A judge of the Newfoundland District County Court allowed *Playboy* magazine to appear as *amicus curiae* in an obscenity prosecution against a drugstore. The store was charged with selling obscene magazines. *Playboy* wanted to argue that its publication, one of the magazines seized, was not obscene. The judge felt this would be of assistance to the court, "particularly where there was no voice before the court on behalf of the publications seized."[7]

A judge of the Exchequer Court (now the Federal Court) permitted counsel for the Attorney General of Canada to appear as *amici curiae* in an application made by a wine company under the Trade Marks Act to prevent the Registrar of Trade Marks from restricting the term "champagne" to certain wines produced in France so that the Canadian company could no longer use it to describe its products. In his judgment he stated that the *amici* "were very helpful to the court on the issues upon which they undertook to assist the court."[8]

An Alberta Provincial Court judge permitted a lawyer to appear as *amicus curiae* when a member of a Mennonite community was charged with committing an offence under the School Act of Alberta for not sending his child to public school. The accused and 49 other Mennonites had withdrawn their children from the public school and started their own school because they did not approve of the values being taught in the public school system. Because of his religious beliefs, the accused refused to be represented by counsel. The judge ruled that the following constituted the scope to be permitted to the *amicus curiae*:

(a) to "call to the attention of the court points of law, or facts that would appear to have been overlooked";

(b) to suggest witnesses that the court might call and questions that the Court might ask of any witnesses;

(c) to make submissions to the court, "either in oral or written form concerning any matter that he thinks should be considered by the court in reaching its finding."[9]

A judge of the Supreme Court of Alberta appointed a lawyer to act as *amicus curiae* in a custody dispute between two parents, in order to obtain independent objective assistance.[10] "Through the medium of the *amicus curiae* one is able to gain help of professional assistance that has not been hired by either side to view the situation."

Why is the procedure not used as extensively in Canada as it is in the United States? Although several reasons can be advanced to account for the differences,[11] two obstacles may be particularly important. First, the rules of appellate courts in Canada are generally restrictive concerning the length and content of written argument. It is possible that an *amicus* brief should be extensive and detailed if it is to have much impact on the outcome of the case. But the court's rules usually prohibit this by requiring parties to set out *briefly* the facts and points of law they intend to argue. A successful appellant before the Supreme Court of Canada was denied an award of costs for the preparation of his written brief because it was 912 pages in length, bound in two volumes, with an 86-page appendix.[12]

Secondly, the Canadian judiciary has, for the most part, continued its reluctance to grant permission for appearances as *amicus curiae*. For example, in 1977, Joe Clark, the Leader of the federal Conservative Party, brought an application in the Supreme Court of Ontario for a judicial review of Canada's uranium regulations. Clark claimed that the federal government had no power to make regulations prohibiting his party from discussing in Parliament the information that Canada was participating in an international cartel to maintain artificially high world prices. The Attorney General of Canada came to court to argue that the regulations were valid, and the Canadian Civil Liberties Association sought permission to intervene *amicus curiae*. The Chief Justice refused permission, stating:

> Subject to statutory or court-made rules, it is my view that interventions *amici curiae* should be restricted to those cases in which the court is clearly in need of assistance because there is a failure to present the issues (as, for example, where one side of the argument has not been presented to the court). Where the intervention would only serve to widen the *lis* [issues in dispute] between the parties or introduce a new cause of action, the intervention should not be allowed.
>
> I concluded, in the present case, that the experience and competence of counsel for the applicants guaranteed a complete canvass of the legal issues involved and that the intervention was therefore not appropriate.[13]

In another decision, a panel of three Ontario Supreme Court judges denied a local residents' group the right to appear in a judicial review application brought by a developer against a municipality for refusing to issue a building permit. The decision stated:

> We are assured . . . that the city corporation, through its counsel, is strenuously and will continue to strenuously resist the application of Ronark, which position it has already taken by the refusal of the building permit and the precipitation of these present proceedings . . . to open the door to interested parties who may indeed be affected by the ultimate result, but who have not a direct interest in the legal rights as between the applicant and the municipal corporation, would create a situation that would in effect turn the court from being a judicial body, into a forum for the advancing of all sorts of political arguments that should form no part of the decision which will have to ultimately be made in this case.[14]

Similarly, another panel of three judges of the Ontario Supreme Court refused to permit the head of a residents' association to be represented in an application by McDonald's Restaurants to force a municipality to issue them a building permit. The dissenting judge, who was willing to hear the residents' group, stated:

> From what is before us it would seem that it was the vigilance of the ratepayers, in this instance, which has resulted in the action of the borough. I do not consider that those who have a very real interest in the enforcement of the bylaw should be precluded from appearing before this court. . . . In this day of bigness, in this day when municipalities have so many conflicting demands upon them and so many interests to represent, when a local community within the municipality comes forward and asks to put its position before the court on a matter directly affecting it, it would seem to me that the discretion of the court should be exercised to permit that to be heard.[15]

In one case, *amicus curiae* status was granted by the court to allow a party who had been deprived of carriage of proceedings by the provincial Attorney General to continue to participate in the proceedings. Magda Rayner, a concerned citizen, had laid charges against a cement company under the provincial Environmental Protection Act. The company argued in defence that the legislation was invalid on constitutional grounds and won. The provincial Attorney General appealed this decision to the Ontario Supreme Court, as did the informant. The Supreme Court upheld the right of the Attorney General to take over carriage of the case, but allowed lawyers for Magda Rayner to participate as *amici curiae*.[16]

In summary, Canada's higher courts, perhaps because they are already overloaded and fear that recognition of *amici curiae* will raise the cost and increase the length of hearings, and perhaps because they are afraid of becoming a political forum, still discourage applications for recognition as a friend of the court. Nevertheless, there is a need to inject a broader perspective into some court cases, and if you feel the parties will not raise important social issues involved in their case, it may be worthwhile to ask the court's permission to raise them yourself.

WHAT OTHER FORMS OF INTERVENTION ARE AVAILABLE?

Some courts use the term "intervenor" or "intervenant" in providing explicitly for participation by people other than parties. There may be some differences between an intervenor under such rules and the traditional *amicus curiae*. For example, the Supreme Court of Canada has made intervention rules under which the court can retain the same discretion it has over the *amicus*; but the intervenor becomes a party to the action and may be awarded or ordered to pay costs, which would not be the case with an *amicus curiae*.[17]

The Supreme Court of Canada has been willing to allow its intervention rule[18] to be used to provide more than just the federal and provincial Attorneys General with access to the court. In the McNeil case, where the right of the Nova Scotia Censorship Board to censor the movie *Last Tango in Paris* was questioned, the Canadian Civil Liberties Association was permitted to intervene in the case and present written and oral argument.[19] In the Morgentaler case, involving the appeal of Dr. Morgentaler of Montreal from conviction under the Criminal Code for performing abortions, six associations including the Canadian Civil Liberties Association and various pro- and anti-abortion groups, were permitted to intervene, file briefs, and be represented by counsel at the hearing to present argument.[20]

The Ontario Court of Appeal recently adopted intervention rules similar to that of the Supreme Court of Canada.[21] Since these new rules apply only to appeals before the Court of Appeal, intervention by public interest groups at trial or in other Ontario appeal courts will continue to be as *amicus curiae*.

However, a task force studying the rules of civil procedure in Ontario has recommended that three forms of intervention be codified: interventions by statute in accordance with the procedures set out in the statute; intervention by permission of the court, where any person other than a party claims an interest in the subject matter of the action, or claims that he may be adversely affected by it; and intervention by any person by permission of the court as *amicus curiae* to render assistance to the court.[22]

In other provinces, interventions will also continue to be as *amicus curiae* except where more specific rules are made.

The opportunities to intervene exist, and they will probably expand if public interest groups take advantage of them. Only through repeated efforts to convince the courts to expand the scope of their inquiry will they become accustomed to the idea that *amici* and other intervenors can assist them in making the fairest decisions. Although the concern among Canadian judges that the courtroom will become a political forum is very much alive, there is some evidence that this concern is giving way to the recognition that public interest intervenors contribute substantially to the judicial process.[23] As groups develop in their sophistication, experience and determination to effect change, intervention in the judicial process may continue to increase and may prove to be an effective legal tool.

Getting the government to bring important matters before the courts: the reference

Another way to bring important matters before the courts is to ask the government to refer important legal questions to the court. Although usually called a "constitutional reference," the reference procedure is not limited to constitutional matters. If the government agrees to the reference, the problems of standing and liability for costs are diminished.

WHAT IS THE REFERENCE?

The "reference" can bring before the courts legal issues that raise important social questions. To initiate a reference, it is not necessary to have a special property or financial interest in the disputed matter, nor must you wait for someone else to launch a suit. It is only necessary to convince the government that the law is unclear, important issues are at stake, and that it would be better for the government to ask the courts for a ruling on the matter than to deprive someone of justice or wait for private disputes to arise.

Although it is often called the "constitutional reference," the authority of government to refer important questions to the court is by no means limited to the constitutional validity of statutes or regulations. The federal government and each of the provinces have passed legislation allowing the Cabinet to refer important questions of law or fact to the courts. The only restriction on what the government can refer is that it must be the kind of issue the courts can normally decide. References have been held not only to interpret the validity or effect of legislation, but also to reopen controversial murder trials, in which there was doubt in the public mind about whether a convicted person was in fact guilty and whether he had a fair trial. The well-known Stephen Truscott case is an example.

In 1959, when Stephen Truscott was 14 years old, he was convicted
of murdering Lynne Harper, a 12-year-old schoolmate. His conviction
was upheld by the Ontario Court of Appeal, but several years later a
best-selling book about his trial raised questions about whether the
facts found by the jury were correct. At the time of the trial, a person
convicted of murder had no right of appeal to the Supreme Court of
Canada on the basis that wrong factual findings had been made, and
could only appeal errors of law. Although the law was changed a year
after Truscott's conviction to allow an appeal on these grounds, the
change came too late to help Truscott. Following the publicity gen-
erated by the book, the federal cabinet launched a reference to the
Supreme Court. The Cabinet ordered the court to review not only the
evidence presented at the trial, but also any new evidence, including
evidence that would have been inadmissible at the original trial. The
court again upheld Truscott's conviction, by a vote of eight to one.[24]

There has also been a reference to determine whether a criminal
court has the power to jail a member of a provincial Legislature for
refusing to disclose the name of an informant. In March 1976, Ed
Ziemba had accused Abko Medical Laboratories and some doctors of
improper laboratory practices in a speech in the provincial Legislature.
Ziemba had earlier received information and documentary evidence
from a confidential source, pointing to possibilities of kickbacks to
doctors from Abko and Abko's involvement in overcharging the Ontario Health Insurance Plan.

Police followed up on allegations, and charges of fraud were laid
against Abko and two of its owners. In proceedings against Abko, Mr.
Ziemba refused to reveal his sources of information during a preliminary hearing. On a resumption of that hearing in June, 1977, Ziemba
again refused to reveal sources and was imprisoned for six days for
contempt of court. He claimed that as a member of the Legislature he
was duty-bound not to reveal his sources. The government referred the
matter to the Ontario Court of Appeal for a ruling. The court discussed
not only Ziemba's predicament, but also what principles and interests
the trial court should consider in determining whether it is in the public
interest to make an MPP disclose his sources.

The decision of the court reference, released in early 1978, ruled
that MPPs have no immunity from answering questions in criminal
proceedings.[25]

At the actual trials of Abko and an individual defendant in September, 1978, and January, 1979, the trial judge ruled that Ziemba's

testimony would not be necessary but only because the identity of his informant was not relevant, not because Ziemba was an MPP.

HOW DOES THE REFERENCE WORK?

Section 55 of the Supreme Court Act, which governs the procedures of the Supreme Court of Canada, is an example of legislation author-izing a reference. Section 55(1) states that:

Important questions of law or fact concerning:

(a)   the interpretation of the British North America Act;

(b)   the constitutionality of interpretation of any federal or provincial legislation;

(c)   the appellate jurisdiction as to educational matters, by the British North America Act, 1867, or by any other Act or law vested in the Governor-in-Council;

(d)   the powers of the Parliament of Canada or of the Legislatures of the provinces, or of the respective governments thereof, whether or not the particular power in question has been or is proposed to be exercised;

(e)   *any other matter, whether or not in the opinion of the courts* ejusdem generis *[similar to, in the same category as] with the foregoing enumerations, with reference to which the Governor-in-Council sees fit to submit any such question*

may be referred by the Governor-in-Council to the Supreme Court for hearing and consideration; and any question concerning any of the matters aforesaid, so referred by the Governor-in-Council, shall con-clusively be deemed an important question.

Under this Act, when the federal Cabinet refers a question to the Supreme Court for its opinion, the court must notify the Attorney General of any province whose legislation is affected or which has a special interest in the question, and allow him to be heard if he wishes. The court may also direct the federal Cabinet to notify any person or the representative of any class of people interested in matters to be raised during the hearing. The Act states that such persons are entitled to be heard. Also, the court may request any lawyer to argue the case on behalf of any affected interest for which no lawyer appears. The federal government must pay the lawyer's fee.

The provincial statutes are similar. Sometimes they are broader, simpler and more to the point. For example, the Ontario Constitutional Questions Act provides that the provincial Cabinet may refer to the

Court of Appeal or to a judge of the Supreme Court of Ontario "any matter that [it] thinks fit." Provincial reference statutes also allow the court to appoint lawyers to argue for one side or the other — for example, the appointment of J. J. Robinet to argue the side of the tenants in the Ontario Residential Tenancy case (described next).

HOW CAN THE CONSTITUTIONAL REFERENCE BE USED?

Two recent cases show how public interest groups can use the reference to raise important issues. Under the Ontario Constitutional Questions Act, the Ontario Cabinet recently asked the Court of Appeal to give its opinion on the legality of proposed landlord and tenant legislation.[26] The draft statute would establish a Residential Tenancy Commission that would have sweeping powers to make orders evicting tenants at the request of landlords. In 1979 when this legislation was introduced in the Ontario Legislature, a committee of the Legislature held public hearings and invited submissions. Group after group representing tenants appeared before the committee to argue that the provincial Legislature had no authority to establish such a tribunal. They argued that the Commission would be exercising powers that, according to the Canadian constitution, are only to be exercised by a court appointed by the federal government. Many of these groups asked the Legislature committee to recommend that the government refer the legality of this question to the court for an opinion.

The government agreed to do so. It placed advertisements in newspapers advising the public that it had referred this question to the courts and inviting any interested parties to apply to the court for standing. The Attorney General of Ontario appeared before the court to argue that the legislation was valid. The court also recognized several tenants' associations, landlords' and developers' associations, community legal clinics and the Law Union of Ontario. Some of these groups argued in favour of the validity of the legislation, and others argued against. The court itself appointed a prominent lawyer to argue against the legislation. The court ruled that the legislation was not valid.

In a virtually identical reference in Alberta in 1978, the Appellate Division of the Alberta Supreme Court ordered the government to give notice of the hearing to the federal government, a tenants' association, a consumer group, a developers' association and two real estate associations. None of the associations was represented at the hearing. The federal government and the Alberta government played only a very small role in the proceedings. The court appointed one lawyer to argue that the legislation was valid and another to argue the opposite position.[27]

IS STANDING A PROBLEM?

As should be apparent from this discussion, no one has an automatic right to a reference. It is necessary to convince the government to ask for one. If the government agrees to ask for a reference, this does not automatically confer standing on anyone, but it is likely that the court will grant standing to the person who requested the hearing and to anyone else who may have a concern about the matter. Although the statutes provide only for references by the appropriate government, in fact, such references are usually made at the request of private individuals or groups. Thus, a request for a constitutional reference may actually be a way around the standing barrier.

WHAT ABOUT COSTS?

As mentioned later in chapter 4, normal civil litigation usually involves the losing party paying a large portion of the legal expenses of the winning party. There is no guarantee that a party who requests a reference, or who intervenes in a reference requested by someone else, will be free from costs if it ends up on the losing side. However, because references usually involve matters of great public importance, it is unlikely that costs would be awarded against the successful party. In fact, scrutiny of about 20 references (a large percentage of the references over the past 50 years) did not reveal a single reference in which the court awarded costs. In most cases, no mention was made of costs in the court's decision. In a few cases, the court explicitly stated that it was not going to award costs.

WHAT KIND OF EVIDENCE CAN BE INTRODUCED IN A REFERENCE?

One of the reasons courts are reluctant to decide matters of broad public interest is that they are not equipped with the resources to decide many such matters. They do not have the resources available to a Legislature for studying the implications of social policies and hearing from all the different kinds of interests that may be affected. Nor are the rules of evidence generally flexible enough to allow a court to take into account economic, sociological, attitudinal, psychological or other studies.

One potential advantage of a reference is the opportunity to introduce social and economic arguments and statistics, both in favour of the validity of legislation and against it. The extent to which such extrinsic evidence may be used to shed light on the legal validity of legislation is very controversial. In a 1950 case, the Supreme Court of Canada appeared to rule that extrinsic evidence may not be used in a reference;[28] nevertheless, this case appears to have been overruled, and in recent references the courts have relied increasingly on this kind of evidence.

In recent years, when governments have turned to the courts to rule on questions of legislative validity that involved such broad social issues as inflation[29] and conservation of natural resources,[30] the courts have considered evidence of the social and economic climate surrounding the passage of the legislation. They did this to determine which level of government had jurisdiction to pass it. Although the courts may not determine whether a law is legal on the basis of whether it is advisable, extrinsic evidence may help them determine the legality of a measure.

For example, the federal government generally has jurisdiction over matters that affect the country as a whole, and the provinces over affairs that affect the people of the province. If a province were to pass laws raising the prices of petroleum or rationing gasoline, the court might look at economic studies to help determine whether this would primarily affect people within that province or people in other parts of the country. The courts have taken an increasingly liberal approach towards the admission of such studies in references.

CONCLUSION

A request to the Cabinet that it refer a matter to the courts focuses public attention on the social issues and on the possible illegality of government actions or legislation. If the government refuses the request, public opinion may force it to justify its refusal. If the government agrees to refer the matter to the courts, it is likely that the social and economic issues will be raised and discussed in a more or less neutral forum. Standing and costs are unlikely to cause problems. The court may provide an opportunity for the introduction of social and economic arguments, studies and statistics. The court itself may appoint top-notch lawyers to argue both sides of the case, saving individuals or groups of modest means from the cost of hiring their own lawyers.

With these advantages, the constitutional reference should be considered a useful public interest advocacy tool.

3.

TEST CASES

Sometimes people take advantage of ambiguous or unclear laws to engage in practices that are oppressive, for example, racial or sexual discrimination. In such circumstances, the "test case" is taken not only to protect the rights of the affected individual, but to clarify the laws for many others in the same position. It can be a useful step towards ending the oppressive or unfair practice.

Perhaps the best-known test cases in Canada were cases taken by civil libertarians on behalf of black people who were refused service in Ontario restaurants in the 1950s. Despite the obvious value of test cases, they may raise practical problems for the litigant and ethical issues for his legal advisors, particularly if the lawyers are active in setting up the factual situation to be used in court.

The test case is a time-honoured tool of public interest advocacy. Test cases are attempts to use a set of circumstances to clarify the law, and to establish the rights or obligations of a broader class of people than the parties. The primary purpose of this kind of legal action is to serve the common interests of a class or group of people, rather than to resolve a dispute between parties, although this may also be a consideration.

WHAT SHOULD LAWYER AND CLIENT DISCUSS BEFORE GOING INTO A TEST CASE?

Because of the special nature of a test case, the lawyer and his client may agree in advance to suspend some of the normal considerations in their case. Normally, because of the great expense of litigation, a lawyer would discourage a client from commencing litigation that has little chance of success, and would encourage the client to accept a reasonable offer of settlement or compromise rather than continue litigation indefinitely. But a test case may be just as useful in clarifying the law whether it is won or lost. Therefore, the lawyer and his client may agree at any time to continue a test case because it could achieve social change, even if a reasonable settlement offer is made. Moreover, since the financial interests of the client are not the primary goal of the litigation, the "generosity" of a settlement offer may not deter the lawyer or his client from seeking a judicial decision on the matter.

There are other differences as well between the case to vindicate private interests and the test case. In the private case, the high cost of litigation and the party-and-party costs (costs that may be awarded against a plaintiff who loses his case) usually make it impossible for the plaintiff to resist an attractive settlement offer. In test cases, there is often a public interest group that is prepared to absorb these costs. Also, it would normally be improper for a lawyer to encourage his client to break the law. There may be an exception when the purpose of breaking the law is to test it rather than to achieve some personal gain.

HOW DO TEST CASES ARISE?

Test cases tend to arise in one of three ways. First, there may be numerous claims against the same defendant, or one plaintiff may have similar claims against different defendants. The claims are all similar in their circumstances and embrace the same questions of law and evidence. In this situation, the parties or the court may select one action to go to trial first, because it is representative of the others. The first case will serve as a test of the rights of the parties in the other cases. Often, all parties will agree to be bound by the result of the test action. For example, if hundreds of women who took the same drug gave birth to deformed babies, and all of them sued the drug manufacturer, they may agree to select one typical case as a test case.

Secondly, public interest groups seeking to advance a particular form of social change may be interested in a situation that exemplifies a particular injustice. If the group becomes aware of someone with a grievance that would make a particularly strong test case, it may assist that person in obtaining legal counsel and may support the litigation. For instance, if a gay person were fired from his job because of his sexual orientation and wanted to sue his employer for wrongful dismissal, he might ask a "gay liberation" group or civil liberties association to provide him with a lawyer. The group would discuss whether the case would advance the cause of gay rights or civil liberties, whether the plaintiff was sincere, credible and likely to stick with the case under adverse circumstances, and would agree to provide the service if this seemed likely.

Thirdly, members of public interest groups occasionally will "set up" a test case situation by deliberately placing themselves in a position where they know they will be harmed by someone else's activities or even by intentionally breaking the law to test whether it applies to that situation. The anti-racial discrimination cases described below are examples of setting up a test case.

Frequently, new laws are passed that appear to expand the rights of some group, but they are resisted by those upon whom they impose obligations. The latter group may resist the law because of its ambiguity, or because they believe that they can ignore it with impunity. When they are rich and powerful and those whom the law was intended to benefit are poor or are vulnerable because of some relationship they have with people resisting the law, new rights may remain unclarified and unenforced for a long time. Landlords and tenants are a good example. Tenants may be afraid of reprisals if they enforce what they believe to be their rights against their landlords. They may not have the financial resources to carry their case to the higher courts, which can make decisions that are binding on lower courts.

In such situations, a test case is needed. It could take a long time, however, for a good test case situation to arise — a situation in which the facts are strongly favourable to the people who have been granted the right, the issues are clearly defined, and the plaintiff has the courage to carry on lengthy, psychologically stressful litigation.

Therefore, public interest advocates have sometimes taken advantage of existing situations that might otherwise have been ignored, or have created situations to test the law.

HOW DO THE COURTS FEEL ABOUT TEST CASES?

Despite the fact that courts have occasionally frowned upon test cases, there does not appear to be anything legally or ethically wrong with a public interest group or lawyer commencing or even "setting up" a test case. The Canadian Bar Association's Code of Professional Conduct, for example, warns lawyers never to assist a client to be dishonest or to violate the law, and to be on guard against becoming the tool or dupe of an unscrupulous client or people associated with the client. However, it goes on to state that:

> A *bona fide* test case is not necessarily precluded by [this rule] and so long as no injury to the person or violence is involved, it is not improper

for the lawyer to advise and represent a client who, in good faith and on reasonable grounds, desires to challenge or test the law, and the test can most effectively be made by means of a technical breach giving rise to a test case.

This appears to mean that although a lawyer cannot assist in dishonesty, he may advise someone whom he knows intends to break the law in order to test it. For example, if the black woman in Birmingham, Alabama, who decided to break the law and be arrested rather than give up her seat on the bus to a white person as required by law had come to a lawyer for advice, he would have been doing nothing unethical by supporting her decision to do this and representing her.

Occasionally, in refusing to provide a remedy or redress, courts have remarked upon the fact that a situation is artificial. However, in none of these cases did the decision actually turn on the fact that someone had deliberately set up a test case. Therefore, they do not stand for the proposition that setting up a test case is improper or ineffective. Certain racial discrimination cases illustrate the way the courts have treated "set up" test cases. In one of the early Canadian cases, a black man in Montreal bought a ticket to the movies.[1] The ticket had written on it that the ticket holder had the option to sit either in the orchestra section of the theatre or in the mezzanine area. When this particular ticket holder took an orchestra seat, a theatre employee appeared and told him to go up to the mezzanine, an area reserved for negroes. He was offered the choice of sitting in the mezzanine or a refund of his money. He refused to move. At court, the trial judge awarded him damages for breach of contract, but the theatre owner appealed to a higher court, which overturned the decision.

The three appeal judges gave several reasons for ruling against the man, based primarily upon the theatre owner's "freedom of commerce." However, one judge noted that the plaintiff "knew at the time he purchased the ticket that he would not be allowed to occupy a seat in the orchestra, and that he had gone to the said theatre and had purchased said ticket for the sole purpose of taking the present action against the defendants. . . . He therefore exposed himself deliberately to the refusal of which he complains in his action."

More than thirty years later, the same issue was raised obliquely in one of a series of test cases under the Ontario Fair Accommodation Practices Act. The Act provided that, "No person shall deny to any person or class of persons the accommodation, services or facilities available in any place to which the public is customarily admitted because of the race, creed, colour, nationality, ancestry or place of origin of such person or class of persons." In 1954, shortly after the Act was passed, black and white civil rights activists went to Dresden, Ontario, to test the law in a number of restaurants. These restaurants allegedly barred coloured people.

Representatives of the Student Christian Movement, the Joint Labour Committee for Human Rights, a reporter for a Toronto newspaper, a resident of Dresden and a black man named Bromley Armstrong drove from Toronto to Dresden to eat in one of these restaurants. The waitress refused to serve them. The local resident, who knew the owner, went to the kitchen and asked him for service. The owner said he was "too busy." Mr. Armstrong laid a charge under the Act and the owner was convicted.

However, on appeal, County Court Judge Grosch overturned the conviction, stressing the fact that this was a test case.

> These four went to Dresden for the avowed purpose of getting evidence as to whether the appellant and others were observing the law, and to obtain evidence for a test case, and it was not, as Donaldson [the newspaper reporter] admitted, a "legitimate or genuine case of people wanting food or refreshments at all." Furthermore, it was not a case of providing service for the residents of a local and surrounding community or for travellers or tourists visiting in or passing through the town, which ordinarily is what service one expects a restaurant to provide.
>
> These seven people did not go to this restaurant at approximately the same time by coincidence, but as a result of and part of a preconceived plan, or as one of the witnesses testified: "This whole thing was a scheme to try and create a situation there," and was planned in Toronto as a test case by the Joint Labour Committee for Human Rights.[2]

Judge Grosch did not base his decision on the fact that the situation was set up, however, but said he was not satisfied there was sufficient evidence that service was denied, or that, if it was denied, this was because of the colour of the informant. On the same day, he also quashed the conviction of another restaurant owner, again stressing that the primary reason for the presence of the informant in the restaurant was not to obtain food but to "see if the Emerson's Restaurant was obeying the law."[3] In this case, the reasons given were that there was insufficient evidence that the food requested was available or that the denial of service was because of race, creed, colour, nationality, ancestry or place of origin. (Judge Grosch, incidentally, was one of a group of landowners who, in a 1949 case, had petitioned the court to enforce a clause in several deeds prohibiting landowners from selling their property to Jews or negroes, although he stated in a newspaper interview that this involvement had not influenced his decision.)

However, County Court Judge Lang in two very similar cases involving the first restaurant owner, two black men from Toronto and the same representatives of the two public interest groups, upheld two convictions for the same offence. Judge Lang apparently was not bothered by the fact that these were test cases.[4]

In none of these cases did the decision actually turn on the fact that someone had deliberately set up a test case. Therefore, they do not stand for the proposition that setting up a test case is improper. The primary purpose of the courts has traditionally been to settle disputes between individual parties, rather than to establish broad social policy. But it is sometimes recognized by the courts that individual cases frequently affect a broad spectrum of the public and serve an important role in clarifying the law for others. This is why, for example, the courts often do not award costs against the loser in court cases that involve matters of broad public interest or the interpretation of legislation that has not yet been tested. The test case, therefore, appears to be a legitimate instrument of public policy and is no less legitimate if it is "set up."

WHAT IS THE KEY TO A SUCCESSFUL TEST CASE?

In order to have a successful test case, you must avoid falling into either of two traps. First, you should know that the courts will not decide questions that are premature or merely hypothetical. The situation is not hypothetical just because it has been set up. However, occasionally a situation involving a *potential* injury or breach of the law may appear to be an ideal test case. Until the injury or breach actually occurs, the court will not consider the case. If you were to ask the court to tell you what your rights or obligations would be if this were to occur, the court would refuse. For example, if the civil rights advocates had simply stayed in Toronto and asked the courts for a decision on whether it would be illegal for restaurants in Dresden to refuse to serve Mr. Armstrong, they would not be heard. Or to take a more current example, if Alberta were to pass legislation setting the price of oil, the courts could rule whether this was within the jurisdiction of the province or the federal government. But if Alberta were to ask the court what it would do if the province were to pass such legislation, the court would refuse.

Secondly, the setting up of a test case might result in the plaintiff or prosecutor being unable to prove one or more of the essential elements of its case. An act or omission that would be illegal if someone were involuntarily subjected to it might not be illegal if the plaintiff or informant voluntarily exposed himself to it.

A recent pollution case that was not a test case illustrates this problem. Toronto Refiners and Smelters, a leading smelting company, was charged with discharging a contaminant contrary to the Ontario Environmental Protection Act.[5] Such pollution offences generally involve some element of causing harm. It is not usually an offence to discharge obnoxious substances if they are incapable of causing or are unlikely to cause any harm. But the same discharge in a harmful quantity or at a location where it is likely to cause harm is punishable. In this case, the company discharged a foul-smelling chemical into the air late at night. No one was present except an inspector from the Ontario Ministry of the Environment. He deliberately entered the visible plume, whereupon his eyes began to water and he had difficulty breathing.

At trial, the company was convicted. However, the Ontario Court of Appeal overruled the company's conviction on the grounds that the discharge wasn't harmful. The court held that the only person affected was the government inspector, and he was affected only because he voluntarily walked into the middle of the area of contamination. Therefore, by deliberately walking into the plume, the inspector vitiated the offence.

The courts have recognized the value of test cases in many ways. If a person breaks the law only to determine a principle, the court can impose a lighter sentence than it normally would.[6] If two litigants in similar lawsuits decide they will treat one of the suits as a test case to clarify the rights of the other person, it isn't maintenance or champerty (see chapter 6) for one of them to support the other's case financially.[7] Test cases fuelled the black civil rights movement in the United States and in Canada. They are likely to be an important part of other movements for social progress in years to come.

CONCLUSION

You are now at the courtroom door. At some point you decided that the court was a good forum to fight in and you overcame the standing barrier. Even though you had no property to defend, you got here through a reference or as a friend of the court. Or perhaps you have a property interest but it is more important to you to use your case as a test case to help others than to settle out of court, which would compensate you for some harm to your own property, but leave others in your situation in doubt about *their* rights.

Using the courts to bring about social change is not an activity for the timorous. Your opponents will often be represented by very successful lawyers, protecting the interests of some of Canada's wealthiest corporations. There are some rules of the game, some traps and tactics, you should know about. If you do, your journey through the courts and tribunals that enforce the law can go smoothly. The next part of this book tells you what to expect in certain situations that often arise before courts and tribunals and how to avoid a few snares for the unwary.

Part II:
Before the Courts and Tribunals

4.

WHO PAYS?

When you consider mounting a legal case, the first question is, "What will it cost us?" The expense will include items like the fees payable to various courts and tribunals, the cost of obtaining documents, photocopying, long-distance phone calls, travel, hiring expert witnesses (if necessary) and paying your lawyer, unless he is providing his advice free of charge. These costs vary greatly from case to case. In addition, in some situations if you lose your case you may be required to pay some of the legal expenses of the other side. These "party-and-party" costs are explained in this chapter.

A particularly insidious aspect of costs is that opposing lawyers will sometimes try to convince a court or tribunal to award costs against a lawyer *personally*, because he has taken a public interest case. The chances of this succeeding are very slim, but it could happen. The circumstances under which a lawyer might be personally liable for costs are described.

WHAT ARE THE COSTS AND WHO IS LIABLE?

There are three kinds of costs involved in any court case: "disbursements" (expenses such as photocopying costs, fees paid to the court to file documents and fees paid to expert witnesses such as doctors, lawyers and actuaries); your own lawyer's fees; and the fees and disbursements incurred by your opponent. These are the "hidden costs" you incur if you lose.

One of the first things a public interest advocate must consider when he thinks about using the courts is the possibility of having to pay part of the legal expenses of his opponent, in addition to paying his own lawyer. Courts, and occasionally tribunals, have the power to order you to pay a substantial portion of the other side's legal expenses if you lose the case or misbehave; the other side may be ordered to pay costs if you win. These awards are called party-and-party costs and they are often a serious deterrent to public interest litigation.

In general, in private prosecutions, Small Claims Court actions and hearings before boards and tribunals, either no party-and-party costs are awarded or the awards are very small. In civil litigation, including judicial review applications, however, the loser is usually ordered to pay costs to the winner, and these costs may be substantial. In these inflationary times, any estimate of costs I can give you will soon be out of date. However, it is not unrealistic to expect to pay $800 to $1,000 for each day of trial, and your lawyer may have difficulty estimating how long the trial will last. Judicial review applications, which primarily involve interpretation of the law, often take one to two days of court time. Other civil cases involving questions of fact — for example, which of ten factories in a polluted area caused the plaintiff's illness — may last for weeks. If a party loses his case on a judicial review application that takes two days of court time, the costs awarded against him may be around $2,000.

HOW DO THE COURTS AWARD COSTS?

Statutes establishing the courts usually provide them with wide discretionary powers to award costs in any way they see fit. Over the years the courts have established a general rule that costs should "follow the event"; that is, the loser must pay the costs to the winner. These costs are calculated according to "tariffs" established for each court. In civil litigation, the tariff usually provides for the loser to pay approximately one-half to two-thirds of the winner's legal fees and disbursements.

Here's how the system works in practice. If you win your case, your opponent will pay a substantial portion of your lawyer's fees and then legal expenses. If you lose, you pay a similar share of his costs. Suppose the loser appeals. If he loses again, he will probably have to pay two sets of costs — the costs of the initial trial and the costs of the appeal. But if he loses the first time and wins the second time, the results can be fairly unpredictable. Success on appeal wipes out the trial judge's award of costs against him. The appeal judges, with their wide discretion, can then award the victor the costs of both the trial and the appeal (the usual result) or of the appeal only (no costs of the trial being awarded to either party). Occasionally, they may leave the original award intact but award costs of the appeal to the victor. Or if each side wins a partial victory on appeal, they may not award costs to either. To complicate matters still further, the decision of the appeal court may be appealed to an even higher court, which may reverse the first appeal court's decision. This court would then have discretion over the costs of all three hearings.

Another result of the wide discretion the courts have is that, except where their decisions on the merits of a case are overturned, higher courts are reluctant to overrule their costs awards. If you feel it is unfair for you to pay the other side's costs even though you lost the case, it is seldom worthwhile to launch an appeal against the costs award.

Because the judges have wide discretionary powers they can depart from the general rule that costs follow the event. The court may decide not to award costs to a successful party if the question at issue is a new one,[1] if a new statute is being interpreted,[2] or if the action is a test case.[3] If a matter of great public interest is at stake, the court may exercise its discretion not to award costs against a public interest litigant who loses.

For example, in the Elora Gorge case, two members of a Conservation Authority sued the Authority and the Municipal Council for an injunction to prevent the construction of a highway and bridge. Both would pass through a park and the bridge would cross the deepest and most scenic part of a unique river gorge in southern Ontario, just north of the City of Guelph. Although the Ontario Supreme Court dismissed the plaintiffs' action, the judge did not award costs against them: "I have expressed the view," Mr. Justice Weatherston said, "that if it had not been for the concern of citizens in the area, no consideration would have been given to the environmental factors . . . councils must learn that they should take all relevant matters into consideration and these were most important considerations which initially were completely ignored. I think that the plaintiffs have done a public service here in bringing this application . . . I make no order as to costs."[4]

On the other hand, the fact that a plaintiff believes he is acting in the public interest is no guarantee that costs will not be awarded against him. The plaintiffs appealed the Elora Gorge decision and lost. The Ontario Court of Appeal then ordered them to pay approximately $16,000 in costs.[5]

Moreover, for every court that takes the attitude of Mr. Justice Weatherston towards a case that is brought in the public interest, there seems to be another court that takes the opposite view. In a case in which residents of Winnipeg sought to overturn a decision of the City of Winnipeg to realign a road in a manner that would have significant impact on the environment, a judge of the Manitoba Court of Queen's Bench said: "I think that this is clearly a case where a few individuals who cannot get the majority of people to see their point of view are attempting to accomplish the same by making an application to this court." The application was dismissed, and costs were awarded against the applicant.[6]

Similarly, in 1978, costs were awarded against a staff member of Pollution Probe who challenged the failure of the Ontario Minister of the Environment to file a timetable for phasing out nonreturnable pop cans, in accordance with an amendment to the Environmental Protection Act that appeared to require him to do so.[7] This section of the Act had never been interpreted before and involved a significant public interest issue, as nonreturnable cans are a source of litter and wasted energy and cause a waste disposal problem. Nevertheless, when the court ruled that the EPA amendment did not require the filing of such a timetable, costs were awarded against the plaintiff. "This is a case of some importance no doubt," Mr. Justice Hughes said. "Nonetheless, the advisors of the applicant must have been well aware and made her well aware of the risks inherent in bringing the application."

ARE THERE LESS EXPENSIVE ALTERNATIVES?

Often the main purpose of a public interest lawsuit is not to recover all the money you have lost as a result of some unjust activity, but to put a stop to that activity. In this case, the small claims court may be the answer to the costs problem.

Small Claims Courts, which decide disputes involving relatively small sums of money, are informal in their procedures and encourage people to be their own lawyers. These courts frequently award no costs. When they do award costs, they are usually limited by tariff to relatively small amounts: for example, a maximum of $50. In some provinces, such as Ontario, it is also relatively inexpensive to appeal a Small Claims Court decision if you lose. If you lose the appeal as well, the tariff limits the costs that can be awarded against you so that they will probably be less than $100.

Because it is inexpensive to sue in this court, sometimes a good strategy is to bring a number of actions in it, each for a small amount of damages, rather than seek an injunction in a higher court.

Sometimes a prosecution in the criminal courts for violating a statute will serve the same purpose as a civil action, without the liability for costs. In the criminal courts, if your complaint is dismissed (that is, if the accused is found not guilty of the offence), usually no costs will be awarded against you in a private prosecution. Even if the judge awards costs to the accused, which you must pay, these will rarely exceed $100, and will usually be only $5 or $10.

ARE THERE COSTS INVOLVED WITH BOARDS AND TRIBUNALS?

Similarly, most boards and tribunals do not award costs either to the applicant or to those opposing him, regardless of the outcome. For example, after the dissident members of the Conservation Authority lost their court cases to stop the bridge being built over the Elora Gorge on legal grounds, two environmental groups exercised their right to a public hearing before the Ontario Municipal Board, at which they opposed the bridge on planning grounds. When the applicants for permission to build the bridge and the highway approaches asked for costs against their opposition, whom they had beaten once again, the Board refused, stating:

> This Board, however, is of the firm opinion that the hearing of this matter, regardless of any delays which may have been occasioned, is the right of the citizens of the Province of Ontario under the Planning Act, RSO 1970, chapter 349, and unless the objection or objections be deemed to be frivolous or without merit, no order as to costs should issue. The objections to the proposal were stated with certainty, clarity and with a great deal of merit, and certainly were anything but frivolous. There will therefore be no order as to costs.[8]

This has been the traditional attitude of the OMB towards costs. Like some other boards and tribunals, however, it has developed a "one-way" costs rule. Although the proponent will never be awarded costs against objectors unless they misbehave badly, opponents will sometimes be awarded costs if they defeat the application.

There appears to be a trend towards giving costs to members of the public to help them defray their expenses in opposing wealthier applicants. One example is a 1977 decision of the Ontario Energy Board, in which it awarded costs for the first time to members of the public opposing rate increases for Ontario Hydro.[9] The award was based on the fact that intervenor participation had been helpful to the Board. Costs were awarded to those intervenors whom the Board considered to have actively participated and put forward intelligent, well-informed and effective interventions.

WHAT COSTS CAN AN ADVOCACY LAWYER FACE?

One of the hazards of being a public interest lawyer is the possibility that lawyers on the other side will attempt to convince a judge to award costs against you personally, if your client cannot afford to pay. For example, this happened in a 1975 test case that involved important points of law and tenants' rights. The case was one of a series of actions under Ontario's newly passed Landlord and Tenant Act taken by Parkdale Community Legal Services, one of the first "storefront" law clinics in Canada.[10] Parkdale acted for a number of tenants fighting a landlord who was notorious throughout Toronto after press coverage of the state of disrepair of his highrise apartment buildings, involving the lack of repair of faulty elevators, garbage and debris, elevator breakdowns, lack of hot water, fires around the incinerator, cockroaches, poor security, breakdown of air-conditioning and water leaking through the ceiling.

The test case was one of a series of cases that attempted to clarify the meaning of certain sections of the new Act. One of these cases went all the way to the Supreme Court of Canada. In this case, the issue was whether the Act entitled tenants who claimed that a landlord was failing to meet his obligations of repairs to withhold their rent and instead pay it into a "trust fund" to be held until the courts determined their rights. When the tenants withheld their rent, the landlord evicted them for non-payment. The tenants challenged the eviction on the grounds that the Landlord and Tenant Act gave them the right to withhold rent under these circumstances. The court held that the tenants had no right to withhold rent to force repairs, and if they did so, the landlord could evict them.

At the conclusion of his argument, the lawyer for the landlord asked County Court Judge Cornish to award costs personally against Mary Hogan, the lawyer for the tenants, who was an employee of Parkdale Community Legal Services. At the time, PCLS was funded by grants from the federal government, the City of Toronto and York University. The landlord's lawyer argued that PCLS staff were the instigators of the "trust fund" idea and were a "controlling force" behind the actions of the tenants in their fight with the landlord. He argued that since Mary Hogan was a solicitor on the staff of PCLS, she could be held responsible for its actions.

The case raises interesting questions about the liability of community legal clinics and public interest lawyers. Although in the end Judge

Cornish refused to order costs against Ms. Hogan, he seemed to exhibit great ambivalence about this:

> There is little doubt in my mind that individual members of lower income groups need protection against the more powerful forces in our society, and the Ontario Legal Aid Plan is a successful thrust in this direction.
>
> It is claimed that there are areas of need for legal services which this plan does not reach and this may well be true. If this is so, then either the plan must extend its scope or other more radically oriented groups will fill the gap. Parkdale Community Legal Services appears to be one such group. . . .
>
> The existence of this organization and the claim for costs in this application against one of its staff lawyers throws into focus a serious problem. On the one hand, we have a group trying to fulfill a social need. On the other hand, there are dangers inherent in an organization undertaking and sponsoring litigation without the need of having any regard to the legal costs incurred.

Judge Cornish not only refused to award costs personally against the tenants' lawyer, but he also refused to award the normal costs against the tenant in whose name the action was brought. Recognizing that she could not possibly be expected to bear the costs of the proceedings, which had consumed eight court days and would normally amount to at least $1,000, he fixed her liability for costs at $200.

In remarking that the request for costs to be awarded personally against the clinic lawyer was "a situation which required consideration by all concerned with the administration of justice," Judge Cornish gave notice that participation of public interest lawyers and community legal clinics in representing the poor in test cases is an unusual situation that may not fit neatly into the normal costs rules.

Lawyers for defendants can be expected to attempt to use this tactic in situations where an impoverished client has put their client to great expense and where a community legal clinic has been more directly involved in planning and implementing their clients' activities than would be expected from the traditional lawyer. Nevertheless, there is substantial evidence that such requests will continue to be unsuccessful.

WHEN WILL COSTS BE AWARDED AGAINST A LAWYER?

The court's discretion to depart from the general rule that the loser is responsible for the winner's costs includes the authority to order the losing party's lawyer to pay the costs personally. An award of costs against the solicitor is an extreme departure from the general rule and would be made only in rare cases. The basis for such an award is the court's authority over its officers. When a solicitor appears before a court, he is an officer of that court. He must balance his duty to his client against his duty to the court. The Canadian Bar Association Code of Professional Conduct states that the lawyer has a duty to treat the court with candour, fairness, courtesy and respect. For example, the lawyer must not abuse the process of the tribunal by: instituting or prosecuting proceedings that are motivated by his client's malice; knowingly assisting or permitting his client to do anything dishonest or dishonourable; knowingly misstating the contents of a document, the testimony of a witness, the substance of an argument or the provisions of a statute; abusing a witness; deliberately neglecting to inform the tribunal of any law or cases relevant to the case at hand.

Sometimes, representing a public interest litigant can place a lawyer in a position in which his duty to his client can be made, by a sharp opponent, to appear to conflict with his duty to the court. For example, many public interest cases have little chance of success because they are based on theories of law and public responsibility not held by most of society, or based on facts that are difficult to prove, for example, the likelihood that a relatively new drug, chemical or technology causes cancer. In such cases, the opposition may be able to convince the court that the advocacy lawyer is deliberately wasting the court's time with a case that has no merit. The conflict between duty to the client and duty to the court may be real in cases where the client demands a "political" defence rather than a "legal" one. Public interest lawyers sometimes walk a fine line. In some instances, the court's common law authority over its officers has been expressed in statute. For example, the Federal Court Act provides that the court may make an order against a solicitor who is responsible for costs that are incurred "improperly or without reasonable cause or are wasted by undue delay or by *any other misconduct or default.*"[11] This rule indicates that in essence the court will not make such an order unless there has been some misconduct.

Costs may be awarded against a solicitor in two very specific situations. First, a solicitor who acts without the authority of his client may be ordered to pay costs if he has negligently failed to obtain a proper retainer.[12] However, he will not be required to pay costs if he has acted in good faith and with the belief that his retainer was sufficient.[13] Secondly, a solicitor may be ordered to pay costs if he acts for a mentally incompetent person or for a person who has been declared incapable of managing his affairs.[14]

For the public interest lawyer, the specific situations described above are unlikely to arise. However, the following cases shed some light on the kinds of "misconduct" that may lead to an award of costs against a solicitor. In one case, the solicitor for the plaintiff was ordered to pay the defendant's costs because of his "obvious disobedience of a court order."[15] In another case, the court made an order of discovery requiring a party to give other parties information, in writing and under oath, describing all documents relative to the case that had been in his possession at any time. Since the client's affidavit of documents was incomplete and misleading, the court held that his solicitor was liable for costs since he had "prepared and permitted his client to make affidavits of documents which were inadequate and false." The court held the solicitor liable even though the affidavits were prepared by a clerk and not by the solicitor himself, since the solicitor had a duty to supervise the work. Therefore, even if a solicitor has delegated the responsibility to someone else, he remains responsible for any misconduct.[16]

In a similar case, a person being investigated by a Commission of Inquiry looking into organized crime asked the court to order the Commissioner to refer a question of law to the Ontario Court of Appeal for interpretation. In support of this application, the client swore an affidavit in which he argued that the Commissioner was biased against him. The court concluded that the affidavit contained "shoddy," "faulty" and "scurrilous" statements, and that the solicitor knew that his client's statements were false. The solicitor's failure to correct these statements was interpreted as a "gross neglect of duty," and the solicitor was ordered to pay costs.[17]

A solicitor was ordered to pay costs in another case because the court felt that examinations for discovery were "reduced to a shambles" either "deliberately or by reason of gross ineptitude." The solicitor was ordered to pay costs even though the examinations had been conducted by another solicitor who was acting on his behalf.[18]

Finally, a solicitor was initially ordered to pay costs when he represented a "plaintiff who had very little chance of success." The trial judge also said that, "where the plaintiff is a poor man, against whom a judgment for the defendant's cause would yield nothing, then a solicitor must act with greater care than he would do if his client was judgment-proof." But the solicitor successfully appealed this order.

Quoting from several leading cases, the Court of Appeal noted that before a solicitor is ordered to pay costs "there must be something that amounts to a serious dereliction of duty, something . . . which justifies the use of the word 'gross.' " Furthermore, "The mere fact that the litigation fails is no reason for invoking the jurisdiction; nor is an error of judgment, nor even is . . . an error . . . which constitutes . . . negligence." The Court of Appeal rejected the argument that the solicitor must act with greater care when he is representing a poor man. It held that such an argument would "transgress one of the very fundamentals of our judicial principles that all men, regardless of wealth or position, stand equal before the law." For lawyers who represent public interest groups it is significant that the court rejected this argument.[19]

CONCLUSION

Before deciding to take legal action, lawyers and clients should carefully discuss the costs involved and take steps to secure funds. It is far easier to raise a "defence fund" before a case goes to court than afterwards. Therefore, it may be as important for any organization intending to launch a test case to have a good fund-raising committee as to have a good legal arm. Moreover, whether you can raise funds to cover legal expenses may be a good test of whether you have an important case. Persistence will usually pay off in more funds than you need if the case is worthwhile. If you are concerned primarily about party-and-party costs that will only have to be paid if you lose, pledges may do the job. Pledges that may never have to be honoured are easier to raise than hard cash — but harder to collect if and when they are needed. Nevertheless, most people honour their pledges.

You should also consider the cost of appeals at the outset. Is the case so important that you should not undertake it unless you are prepared to go all the way to the Supreme Court of Canada? Or will you have made your point even if you lose and don't appeal the decision?

If some member of your group is willing to be the plaintiff, he will be responsible for the costs if the case is lost. Can he afford this if the fund-raising efforts aren't successful?

If you are a lawyer for a public interest litigant, consider whether you will have to use the kinds of tactics that will tempt the court to award costs against you personally. If you anticipate this, you should consider the effects such an award may have on your reputation in the general legal community. Are you willing to pay this price to prove a point or defend a principle? Do your clients understand that this is a possible outcome of your strategy or tactics, and are they willing or able to cover costs awarded against you? If they say they are, you may want to get it in writing. In other words, you may want your clients' authorization to use the specific tactics and their agreement to indemnify you against any costs arising out of those tactics. Of course, you should be aware that any time you breach your duty to the court you may also face disciplinary action by the governing body of the legal profession in your province in addition to any costs awarded.

In summary, as litigant or lawyer, you need to assess realistically your responsibilities and liabilities before issuing a writ and plan for them.

5.

WHAT TO DO AND SAY AND WHAT TO AVOID

In public interest cases, groups and their lawyers are often approached by the press for comment, and groups will ask their lawyer what they can and cannot say. It's a difficult question because it is necessary to keep a balance between the right to exercise free speech and the need to be respectful to the court and fair to other parties. In addition, the other side can use contempt as a weapon to intimidate public interest groups and their lawyers. Chapter 5 provides some guidelines on contempt.

WHAT IS CONTEMPT?

Contempt of court is any act that is likely to embarrass, hinder or obstruct a court in administering justice, or is likely to lessen the authority or dignity of the courts.

CONTEMPT, PUBLIC INTEREST GROUPS AND THE MEDIA

Here the focus will be on the relationship of public interest groups and their lawyers to the courts and to the media during judicial proceedings. The rules that apply to groups and their lawyers are frequently similar to those that apply to the media, but the circumstances of public interest advocates differ in some ways.

Even before deciding to launch a legal action, public interest groups and their lawyers must consider the impact it may have on their right to inform the public about the issues involved. You must understand that once a matter is *sub judice* (under consideration by a court), your ability to speak freely about the issues without fear of being cited for contempt will be severely curtailed. Even if you are willing to continue discussing the issues, the media will be reluctant to report what you say for the same reason. Thus, if launching legal action is likely to tie up a matter in the courts for years, public interest advocates may be reluctant to enforce their legal rights. The trade-off of public discussion for the possibility of a favourable court decision may be too great. Once an issue is before the courts, the media may back off and the opportunity for valuable exposure will be lost.

Of course, the problem of contempt is particularly acute for the media, whose job is to report the news. On the one hand, it is in the public interest to allow the press to publish accurate and objective reports of trials. Moreover, under normal circumstances it is very important to have a press that is willing to discuss and evaluate the kinds of important social issues that might arise during a trial, such as the safety of automobiles or the rights of minorities. On the other hand, the parties are entitled to a fair trial, uninfluenced by outside events. Should the mere existence of a legal dispute have the effect of removing all legitimate discussion of such social issues from the media? If not, where should society draw the line?

A recent case is illustrative of the problem faced by both the media and citizen advocates. The Supreme Court of Ontario called the Toronto *Globe and Mail* before it to explain why the newspaper should not be cited for contempt of court for publishing an article about a professor who was fired by McMaster University. The article had appeared on the very morning the court was to begin hearing the professor's application to strike down the university's decision to dismiss her. It said that the professor was an expert in women's studies, a new discipline which people interviewed described as unconventional and controversial. People were quoted who said the professor was recognized to be a good teacher, but the university had questioned the quality of her research.

Mr. Justice Henry said, "Those of us who have read it feel it is a slanted article and have quite strong reservations whether we should hear the case at all." *The Globe*'s lawyer argued that the newspaper had printed the article because it believed the case to be "only part of a wider problem which is clearly a matter of public interest — that is, the struggle between teaching and research at McMaster and its bias against unconventional subjects." He said that *The Globe* did not think the article would influence Supreme Court judges. The court decided not to cite *The Globe* because it found that the newspaper did not intend to interfere with the judicial process.

About two weeks later, the Attorney General of Ontario asked the Ontario Supreme Court to cite the same newspaper for contempt, this time because of an editorial it published during the course of a trial to determine the validity of writs authorizing the Sheriff to evict 250 residents of the Toronto Islands from their homes. The Sheriff's Office had refused to serve the eviction notices on the basis of a legal opinion provided by the Attorney General Ministry that the writs had expired. In its editorial, *The Globe and Mail* commented, "not two weeks ago, in as shabby an act of political opportunism as we ever want to witness, the Attorney General's Office sought to obstruct the serving of eviction notices upon the residents of Toronto Islands, and, in so doing, it plainly and simply interfered with the due course of the law." The Attorney General's representative said the government department was merely fulfilling the proper function of providing legal advice to one of its branches — the Sheriff's Office.

Was this a fair comment for a newspaper to make, or was it, as the Attorney General's representative argued, an "unprovoked, unjustified, libellous and scurrilous attack by *The Globe and Mail* on the Ministry of the Attorney General, which includes the Sheriff's Office"? And if in fact it was libellous, should the Attorney General be required to sue for defamation rather than invoke the judicial remedy of contempt?

A courageous newspaper must face the question of contempt whenever it decides to comment or take a stand on any matter that is before the courts, or where judicial proceedings are imminent. Indeed, some lawyers routinely send notices to the media advising them that a matter is *sub judice*. Such notices could be viewed merely as an attempt to inform the media of a relevant factor to take into account when reporting on these issues, or as a blatant attempt to intimidate the media. The present law of contempt may appear to be grossly oppressive. It may seem to make little sense that a matter that is the subject of legitimate public discussion before legal proceedings begin should be any less freely discussed just because a court is considering some aspect of it. The reason for the doctrine of contempt is to protect the image of the judicial system, to allow courts to run smoothly and harmoniously and to protect the parties to judicial proceedings from outside interference or "trial by the press."

Although not everyone finds the courts competent and unbiased, they are usually a better mechanism for settling disputes than some of the alternatives, such as violence and political manipulation. To a large extent, the courts are independent of politics, and are often the only place where the rich and poor may appear on a relatively equal footing. For these reasons, there is a legitimate public interest in protecting the judicial system from unwarranted abuse. However, at times the contempt power may go too far in curtailing freedom of speech; for example, if it prohibits statements that do not interfere with the proceedings of a specific court or harm the chances of success of any party, but merely cast doubt upon the integrity of the judges in general, as happened when the editors of a student newspaper were cited for contempt for writing that the New Brunswick courts were "tools of the corporate elite."[1]

Whenever they are involved in litigation, public interest groups and their lawyers find themselves faced with the problem of finding the delicate line between legitimate comment and contempt of court. Contempt ranges from throwing a rock at a judge to reporting only one side of a case. Like many of the doctrines discussed in this book, contempt is vague and therefore open to abuse. But despite the grey areas, there are extremes at each end of the spectrum that are clearly contempt or clearly not contempt. A discussion of the principles involved should help public interest advocates to recognize those extremes and help their lawyers give advice quickly when necessary.

WHAT KINDS OF CONTEMPT ARE THERE?

There are several kinds of contempt. Some are based primarily on one of the policy considerations mentioned above, such as ensuring that the parties get a fair trial, while others focus on another, such as protecting the public image of the courts. Often, these considerations, as well as the different kinds of contempt, overlap.

Civil contempt

Contempt can be divided into criminal contempt and civil contempt, although the actual dividing line between the two is far from clear. Civil contempt consists primarily of one of the participants in a lawsuit failing to comply with an order of the court. It also applies to anyone else who has knowledge of a court order and causes it to be breached; for example, individual employees who picket a factory knowing that the court has issued an injunction against picketing to the union.[2]

The leading English text on the law of contempt describes civil contempt as a private wrong — a wrong done to the person who is entitled to the benefit of the court order — and thus an offence against that person.[3] But in Canada it also appears to be a public wrong. The distinction between the "private" and "public" nature of this offence becomes blurred when one considers that contempt applies not only to the parties but also to others who breach the court's order. Because civil contempt is a "private" matter, contempt proceedings are usually initiated by the person suffering the harm rather than by the court. However, the Supreme Court of Canada has ruled that in some cases the court itself may initiate the proceedings for contempt.[4] Therefore, there is a strong argument that refusal to obey a court order is also a "public" wrong, because it is an offence against the court that made the order.

Clearly, if people were free to ignore court orders, confidence in the effectiveness of the entire judicial process would be quickly undermined. This form of contempt therefore also serves a legitimate *public* interest.

In most cases, defiance of a court order is no more effective than standing up in court and hurling invective at a judge. This is not normally a reasonable tactic to use. However, there may be cases where the court issues an injunction (for example, against a peaceful civil liberties march or against a union picketing) that appears so unfair that public interest advocates are sorely tempted to defy it. History will likely record that Martin Luther King was right, and the judges wrong, when he and thousands of blacks defied court orders against their peaceful protests in the southern states.

Criminal contempt

Criminal contempt may be committed in the presence of the court ("contempt in the face of the court" or "contempt *in facie curiae*") or outside of the courtroom ("constructive contempt" or "contempt *ex facie curiae*"). There are borderline cases, such as a noisy demonstration on the courthouse steps or in the corridors of a courthouse, that could be considered as either contempt in the face of the court or constructive contempt because it is unclear whether they are committed in the judge's "presence."

WHAT ACTIVITIES ARE CLASSIFIED AS CONTEMPT?

There are five main activities that can be classified as contempt:

- misbehaving in court
- obstructing justice
- scandalizing the court

- disobeying a court order

- making statements that are likely to influence the outcome of a trial or to influence the public perception of the trial (the *sub judice* rule)

These forms of contempt are improper whether done in the context of a criminal trial or a civil one. In this sense, the term "criminal contempt" is confusing. "Criminal" and "civil" in this context refer to the kinds of actions the "contemptuous" person engages in, rather than the forum towards which he is contemptuous. The reason these forms of contempt are considered criminal rather than civil is that the wrong is primarily a public wrong, an affront to the public interest in maintaining the proper administration of justice.

Even this statement must be qualified, however. Just as civil contempt may have a public aspect, criminal contempt has a private aspect, as the purpose of criminal contempt is not only to protect the image and smooth functioning of the courts, but also to ensure that the parties to the legal proceedings have a fair trial, free from interference. Thus criminal contempt may also have both public and private aspects, which acquire different emphasis in different circumstances.

Misbehaving in court

This offence is traditionally described as making noise or causing any disturbance that interrupts the courtroom proceedings.[5] The disturbance would obviously include singing, shouting, taking off one's clothes or throwing a book at the judge after he has "thrown the book at you." It could also apply to less overt action such as exaggerated coughing, making faces or even applauding.[6]

The offence may also be committed by actions that do not actually interfere in any way with the physical flow of proceedings, but which nevertheless detract from the dignity of the court, such as an accused refusing to stand as the judge enters the courtroom, a lawyer asking the judge to disqualify himself without giving reasons, or even smoking or wearing a hat in the courtroom contrary to a court order to refrain.[7]

There is obviously a danger in extending the concept of misbehaviour from physical disruption to more subtle forms of disrespect. The danger is enhanced by the fact that misbehaviour committed in the presence of the judge may be punished immediately by that very judge (subject, however, to a right of appeal from both the judge's decision and his sentence). Because the courts are aware of this danger, it is unlikely that any judge will proceed to punish someone for this form of contempt unless it is flagrant or continued, and unless the judge has first given warnings that he considers it contemptuous. Again, this is not of too much concern to us, because it would be rare for a public interest advocate to consider the tactic of disrupting courtroom proceedings.

Disobeying a court order

In addition to being a civil contempt, disobeying a court order can be a criminal contempt. It is a criminal contempt if the order is one made by a criminal court. In fact, disobeying a court's order in a criminal case is also an offence under sections 8 and 116 of the Criminal Code.

Obstructing justice

Obstructing justice has been described as ''those acts having the effect of interfering with the orderly administration of justice by corrupting, perverting or defeating its course.''[8] Even an unsuccessful attempt to do this could be contempt. Most forms of obstructing justice are dealt with in specific sections of the Criminal Code, which creates offences such as bribery of judicial officers, perjury and swearing false affidavits. A partial list of such offences can be found in the Law Reform Commission of Canada's *Working Paper on Contempt of Court*. Obviously, such offences would also be contempt. It is quite likely that there are similar offences not specifically referred to in the Criminal Code that could also be considered contempt because they have the effect of obstructing justice. This form of contempt is also of little interest to public interest groups. Obviously, anyone who attempts to bribe a judge or a witness deserves whatever he gets.

Because they straddle the thin line between legitimate comment and abuse of the judicial process, the offences of scandalizing the court and improper discussion of a matter that is *sub judice* are of greater interest.

Scandalizing the court

The Law Reform Commission describes this as any insulting, abusive or slanderous remark directed against the judge, as well as comments casting doubt upon his impartiality.[9] This applies to remarks made either inside or outside the courtroom. Borrie and Lowe, learned authors on contempt, break this offence down further into scurrilous abuse of a judge or jury and allegations of bias that impugn the neutrality either of a judge or of the judicial system as a whole.[10]

However, legitimate criticism of a judge's decision, or indeed of a judge in his personal capacity rather than in his judicial capacity, is not contempt. As one judge put it, ''Provided members of the public abstain from imputing improper motives to those taking part in the administration of justice, and are genuinely exercising a right of criticism, and not acting in malice or attempting to impair the administration of justice, they are immune."[11] Criticism may be vigorous, provided that it is made with reasonable courtesy, in good faith and without malice.[12]

As a public interest advocate, you will sometimes be asked by the press for your reaction when a judge's decision is handed down. You will not always have time to reflect upon what you want to say, and sometimes the press may even try to put words into your mouth. If you are happy with the decision, there is nothing wrong with saying so. If you are unhappy with the decision, as a rule of thumb, you should be safe if you criticize the judgment itself, rather than the judge. There is nothing wrong with saying you are "disappointed" or that you are considering appealing the decision or advising your client to appeal. Nor would it be improper to state what your arguments to the judge were, or give your reasons for thinking a different decision would have been in the public interest; for example, telling the press that a decision of the courts that the Canadian Bill of Rights does not prevent discrimination against Indian women will create great hardship. It appears that "reasoned argument or expostulation"[13] is not contempt. One eminent judge has suggested that it is even appropriate to say that judges are mistaken and their decisions are erroneous; all he would ask is "that those who criticize us will remember that, from the nature of our office, we cannot reply to their criticism."[14]

Scandalizing the court is a form of contempt in which certain forms of expression are clearly appropriate and others are not. To say that a certain decision will do great harm to large groups of people is appropriate. To say that the judge could not have reached that decision unless he was crazy or corrupt is clearly inappropriate. Between the two is a grey area.

You may be approached for comment at a time when your emotions are running high. Unless you are particularly upset and throw caution to the wind, or unless you know the reporter very well and are being much "freer" in your conversation with him than you would normally be with a member of the press, it should not be difficult to avoid the grey area that may get you into trouble.

If you initiated the proceedings, remember that you chose the forum, and must be prepared to live with the results of your choice of strategy. If you are a defendant or a lawyer for a defendant, you are not before the courts voluntarily; but if your group has chosen to initiate a prosecution or an application for judicial review, you presumably have considered this a better way to achieve your goal than the alternatives, such as political lobbying and community organizing. If you lose, your remedy is to appeal, not to carp.

The *sub judice* rule

This is the most difficult aspect of contempt for public interest advocates. It is the rule that restricts the right to report facts or express opinions on matters that are before the courts. It may also apply to some tribunals. The *sub judice* rule has given rise to more case law than any of the other branches of contempt. However, it is not clear to what extent it affects public interest litigants and their lawyers. Almost all of the litigation concerns newspapers and radio and television stations. Whether these restrictions also apply in the same way to public interest groups is a question that can and should be debated.

The Body Politic case, however, was indicative of a situation where civil rights advocates placed themselves in some jeopardy of being found in contempt.

In 1978, *The Body Politic*, a newspaper serving Canada's homosexual community, published an article entitled "Men Loving Boys Loving Men." It discussed sexual relations between men and boys. Unfortunately, the article appeared after a group of homosexual men had tortured and killed a 13-year-old boy in Toronto. The publishers were charged under the Criminal Code with using the mails to distribute "immoral, indecent or scurrilous" material, and the Toronto police seized the magazine's subscription records, its commercial lifeblood. Many viewed this charge and the seizure of the records as part of a pattern of harassment of homosexuals in the Toronto area by police.

In such a highly charged situation it was inevitable that the case would be the subject of public comment. During the trial, a public rally was organized to express moral support and help raise a legal defence fund for *The Body Politic*. Several prominent people spoke at the rally, including the then Mayor of Toronto, John Sewell. Mayor Sewell said nothing about the trial itself, the charges or their merits. But his expression of support for the rights of homosexuals, while condoned by many, raised suggestions of impropriety in other circles. There was widespread comment on the timing of his statement and concern about whether it could influence the outcome of the trial.

The court battle was lengthy and costly for the non-profit gay community newspaper, but in the end, Judge Sidney Harris acquitted the publishers, remarking that on the basis of the issues before him, *The*

Body Politic was a "serious journal of news and opinion." Supporters of freedom of the press and gay rights were pleased by the verdict.

Some weeks later, however, the Attorney General of Ontario decided to appeal the verdict. On February 6, 1980, an advertisement covering almost a full page appeared in Toronto's *Globe and Mail.* In the centre was a bold black headline: "We urge the Attorney General of Ontario to drop the appeal against *The Body Politic.*" In small type, the ad said:

> This decision to appeal is an attack on the freedom of a minority to express its views. It will drain the energy and financial resources of the gay community's principal newspaper and will further weaken that community's capacity to make its views known. Moreover, the effect of this appeal, whatever the intention, will be to punish people who have been found *not guilty* in the courts.
>
> We urge the Attorney General to drop the appeal and to restore the reputation of his department for the fair and equal treatment of minorities.

The ad included the names of approximately 800 individuals and organizations. It was paid for by the signatories and was placed by *The Body Politic* Free the Press Fund. At the bottom was an address to send donations to the fund, care of a Toronto law firm.

Mayor Sewell's statement was carefully scrutinized by a lawyer to ensure it was not in contempt of court, and so, undoubtedly, was the newspaper advertisement. Nevertheless, the activities of Mayor Sewell, the organizers of the public rally, the signatories of the advertisement and *The Body Politic* Free the Press Fund raise the question of what the public can and can't say during the course of a trial or public inquiry, and what statements or activities may leave them open to a citation for contempt of court.

THE *SUB JUDICE* RULE IN DETAIL:

What is a prejudicial statement?

In general, any statement that prejudices the course of civil or criminal proceedings is contempt. However, it is next to impossible to prove that any particular statement has actually prejudiced a judge or jury. Therefore, the cases speak of statements "calculated," "tending" or "likely" to prejudice the court. Even if it turns out that the court has not actually been prejudiced, a statement may be contemptuous if it imposed a real risk of prejudice.

A statement is at greater risk of being considered contemptuous if there is a jury, which may be impressionable, than if the case is being heard by a judge alone, who is presumed to be somewhat resistant to this kind of influence. Similarly, a statement is more likely to be prejudicial if it is made before or during a trial rather than after it. There is presumed to be more likelihood of prejudice before a trial than between the time of the trial decision and the outcome of an appeal. Moreover, the closer the timing of the statement to the actual trial, the more likely it is to be considered prejudicial.

Because of the greater stigma, potentially stiffer penalties, and because the accused is before the court involuntarily in criminal proceedings, statements made about criminal trials are likely to be scrutinized more carefully than those made about civil proceedings.

If there is a real risk of prejudice, a person may be cited for contempt even if he did not intend any prejudice, and, in fact, even if he did not know about the existence of the judicial proceedings. But if there is neither any real likelihood of prejudice nor any intention to create prejudice, statements will not be considered contemptuous.

What is the difference between reporting and commenting?
In determining what is likely to prejudice proceedings, you must make a distinction between reporting and commenting. Once proceedings are "imminent" or "pending" (the exact point at which a statement can be considered prejudicial is questionable) and while they are in progress, it is permissible to provide an accurate and balanced report of the proceedings, but you cannot publicly express opinions about them. There is no doubt that once a trial has actually started, the media may report what is actually said in the courtroom in a balanced and factual manner, unless the judge imposes a ban on publications, holds the hearing in camera, or is holding a hearing into the voluntariness of a confession or admission by a defendant. After proceedings are finished (again, the exact point when this occurs is unclear), it is permissible to comment.

There are several good reasons for suppressing comment during the course of proceedings and for ensuring that reporting is factual and balanced. The law of evidence carefully screens the facts to ensure that only evidence that is useful to prove guilt or innocence comes to the attention of the judge or jury. If the media were permitted to bring inadmissible evidence to their attention, this could undermine the judicial process. Moreover, any newspaper report that tells only one side of the story or prejudges the very issues the judge and jury are to determine also undermines the process.

What is the proper conduct for an individual in regard to contempt?

Although there are many cases discussing the proper conduct of the media, there are very few that consider what is appropriate behaviour of others. It is difficult to say whether the rule that both sides of the story must be told, and that no comments can be made during the course of the proceedings, applies only to the media, or also to parties to the proceedings, witnesses or prominent individuals who might be asked to comment. An examination of cases where this issue has arisen does provide some insights.

In one case, a police officer in the public relations bureau of the Montreal police force issued a press release about a case.[15] The release said that, following lengthy investigations by the bureau responsible for organized crime, charges had been laid against a person who had been seen with members of the Mafia many times, and that more charges would soon be laid. The court held that this was contempt. Even if the facts were true, the publication of them abused one of the parties to the action and could have prejudiced the public against him before the case was heard. The court held that the truth of the published facts is not a defence to contempt if the fact is likely to prejudice a party, to prejudge the case or to prevent justice being done.

The court did not criticize the fact that the police issued a press release stating that charges had been laid or setting out the contents of those charges. But because the release mentioned that more charges would be laid and made a connection between the accused and organized crime, it was contemptuous. "It would be difficult," the judge said, "to imagine a more flagrant example of an attempt to discredit a party in an action and to have a cause prejudged by public opinion."

The court added that in this case there was no need to resolve the conflict that often arises between the fundamental principles of freedom of the press and the right of citizens to be tried by an impartial court free of undue pressure. The police had a direct interest in prosecuting the accused and the tone of the release indicated "a desire to poison public opinion and convince the community that the accused was guilty." The court stated that the police have a more demanding duty towards the administration of justice than the average citizen, and therefore they must be more careful about what they say.

In another case, a lawyer who was representing a person accused of a criminal offence was cited for contempt as a result of a television interview he gave during the trial.[16] In the interview, he had merely repeated the contents of an argument he had made in court before the judge. The judge hearing the contempt charge stated that although he did not condone the lawyer's "thoughtless" interview, he did not consider it to amount to contempt. He added that the possible consequences of such an interview could in some circumstances include contempt of court. He also hinted strongly that, although the lawyer's conduct did not amount to contempt, it might violate the "traditions or the customs of the Bar, or any rule of the Law Society that might govern interviews between lawyers and the press." By this time, the lawyer himself was acknowledging that in retrospect his decision to be interviewed had been "inappropriate."

What about individuals and the media?

There are also several cases involving individuals who gave interviews to the media. In one case, the mother of a mentally retarded child who was charged with killing his teacher gave an interview to a radio station. The interview was part of a program commenting on the need for better facilities to treat disturbed children. In the interview, the boy's mother made numerous statements that indicated that he was guilty. Many of her statements would not have been admissible in court, according to the rules of evidence. The radio reporter took some care not to reveal the identity of the mother or child, but the case was so notorious that anyone who had read the newspapers would know who the boy was. The mother was not held in contempt, but the reporter and his employer were. The court said that if an experienced reporter conducts an interview with a well-meaning but unsophisticated person, the reporter and his employer must take responsibility not only for the reporter's statements, but also for any remarks made by the person responding to his questions.[17]

In other similar cases, neither the interviewer nor the person being interviewed was found guilty of contempt. In one such case, a person gave a speech that was reported by the press.[18] In another, a witness to a murder described to the press what she had seen and heard, and they reported it.[19] Also, a member of the Toronto municipal council gave two interviews to the media. In 1968, a group of hippies held a sit-in on Yorkville Avenue, centre of Toronto's "counter-culture." They wanted the city council to close the street to traffic and turn it into a pedestrian mall. Every night the street was one long traffic jam, as tourists and suburbanites drove through gawking at the colourful inhabitants of the area. In the first interview, the former Toronto mayor Alan Lamport said that he was going to "urge" the courts to impose a heavy penalty against the demonstrators, who had been charged with blocking traffic. In the second interview, he said he "hoped" a heavy penalty would be imposed.[20] In all these cases, the court found that there was no real likelihood of prejudice to the accused.

What is the liability of the speaker?

Do the same restrictions that apply to the media also apply to someone who talks to the press or makes a speech? There are too few such cases for any clear principles to emerge. If the term "publish" is used in the same sense that it is used in defamation actions (see chapter 10), that is, making any public statement to a third party, it is possible that the same rules would apply to both the person making the statement and the person reporting it. The case involving the Montreal police attributed this meaning to the word publication. The court said that even if the newspapers did not use this press release in writing their stories, it was "published" as soon as the information was delivered to persons by any means. Even so, this case does not suggest that the interviewer and the person who gives a speech that the newspaper reports would be treated exactly alike. In the Montreal police case, the judge imposed a more stringent duty on the police, who have a direct interest in the outcome of the case, than on the press. On the other hand, in the case involving the retarded boy and his mother, the court absolved the mother from all responsibility for any effect her statements might have on the fairness of the trial and imposed it on the reporter and the radio station. Thus, it would seem that in some cases the duty of the person making the statement may be greater than that of the media and in other cases it might be less.

Whether the person making the statement or the media reporting it are responsible for the contempt would vary with the circumstances in each case. The more sophisticated and experienced the speaker, and the more he is involved in the case and affected by its outcome, the more likely he is to have some responsibility for any contempt caused by the publication of his statement.

The liability of a speaker may depend to some extent on whether he is considered to be the "publisher." If publication is given the meaning it has in defamation cases, it would include almost any public utterance. On the other hand, if publication is given its more commonplace meaning, then the same rules should not necessarily apply to speakers as to reporters. To determine this will require a ruling from higher courts on whether the ruling of the judge on the meaning of "publication" in the Montreal police case is correct. Borrie and Lowe, who have written the most up-to-date book on contempt, refer to the *sub judice* rule as "contempt by publications," implying that only those involved with publishing the statements (i.e., the media) are subject to this rule. Another English text, in listing classes of individuals who are liable for this form of contempt, mentions newspaper reporters, editors and others associated with the production of publications, but *not* their sources.[21]

Yet the Law Reform Commission of Canada states that the purpose of the *sub judice* rule is to prevent publications or *public statements* that take a position on a current trial and thereby affect the climate of impartiality, or directly influence court officials or the public. The Law Reform Commission has described the offence as "attempting to influence the outcome of a trial." If this definition is accepted, then anyone who attempts to influence the outcome of a trial by making statements calculated to bias the judge or jury or intimidate witnesses would be subject to contempt proceedings regardless of whether the comments are published.

The extent to which the *sub judice* rule is restricted to the media or applies to anyone who makes a statement in someone else's presence is therefore still an open question.

There is a problem in deciding what you should say or not say between the time when you consider launching a legal action and the time when it comes to court. If the matter is one of broad public interest, it would seem sensible for you to have the right to issue a press release announcing your intention to issue a writ or announcing the actual issuance of the writ. It would also seem reasonable for you to respond to factual questions from reporters about the issues in the case and your reasons for bringing it.

Probably, if you do not cast any aspersions on the court itself or attempt to prejudge the issues or prejudice the outcome of the case, you are on safe ground to inform the press of the issues without expressing opinions about their merits. You should try to refrain from commenting on the very issues that the court is to decide, or otherwise attempt to "puff" the merits of your case or denigrate the merits of the opposite party's case.

Nevertheless, since the purpose of contempt is not only to protect the reality of justice but also the appearance of justice, and to protect the abstract image of courts in general as well as particular judges and litigants, there is always a danger of crossing the fine line between factual statements and opinion, or between fair comment and scurrilous criticism. The liability of public interest groups with respect to contempt is largely unexplored territory. If you are asked to give an interview about your own case or someone else's while it is being heard, it would be wise to get a legal opinion first.

CONCLUSION

The possibility of being cited for contempt is not generally a serious threat to public interest advocates. Nevertheless, as public interest groups and their lawyers continue to bring key issues into the courts, it is likely that their opponents will attempt more and more frequently to silence them. The best way to avoid contempt is to discuss public statements with your lawyer before you make them if there is any possibility that they could influence the outcome of a hearing or upset a judge.

6.
LEGAL TRAPS AND TACTICS: MAINTENANCE AND CHAMPERTY

WHAT ARE MAINTENANCE AND CHAMPERTY?

Few people could engage in any form of public interest advocacy, be it litigation, leafletting, organizing demonstrations or running for public office, without the help and support of other members of the community. It is normal and desirable for caring people to lend a hand to advance a worthy cause or alleviate injustice in our society. However, individuals and groups who promote or support public interest litigation run the risk of being sued by the party on the other side of the lawsuit. The risk of such a suit is very small and has not materialized; nevertheless, because maintenance and champerty suits are a potential harassment technique, you should know something about them.

Organizers of a "defence fund," lawyers and expert witnesses who donate their services, and individuals and groups who donate money to defray legal costs should be aware of the torts of maintenance and champerty. Maintenance is the promotion or support of contentious legal proceedings by a "stranger" — a person who has no direct interest in the suit. Usually this "officious intermeddling" consists of providing financial assistance to one of the parties to a lawsuit, but it may also involve providing services.[1] It is possible that actively encouraging a party to continue legal proceedings that have little merit, or providing moral support because of malice towards the defendant, might also be considered maintenance.

Champerty is an aggravated form of maintenance, in which the meddler's reason for supporting the lawsuit is that he has an agreement with one of the parties that he will get a share of the proceeds of the lawsuit or other profits that might be gained as a result of the suit.

Like contempt, malicious prosecution and abuse of process, maintenance is a form of abuse of legal procedures. It was formerly a crime as well as a civil wrong, but the prohibition against maintenance in Canada's Criminal Code was repealed long ago. We are concerned now only with the possibility that the opposite party in a lawsuit may launch a suit for damages against those who helped an individual or public interest group take legal action. Examples of maintenance include a director of a company that had retained an expert to prepare a report about appliances sold by the company providing the expert with money to sue a newspaper for libel after it had criticized the report,[2] and a trade union bringing a libel action in one of its member's names against someone who had allegedly defamed the member.[3]

The tort of maintenance has a valid basis in historical conditions. Maintenance "stems from a time when officious interference in litigation was a widespread evil, practised by powerful royal officials and nobles to oppress their vulnerable neighbours."[4] Like the law of contempt, the rule against supporting civil litigation is based on a desire to be fair to the parties in lawsuits, whose cases should be decided on their merits. The outcome should not be affected by such extraneous considerations as the malice of some third party.

Although it made sense in older times, the rule of maintenance may be an anachronism today. According to Fleming, a leading authority on the law of torts, "its survival in modern law, though in greatly attenuated form, must be attributed to a persistent, if perhaps exaggerated, fear that it is still needed as a safeguard against blackmail and speculation in lawsuits prone to increase litigation."[5]

Unfortunately, however, the survival of the maintenance action may also stem from a very narrow view of the role of the courts. Traditionally, judges have acted as if lawsuits involve only private interests and their outcome is of concern only to the parties. Courts and other public institutions have often been excessively concerned with private property and financial interests, to the detriment of broader social issues. While many lawsuits may be of interest merely to the parties, it is no longer true, if it ever was, that private lawsuits only raise issues of importance to their parties. Private lawsuits may raise issues of great interest and importance to the general public.

Maintenance actions are rare today and there may be little justification for the continued existence of the tort. One possible justification is that maintenance may yet find a new use in deterring powerful interests from promoting "harassment suits" against public interest advocates. For example, a trade association, in an attempt to silence a critic of harmful or dangerous practices by its members, might financially support a frivolous libel suit launched by one of its members against the critic. In such cases, it might be reassuring to know that a maintenance suit against the trade association is available to the critic.

Of greater concern, however, is the possibility that wealthy defendants in public interest suits may use maintenance to sue storefront legal clinics, public interest groups, lawyers or others who support public interest plaintiffs. Maintenance could be used to harass and intimidate such groups.

ON WHAT GROUNDS CAN A MAINTENANCE SUIT BE LAUNCHED?

The following information will help you to determine whether you are open to a maintenance suit as a result of assisting in public interest litigation.

1. A person being prosecuted for a criminal or quasi-criminal offence cannot sue in maintenance.[6] Thus, the private prosecutor and those who assist him need not fear this action. If a defendant feels he is being persecuted, his proper remedy is a suit for malicious prosecution, which is very difficult to prove. Malicious prosecution is a tort that allows an accused who has been acquitted of a criminal charge to sue the person who laid the charges for damage to his reputation caused by the unfounded nature of the criminal charges. Recognizing the value of private law enforcement, the common law requires the defendant to prove two essential elements before the tort of malicious prosecution is established:

    (a)   The informant must be found *not* to have had "reasonable and probable" grounds for laying the charge;

    (b)   in addition, the informant must have acted with malice.

2. There is authority that the law of maintenance is confined to cases where a person improperly and for the purpose of stirring up litigation, encourages others to *bring* actions or to put forward defences that they have no right to make. Some courts have said that if an action has already been commenced before the assistance

is given, there is no "stirring up" of litigation. Thus, the timing of the assistance may be relevant.[7]

3.   In maintenance cases, the conduct of the person giving the assistance has usually been central, if not essential, to the existence of the litigation. Therefore the question is whether the litigation would have occurred without this assistance. If so, it is probable that a suit for maintenance cannot be brought against the assistor.

4.   The person bringing a maintenance action cannot succeed without proof of actual loss.[8] Thus, unless the person suing for maintenance can actually show that he lost the original case and was put to additional expense or suffered some other loss as a result of the third party's involvement, his action will be unsuccessful. Of course, if his true purpose in bringing the maintenance action is to harass someone, and he is willing to pay the costs when he loses, winning won't matter to him.

5.   Maintenance must be brought as a separate legal action and cannot be pleaded as a defence to an action.[9] If a defendant inserts an allegation of maintenance into his pleadings, it can be struck out as frivolous and vexatious.

6.   The question of who initiates the helping relationship may be an important consideration.[10] If a person involved in legal proceedings approaches a potential benefactor and requests assistance, the benefactor seems less likely to be subject to a successful maintenance suit than if he had offered unsolicited assistance. By the same token, the benefactor will be in a better position to resist a maintenance suit if the idea of suing came from the plaintiff than if he suggested it to the plaintiff.

7.   Most importantly, the motives of the person supporting litigation are an important consideration in determining whether he is acting properly. Both selfish and unselfish motives may justify support of litigation. Selfish motives are usually justified in terms of protecting one's own "interest." Unselfish motives are described as "charity." A special relationship with the person being supported also justifies help. Whether this special relationship is an additional justification or evidence of the benefactor's charitable motives or legitimate interest is far from clear.

The law states that if a person has a sufficient interest in the subject matter of the proceedings, his support of a party is justified or "privileged." Like suits for inducing breach of contracts (see chapter 9), a property or financial interest in the matter is sufficient justification for involvement. The interest may be indirect. For example, a trade union may support an employee's claim for lost wages,[11] or a trade association might properly support a manufacturer.[12] The person assisted doesn't appear to have to be in danger of personally losing money or property as a direct result of losing the case in order to justify the assistance.

Charitable motives may also justify intervention. In the case of inducing breach of contract and conspiracy, discussed in chapter 9, you will see that although selfish motives clearly provide a justification for interference with someone's business, it is uncertain whether altruistic motives would be given the same weight. In the case of maintenance, however, it is clear that someone who assists a pauper or a person who could not otherwise afford to assert his rights in court is doing nothing wrong, provided that his motives are sincere.[13]

This still leaves several questions unanswered. There might be mixed motives — both a desire to advance the public interest and a desire to hurt the defendant. What then? Like inducement to breach a contract, perhaps the liability of the person providing help will depend upon which of the plaintiff's motives the court considered to be paramount.

Another problem with justifying support of litigation on the grounds of "charity" is that charity has several different meanings. To some it only means helping the poor. To others, "charity" means any act of kindness or altruism. In some legal contexts, it has a very specific meaning restricted to such things as religious activities, providing educational facilities and helping the poor.

Is the justification for assisting someone with litigation on the grounds of "charity" restricted to the traditional charitable objects of the relief of poverty, educational purposes and religion? On the basis of the cases decided to date, the answer is that it may be even narrower. "Charity" may be restricted to the relief of poverty. Probably the most that can be said is that, as Fleming puts it, the category of exceptions to maintenance is not closed.[14]

WHAT ABOUT THE LIABILITY OF THE LAWYER?

A public interest lawyer who provides free legal services to an individual or group is on fairly safe ground. Not only are his motives usually unimpeachable, but various legal codes of ethics support the right, and even the duty, of a lawyer to assist the poor and to take on unpopular clients or causes, or cases that raise novel and difficult legal issues.

A lawyer may provide free legal advice. Or, in appropriate cases, he may agree to reduce or waive his fee if the client loses his case, but charge the full fee if the client wins. The Canadian Bar Association Code of Professional Conduct, which has been adopted in whole or in part by several provincial Law Societies, says that it is in keeping with the best traditions of the legal profession to reduce or waive a fee in a situation where there is poverty or hardship, or the client or prospective client would otherwise effectively be deprived of legal advice or representation. Orkin, a writer on legal ethics, states that "it has always been proper for a solicitor to advance money for disbursements out of his own pocket or take a case without remuneration out of friendship or charity."[15]

This is very different, however, from arranging with a client to take payment in the form of a share or percentage of the proceeds of the action. This so-called "contingency" fee is popular in the United States. However, in Canada it is champertous, except in provinces where it is permitted by legislation, subject to stringent rules to prevent abuse.

These special considerations to mitigate against the possibility of a solicitor being sued for maintenance are all the more reason for the lawyer to be careful to separate his function as a legal advisor and his role as a participant in public interest activities. If the lawyer's activities can be seen as those of a client or meddler, rather than of a solicitor advising a client, he may lose this protection.

For example, what is the proper characterization of organizing a defence fund? Is this a legitimate legal service to provide on behalf of an indigent client, friend or worthy cause — or is it an unjustified interference in someone else's action? Does the answer depend on whether the lawyer has been retained by one of the parties to the suit and is authorized by this "client" to provide this fund-raising service? If the lawyer is also before the court representing this party, is his position affected by whether his fee will be paid out of the money raised by the defence fund? The answers to such questions may depend on the circumstances of each case.

WHAT IS THE LIABILITY OF THE LEGAL CLINIC OR PUBLIC INTEREST GROUP?

What if the lawyer representing a public interest litigant is a salaried employee of a public interest group or legal clinic that raises the money to cover disbursements in the suit, while the lawyer provides his services free of charge? It is an open question whether the organizations that employ ''poverty law'' and other ''public interest'' lawyers, such as civil liberties associations, native organizations, law school student legal services clinics and legal information, advice and assistance centres, could invoke the lawyer's obligation to provide access to the law in defence of a maintenance action against them for making the lawyer's services available, just as it is questionable whether they are bound by the lawyer's ethics. In many ways, these clinics are to the public interest lawyer what the law firm is to the private lawyer — the structure and framework in which he practises. Yet, while statutes, rules and codes of ethics define the relationship between the private law firm and each of the lawyers in it, they often fail to consider the relationship between the publicly funded ''clinic'' and its staff of lawyers and community legal workers.

SOME TROUBLING ASPECTS OF MAINTENANCE

There are two troubling aspects of maintenance. One is that it is unclear whether the justification for helping with a lawsuit is restricted to cases that fit into one of several common ''pigeonholes,'' or whether it will be judged in the context of the individual case. In cases where the courts have found that an agreement was not maintenance, legal scholars usually explain this finding on the basis that the conduct was justified by ''kinship,'' ''common interest'' or ''charity.'' For example, if a person out of concern and affection assists his brother in litigation, the commentators would be inclined to explain why this is not maintenance by placing his relationship in the ''kinship'' category rather than by considering his motivation.

This isn't necessarily the most logical way to justify the assistance or to explain the results of cases. Using this approach, a suitor who assists his fiancee would be guilty of a tort, while a brother assisting his sister for the same reason would not. What should matter in such a case is the person's motivation, not his or her bloodline. This distinction is important in public interest cases, since the good samaritan will have a greater chance of defeating a maintenance action if the law considers the purity of his motives or the public importance of the issues in the case. If he can only justify his beneficence by fitting himself into a particular pigeonhole of common interest or kinship such as ''brother,'' ''father,'' ''trade union,'' ''trade association'' or ''lawyer,'' he has less chance of success.

The second troublesome aspect is that, while some descriptions of the law merely state that stirring up litigation in which one has no interest is maintenance, others add that it is wrong to encourage people to enforce rights that they may not otherwise be disposed to enforce. The latter description, if it is accurate, is cause for concern by all public interest groups involved in litigation and their supporters. In public interest cases, the harm to the plaintiff is often not great enough to justify his bearing the financial burden of the case alone. It is a simple fact that most public interest lawsuits would not be taken without the support and encouragement of public interest groups, legal aid clinics, public interest lawyers and the like. The most important aspect of a public interest case is either the social issues it raises or clarification of the law — not the plaintiff's private interests.

CONCLUSION

Although the non-lawyer who gives financial support to public interest litigation does not have the lawyer's code of conduct to fall back on, so far there seems to be little evidence that maintenance suits are a serious threat to the good samaritan. The behaviour that has led to maintenance suits has usually involved assistance that is essential to the litigation. Frequently it is a business arrangement. It is doubtful that many donors to a defence fund, volunteer organizers of a fund-raising event, or others who support litigation because they feel it involves some issue of great public importance, would be playing the kind of role that would make them subject to a maintenance suit. Nevertheless, whenever possible you should structure your involvement in such a way as not to lead anyone into the temptation of using maintenance or champerty as harassment techniques.

7.
SEEKING AN ADJOURNMENT

Obtaining an adjournment (postponement of a case) can sometimes be crucial to mounting an effective case. Adequate notice is seldom a problem in the courts, but when someone applies to a regulatory board for a licence or permission to undertake some activity, you might not have much warning. You might not have enough time to prepare your case, get legal aid funding or raise other funds to cover the cost of witnesses and lawyers.

Under these circumstances, you may have no choice but to ask for an adjournment. Yet by asking for an adjournment, you might inconvenience the board and the other parties and appear to be deliberately delaying and disrupting the proceeding. Unless you approach the question of an adjournment very carefully, you may make a serious error in judgment.

WHY SEEK ADJOURNMENTS?

When you bring important issues before courts and tribunals on your own initiative, you have a great deal of freedom to choose the timing of making an application, laying a charge or issuing a writ. Subject to limitation periods that range generally from six months to six years, you can prepare your case to your satisfaction before starting the court or hearing process rolling.

However, many examples of public interest advocacy occur in the context of an individual or community group reacting to the initiatives of government agencies or private businesses. For example, a government agency may decide to extend a noisy highway through one's neighbourhood. The government may decide to cut off someone's unemployment insurance benefits or deny an injured worker compensation. A developer may apply for a licence to operate a polluting factory or for approval to build a housing subdivision on prime agricultural land.

In these situations, you are often entitled to appeal the decision to a tribunal or request a hearing before a board. But in such circumstances, you are reacting to someone else's initiative: that of the government agency that made the adverse ruling or the person who applied for the licence or permit. There is usually a limited time in which to launch an appeal from a government decision — for example, you have thirty days to appeal a decision of the federal government to refuse you unemployment insurance benefits. If the law or government policy allows objectors to have an opportunity for a hearing before a licence or permit is issued, the board that holds such hearings may set a date for the hearing as soon as it receives the application, without consulting the objectors. This often means that, to protect your private interests or to further the public interest, you are required to meet the case against you or to argue against the case for issuing the licence on very short notice. Organizing the community, raising money, obtaining information and hiring a lawyer between the time when you first learn about the opportunity for an appeal or a hearing and the date on which it is scheduled can be a difficult or impossible task.

The amount of notice that boards, government departments or applicants are required to give varies greatly. Sometimes a minimum notice period is required by law and other times it is a matter of policy. Frequently, the notice is relatively short. It may be adequate for a simple situation, but completely inadequate for a complex case. As a result, individuals and groups often do not have time to prepare their case properly, collect evidence and marshall witnesses. If a public interest group is not well organized or adequately funded, it may have to hire a lawyer at virtually the last minute. Occasionally, the group does not even have time to hire and properly brief counsel.

Consequently, individuals or groups may come before the board on the appointed date for the hearing requesting an adjournment: a postponement of the proceedings until a later date. The reason may be that the person needs more time to hire a lawyer. Or the group's newly hired lawyer may ask the board for an adjournment because he has not had adequate time to prepare his case. If the board's rules or procedures do not provide a right to information about the opposite party's case, it may be necessary during the course of proceedings to ask for further adjournments to obtain evidence to rebut evidence or respond to issues that could not be anticipated.

HOW DO COURTS AND BOARDS RESPOND TO REQUESTS FOR ADJOURNMENTS?

Boards are often reluctant to grant adjournments. Adjournments inconvenience the board and the other parties, particularly if the board members and many of the lawyers have had to travel long distances to be present at the hearing and if the request is made at the last minute. Therefore, requests for adjournment should be avoided wherever possible. Even if the need for the adjournment results from matters beyond the control of the party requesting it and the board realizes that it must grant the adjournment to be fair, board members may unconsciously blame the party seeking the adjournment for the inconvenience this causes.

Furthermore, if the community group appears to be continually seeking adjournments, its members may create the impression that they do not wish to deal with the case on its merits, but rather intend to delay and disrupt the proceedings in the hope of delaying the development. This perception can damage the credibility of the group and its counsel in the eyes of board members.

The problem, of course, is not usually caused by any intention to obstruct, but by lack of funding, lack of information and inadequate notice. Boards are accustomed to giving the same amount of notice in every case, even though some cases are extremely complex and require a long time to analyze technical issues, while others are simple. In reality, it is often the inflexibility of the system that creates the need for adjournment; but because public interest advocates so frequently find themselves being forced to ask for an adjournment, the situation creates the impression that they are always seeking delay, and brings community groups into disrepute.

One example of the acrimony this can lead to was featured in Toronto newspapers early in 1980 when the Canadian Transport Commission decided to hold public hearings before approving plans by Canadian Pacific to build a railway track through a residential area of Etobicoke. The residents feared that the track would increase rail traffic, noise and the chances of a major accident. On the first day of the hearings, the secretary of the local ratepayers' and residents' association told the tribunal that his group wanted an adjournment so that it could examine important facts that it believed were missing from the application by CP. The secretary also said his group was not given enough time to prepare its case and needed at least two months to raise enough money to hire a lawyer.

The chairman of the hearing denied the request. The outraged spokesman for the residents told the press, "They kicked us when we were down. I never dreamed that they would do this. After all, they wouldn't have had a hearing at all if we hadn't made a fuss." He called the hearing "a miscarriage of justice that verges on the grotesque."

When these statements were read into the record, the residents' spokesman refused to retract the comments and told the chairman to his face that the hearing was a miscarriage of justice. "Never in my eleven years," said the chairman, "have I heard a remark like that. Go to the Federal Court of Canada if you don't like my conduct in the hearing."

The ratepayers went without an official spokesman for most of the hearing, while CP had a staff of twelve, including a lawyer and a battery of technical experts to defend its application.

It is far better to ask for an adjournment than to present a poorly prepared case. However, if at all possible, you should avoid seeking an adjournment. A request for an adjournment should be made only after every reasonable effort has been made to eliminate the need for the adjournment.

HOW SHOULD AN ADJOURNMENT BE REQUESTED?

If you cannot avoid asking for an adjournment, you should make your request as early as possible and you should never wait until the day of the hearing to make your request known to the board and the other parties.[1] If possible, you should seek the adjournment with the consent of the other parties.[2] If all parties agree to an adjournment well before the hearing date, and the board is informed of this, it is likely to grant the adjournment and reschedule the hearing for a later date. If the parties do not agree to an adjournment, check with the board to find out the procedure for requesting one, notifying the parties officially of your request and arguing for the adjournment. Often, the board will arrange a hearing at which you can argue for the adjournment, other parties can argue against it, and the board can make a ruling well in advance of the date scheduled for the hearings.

There are two important reasons for making your request well in advance and informing the board and the other parties of your needs. The first, obviously, is courtesy. The second is that this will strengthen your case should it be necessary to challenge a board's refusal to grant an adjournment in the courts.

WHAT HAPPENS IF THE REQUEST FOR AN ADJOURNMENT IS DENIED?

If your request for an adjournment is denied, you have three choices. You can proceed and do your best under the circumstances; you can withdraw from the hearings; or you can challenge the decision to refuse an adjournment in the courts.

If it is possible to proceed without greatly prejudicing your case, this may be desirable. If it is impossible, it may be preferable to withdraw or to challenge the board's decision. However, if you withdraw from the hearings, this may preclude a later challenge of the board's procedures in the courts.[3] If you intend to ask the court to challenge any aspect of a board's hearings, it may be better to continue as a participant in the hearings pending the hearing by the court.

If you decide to ask a court to order the board to grant the adjournment, you may be successful in certain narrow circumstances. In general, boards have the right to control their proceedings to ensure that they flow smoothly.[4] No party has an absolute right to an adjournment. The board can refuse any request for an adjournment as long as the refusal does not violate the rules of "natural justice" or any of the statutory provisions and rules of procedure that govern its conduct.

When a board is required to hold a hearing, depending upon the nature of its functions, it must conduct the hearing either in accordance with the rules of natural justice or with the requirement that it act fairly.

The rules of natural justice include the *"audi alteram partem"* rule ("hear the other side"). This simply means that the board has a duty to give each party a reasonable opportunity to present its case.[5] In some cases, a refusal to grant an adjournment has been interpreted as a breach of this duty. Whether a refusal to grant an adjournment is a breach of the rules of natural justice depends upon the particular circumstances of each case.[6] Other rules of natural justice include the requirement that a board not be biased in favour of one of the parties, and that it not act capriciously, wantonly or arbitrarily.[7] A board cannot be accused of arbitrary action in refusing an adjournment if it weighed the need for an adjournment against the rights of other parties to an expeditious decision.[8]

Where a board is not required to hold a hearing, but does so anyway, it may not be required to follow the rules of natural justice, but it may have a duty to act "fairly." The requirements of fairness vary from board to board depending on the nature of its functions and the circumstances of each case. The fairness requirements are less stringent than the requirements of natural justice, and it is impossible to say exactly what fairness requires, because the courts have interpreted it differently in the last year or two from the way they treated it in the past, but in some circumstances the requirement of fairness will probably encompass a right to an adjournment.

When a request for an adjournment is based solely on the convenience of his lawyer, the party who is denied an adjournment cannot successfully argue that the board's refusal is a denial of justice. On the other hand, the board may not base a denial merely upon its own convenience.[9]

CAN A DENIAL BE SUCCESSFULLY CHALLENGED?

A challenge of a board's refusal to grant an adjournment is most likely to succeed if the request for the adjournment was based on factors beyond your control. For example, you may successfully argue that an adjournment was justified under the rules of natural justice if you had not received important information and had made prompt and reasonable attempts to obtain the information. Similarly, if an important witness is not in attendance and you have taken prior steps to secure his attendance, a refusal to grant an adjournment may be a denial of natural justice. For this reason, it is important to place all witnesses, even cooperative, reliable ones, under subpoena, if the board has the power to issue subpoenas. This way, you can show the board (and if necessary the court) that you made reasonable attempts to ensure that the witness would be there.

If the court agrees that you were not given sufficient prior notice of hearings and consequently did not have a reasonable period of time to prepare, it may order an adjournment. What constitutes "sufficient notice" will vary from case to case. To a large extent this will depend upon the complexity of the issues before the board.

Finally, the necessity and reasons for an adjournment must be made very clear to the board. When arguing for an adjournment before the board, keep in mind that these arguments, any arguments made against your request for an adjournment by other parties and the board's comments and ruling may be the only material a court gets an opportunity to review. Once you go to court, it may be too late to change or amplify your reasons for requesting an adjournment. A court will not respond favourably to a party that has asked a board for an adjournment for one reason but argues before the court that the adjournment should have been granted for other reasons that were not presented to the board.

As a matter of strategy, in making your arguments before the board and the courts, you might compare the amount of notice you were given with the length of time the proponent had to prepare his case. Although there is no legal authority to support the proposition that this is grounds for a court to overturn a refusal by a board to grant an adjournment, it may help persuade a court or board that your request is reasonable. Try to find out before the hearing how long the applicant took to prepare his application, the length of time between the date when the applicant first submitted an application for a licence and the date on which the applicant or the government formally requested a public hearing, and how long the government agency or agencies involved took to review the matter at hand.

CONCLUSION

The courts have been extremely reluctant to find that a board acted improperly by refusing to grant an adjournment. On the rare occasions when the courts have found impropriety, this has been based on a denial of natural justice; particularly the aspect of natural justice that requires a board to hear *both* sides of a case.

If you hope to persuade a court that you have been denied natural justice, you must demonstrate that you have acted reasonably in seeking the adjournment. Generally, you should avoid asking for an adjournment if at all possible. If an adjournment is essential, you must make the request promptly and on the basis of factors beyond your control. If you are denied an adjournment, acting reasonably may entail continuing to participate in the hearings, since the board would be free to continue with the hearing and render a decision in your absence if you were to withdraw. If you think you may have a reasonable chance of success before the board without an adjournment or success in having the court order the board to grant an adjournment, it is advisable not to withdraw.

Remember that success before boards and tribunals is often a matter of degree. You may not get all the benefits or compensation you feel you are entitled to, but you may be awarded a portion of them. You may not succeed in having an application refused, but you may succeed in having stringent conditions attached to the licence. Withdrawal may be the best strategy only in unusual circumstances: for example, where you feel that you would be hopelessly prejudiced by your lack of resources, or reforming the process of the board by bringing its unfairness to the attention of the public is more important than success on the specific application. If it is more important to successfully challenge a refusal to grant an adjournment than to embarrass the board by withdrawing, it is necessary to show the court that you have acted in a responsible and credible manner.

Part III:
Keeping Out of Court and Out of Trouble

8.

DEMONSTRATIONS, PROTEST AND THE LAW

The 1960s and 1970s were periods of social revolution, marked by protest marches and demonstrations sometimes involving millions of people. Public interest groups took to the streets to publicize and advocate their cause. People protested in favour of civil rights for black people, women, gay people, and against such things as nuclear weapons tests, nuclear power plants, the Vietnam War and the mass slaughter of whales and baby seals.

Arrests or charges during demonstrations can be the result of police harassment, ignorance of the law or a deliberate decision to engage in civil disobedience. It is important to be able to judge whether you are being harassed by the police or legitimately charged because you are impeding traffic. Chapter 8 deals with some of the legal, ethical and practical problems that can surface at demonstrations.

Demonstrations and picket lines are prime examples of advocacy techniques that can land you in court. Such situations are highly charged, things can happen very fast, and it is easy to break the law or to be wrongly accused of breaking the law. People are often ignorant of the law until it's too late. You may not think about being arrested or charged with an offence because you are organizing or participating in a protest. If you do think about it in advance, there are many steps that can be taken to avoid problems.

WHAT RIGHTS DOES A DEMONSTRATOR HAVE?

A peaceful demonstration, rally or picket line is a perfectly legal method of making a point, as long as it stays within the law. The rights to demonstrate and picket arise from fundamental civil liberties: freedom of speech and freedom of assembly. Written information can be displayed on signs or placards, or handed out in the form of pamphlets, on the basis of a right closely related to freedom of speech: freedom of the press.

Theorists disagree about whether these so-called "fundamental" rights are universal, absolute and immutable or subject to qualification. But for practical purposes, these rights or liberties must be treated as qualified rights. The Supreme Court of Canada has put it this way:

> It is to be remembered that the human rights and fundamental freedoms [are] the rights and freedoms of men living together in organized society subject to a rational, developed and civilized system of law which imposed certain limitations on the absolute liberty of the individual.[1]

Thus, every person is free to say or do anything the laws do not forbid. He may associate with anyone with whom the laws do not forbid him to associate. Groups may assemble for any purpose, and at any time or place not prohibited by law. Since the limits of free speech, freedom of the press and freedom of assembly are largely determined by what is forbidden, the only practical way of describing their scope and limitations is to outline what a person may *not* do or say and assume that everything else is permitted.

The laws that limit what can be done or said during a demonstration will be briefly described below. First let me describe some of the practical limitations of demonstrations that lead to the danger of a legal demonstration becoming in part illegal or becoming an opportunity for the arrest of innocent people, even though they have not broken any laws. Frequently, neither the organizers nor the participants have much control over who might attend and attempt to manipulate the demonstration. Although most demonstrations remain peaceful and orderly and there is frequently good cooperation between demonstrators and the authorities, some demonstrations have led to protesters being injured and even being killed by police. Others have led to mass arrests. And lawyers attending demonstrations to advise their clients have not been immune from arrest.

LAWYERS AND DEMONSTRATIONS

Demonstrations can lead to violence. Counter-demonstrators, radical fringe groups or individuals, the person or corporation whose activities are being protested or whose property is being picketed, police or other authorities and the demonstration organizers themselves may deliberately or innocently cause trouble.

A demonstration is, by its very nature, a potentially explosive situation. It consists of a large gathering of people who are deeply committed to an issue or a point of view. There is often a program of speeches designed to intensify their conviction. Since the demonstration's purpose is to bring attention to the issue, the media, invited or uninvited, often attend. The demonstration occurs in a public place where anyone can intrude and sometimes in a confined, crowded area. The police attend to keep the peace, in the expectation of trouble, and the "other side," the object of the unhappiness of the demonstrators, may often be nearby.

The situation is particularly perilous for the public interest lawyer, who faces the double jeopardy of criminal conviction and discipline or disbarment. If he endeavours to assist his client at the demonstration, he risks circumstances that could place him in a position of breaking the law or of being arrested and possibly convicted of an offence he did not commit. Although most police in most Canadian cities are fair-minded, even-tempered people trying to do their job, some panic in situations like demonstrations. Others dislike demonstrators and particularly resent the presence of lawyers at demonstrations.

In 1970, Clayton Ruby, a Toronto lawyer, was arrested at a demonstration and charged with obstructing police. A well-known civil liberties lawyer whose clients often espoused unpopular causes, he was an obvious target for police resentment. While representing clients at an anti-Vietnam War demonstration, Mr. Ruby was trapped by a throng of demonstrators fleeing mounted police. According to Mr. Ruby, he was assaulted by a police officer who had removed his identification badge. When Mr. Ruby demanded to know the officer's badge number, the officer arrested him. Of course, the police officer had a different version of events. Fortunately, there were witnesses to the incident. At the trial a Provincial Court judge accepted the lawyer's version of events and that of his witnesses over the version of the arresting officer, and acquitted him on the basis of credibility.

In 1977, a lawyer representing members of the Greenpeace Foundation accompanied his clients to the ice floes of Newfoundland, where the Greenpeacers were protesting the seal hunt. Although he was there merely as a legal advisor, when one of his clients seized a seal pup to "save" it from the hunters, the lawyer was charged along with his client for "interfering with the seal fishery" contrary to regulations under the Fisheries Act.

He too was acquitted. At his lawyer's request, Judge G. W. Seabright wrote a letter setting out his reasons for acquittal:

I found the involvement of Mr. Ballem was one of solicitor and client relationship. Mr. Ballem at no time contravened the laws of the country. As I observed, one may look with envy upon the vigour with which Mr. Ballem fought to protect the rights of his client [the Greenpeace Organization] and his endeavours to obtain permits, so that he might accompany his clients to the ice.

The Crown contends because of the foregoing, that the actions of Mr. Ballem should be considered under section 21(2) of the Criminal Code. I disagree with this argument and dismiss all charges against him.

I should also like to comment on his willingness to attend court, and as well his conduct in court which I found to be impeccable.

The only sin committed by Mr. Ballem, if one wishes to use that term, is that the vigour with which he protected his clients' rights can be the envy of the practising bar, and rather than to bring any disgrace on himself should certainly in my opinion bring honour.[2]

The case of the solicitor, Peter Ballem, is merely the tip of the iceberg. The legal problems that protest attracts are not limited to violence or to mass marches. The strategies used by the Federal Government against Greenpeace illustrate the difficulty in staging a lawful protest if the government or some other powerful interest group decides to impede a group's efforts. Even if the protest only involves a few people, authorities can make it difficult or impossible for them to stay within the law.

WHAT DOES THE LAW SAY ABOUT THE RIGHT TO DEMONSTRATE?

The right to demonstrate is based upon freedom of speech, freedom of the press and freedom of assembly. The limitations on these freedoms are both criminal and civil. The limitations on freedom of speech and the press are a hodgepodge that defies categorization. But in general they prohibit statements that untruthfully harm the reputation of a person or group, and prohibit encouragement of criminal activity and encouragement of violence against individuals or the state.

Freedom of assembly is concerned more with the choice of time and place and the physical activity of groups than with what they say. Limitations on freedom of assembly generally involve laws against interference with the movement of pedestrians or traffic and interference with public or private property.

Freedom of speech

One of the most eloquent descriptions of the nature of freedom of speech was made by Lord Coleridge in 1909. It is equally valid today.

> A man may lawfully express his opinions on any matter, however distasteful, however repugnant to others, if, of course, he avoids defamatory matter, or if he avoids anything that can be characterized as blasphemous or as an obscene libel. Matters of state, matters of policy, matters even of morals — all these are open to him. He may state his opinion freely, he may buttress it by argument, he may try to persuade others to share his views. Courts and juries are not the judges in such matters. For instance, if he thinks that either a despotism, or an oligarchy, or even no government at all, is the best way of conducting human affairs, he is at perfect liberty to say so. He may assail politicians, he may attack governments, he may warn the executive of the day against taking a particular course; he may seek to show rebellions, insurrections, outrages, assassinations and such-like are the natural, the deplorable and the inevitable outcome of the policy which he is combatting. All that is allowed, because all that is innocuous; *but, on the other hand, if he makes use of language calculated to advocate or to incite others to public disorders, to wit, rebellions, insurrections, assassinations, outrages, or any physical force or violence of any kind, then, whatever his motives, whatever his intentions, there would be evidence on which a jury might, on which I should think a jury ought, and on which a jury would decide that he was guilty of a seditious publication. . . .*[3]

More specifically, freedom of speech during demonstrations is subject to the restrictions set out below. Disturbing the peace, mischief and obstructing police are charges that frequently arise out of demonstrations and picket lines. Other charges such as threatening and intimidation are much rarer.

● *Disturbing the peace. (Sections 171 and 172 of the Criminal Code.)* Disorderly conduct in a public place, such as "fighting, screaming, shouting, swearing, singing, or using insulting or obscene language," or disturbing the peace and quiet of occupants of a dwelling (other than one's own home) is illegal. So is disturbing a religious service or a group gathered for some "moral, social, or benevolent purpose."

● *Obstructing Police. (Section 118 of the Criminal Code.)* This section provides, in part, that:

Everyone who

(a)   resists or wilfully obstructs a public officer or peace officer in the execution of his duty or any person who is lawfully acting in aid of such an officer

(b)   omits, without reasonable excuse, to assist a public officer or peace officer in the execution of his duty in arresting a person or in preserving the peace, after having reasonable notice that he is required to do so . . .

is guilty of . . .

(c)   an indictable offence and is liable to imprisonment for two years, or

(d)   an offence punishable on summary conviction.

Although, under this section, a variety of public officials (for example, gamewardens) may be "public officers" or "peace officers," the official most likely to be encountered during a demonstration or protest is the police officer. Clayton Ruby, a prominent criminal lawyer, discusses this in an article on "Obstructing a Police Officer." Ruby says it is unfortunate that our civil liberties are so often determined in the context of obstructing police and other similar charges, because "a judicial tendency to support police actions overshadows a need for a sensitive understanding of the problems of a society where human rights and individual liberties are preserved by law." According to Ruby:

> Political demonstrations may disclose a content that is anathema to the individual police officer. Many police officers have a need to "teach a lesson" to those who do not display the proper humility and respect, or to those who question police authority. It is not accidental that these charges are used disproportionately against the young, the long-haired, the political and racial minorities. The charge is open to use as a "coverup" for assault by the police in that it explains injuries suffered by accused persons.[4]

"Obstructing" may consist of words or actions. Anyone arrested has a right to know the reason for his charge. If an arresting police officer refuses to tell the reason for the arrest, it appears that the arrested person has a right to resist arrest verbally and, within reason, even physically. However, it's usually safest and wisest not to use physical force to resist arrest. Moreover, a friend or a lawyer cannot help a person being arrested to physically resist an unlawful arrest. Anyone who interferes with someone else's arrest is in danger of being charged himself with obstructing police.

However, mere criticism or questioning of a police officer is not an obstruction, whether it is done by the arrested person, his lawyer, a friend or a stranger.[5] Inciting a crowd to rescue someone being apprehended by police, on the other hand, is likely to be obstruction. You are not obstructing merely because you insist on explaining to the officer why you should not be arrested. You may make "inquiries, arguments and protests."[6] The person being arrested or someone speaking for him can't be charged with obstruction because he asks the reason for arrest or tries to make a statement in answer to the reason he is given, unless this right is exercised in a manner that is intemperate, unduly persistent, irrelevant or made in an unreasonable manner.[7]

If a police officer is abusive or threatening during a demonstration or exceeds his legal power, it is probably unwise to argue with him even though you have a right to do so. Deal with his superior if possible. Get his badge number and, if possible, his name. It is better to deal with his behaviour in another forum and at a later date than to risk escalating a disagreement into an arrest or charges against you. If you are arrested, you have the right to remain silent, except that you must give your name if requested to when you are found committing an offence. Whether the alleged offence is a minor (summary conviction) offence or a major (indictable) one, refusing to answer an officer's question as to your identity may constitute an obstruction. Earlier cases led many lawyers to believe that in summary conviction cases it was not an obstruction to refuse to identify yourself to a police officer, and so advised their clients. But in 1978 the Supreme Court of Canada ruled that a person stopped *while committing an offence* must identify himself to the police officer, even if the alleged offence was merely riding a bicycle in contravention of the traffic laws.[8]

If the police stop you some time before or after an alleged summary offence is committed, rather than during its progress, it appears that you do not have to identify yourself. For example, let's say that someone had been seen riding a red bicycle through a stop light several hours before you entered a street walking alongside your bicycle — a scarlet-coloured one — and police stopped you to question you. It would be difficult for a police officer to establish that you were detained in the process of committing an offence, and it would not be "obstruction" if you refused to identify yourself to him. Nevertheless, if there is any doubt whether you were detained during the course of an offence, the courts will undoubtedly resolve it in the police officer's favour.

Beyond giving your name and address if questioned by the police, in most cases it is wisest to remain silent until you have consulted a lawyer. This is your right. It is always better to remain silent than to tell police a false story. This in itself may constitute obstruction of police, even if you have done nothing else wrong.

As a good citizen, by all means be cooperative with police wherever possible. But if you are arrested or charged with an offence, unless you are sure the charge is a very minor one, a good policy is to tell the police politely and firmly, "Officer, I would like to cooperate with you as fully as possible, but under the circumstances, since I understand that you may use anything I say against me, I would like to discuss this with a lawyer before discussing it with you."

● *Mischief. (Section 387 of the Criminal Code.)* This offence is committed by wilfully doing an act that "obstructs, interrupts or interferes with the lawful use, enjoyment or operation of property, or obstructs, interrupts or interferes with any person in the lawful use, enjoyment or operation of property" (or by wilfully refraining from doing some act with the same result). This offence usually consists of damaging or destroying property, but obstructing access to property might also qualify.

● *Threatening. (Section 745 of the Criminal Code.)* Section 745 is often referred to as the "threatening" section of the Code, but it does not create a punishable offence or even mention threatening. It says that "any person who fears that another person will cause personal injury to him or his wife or child or damage his property, may lay an information before a Justice."

The section applies only when someone has spoken words that might reasonably be construed as a threat and when the person who heard the words actually believes he is in some danger. Mere gestures are not "threats." If the Justice believes there is a potential danger, he may order the defendant to enter into a recognizance to keep the peace for up to a year. He may also impose any other reasonable condition the court considers desirable for securing the defendant's good conduct.

● *Intimidation. (Section 381 of the Criminal Code.)* The actual "threatening" or "intimidation" section of the Code is section 381. The portions of that section that are relevant to freedom of speech are as follows:

> Everybody who, wrongfully and without lawful authority, for the purpose of compelling another person to abstain from doing anything that he has a lawful right to do, or to do anything that he has a lawful right to abstain from doing,
>
> (a)   uses violence or threats of violence to that person or to his wife or children, or injures his property,
>
> (b)   intimidates or attempts to intimidate that person or a relative of that person by threats that, in Canada or elsewhere, a violence or other injury will be done to or punishment inflicted upon him or a relative of his, or that the property of any of them will be damaged . . . is guilty of an offence punishable on summary conviction.

● *Sedition and Seditious Libel. (Sections 60, 61 and 62 of the Criminal Code.)* Everyone who speaks seditious words, publishes a seditious libel or is a party to a seditious conspiracy is guilty of an indictable offence and is liable to imprisonment up to 14 years. A person is assumed to have a seditious intention if he teaches, advocates, publishes or circulates any writing that advocates the use of force as a means of accomplishing governmental change in Canada.

However, no one is deemed to have a seditious intention if he only intends, in good faith,

(a)   to show that Her Majesty has been misled or mistaken in her measures;

(b)   to point out errors or defects in (i) the government or constitution of Canada or a province, (ii) the Parliament of Canada or the Legislature of a province, or (iii) the administration of justice in Canada;

(c)   to procure, by lawful means, the alteration of any matter of government in Canada;

(d)   to point out, for the purpose of removal, matters that produce or tend to produce feelings of hostility and ill-will between classes of people in Canada.

● *Obscenity*. Under Section 159 of the Criminal Code, everyone commits an offence who:

(a) makes, prints, publishes, distributes, circulates or has in his possession for the purposes of publication, distribution or circulation any obscene written matter, picture, model, phonograph record or other thing whatsoever, or

(b) . . . a crime comic.

Section 159(2) provides in part, that

Everyone commits an offence who, knowingly, without lawful justification or excuse,

(a) sells, exposes to public view or has in his possession for such a purpose any obscene written matter, picture, model, phonograph record or any other thing whatsoever,

(b) publicly exhibits a disgusting object or an indecent show.

To be obscene, a publication must have as a dominant characteristic "undue exploitation of sex, or of sex and any one or more of the following subjects, namely, crime, horror, cruelty and violence."

The motives of an accused are irrelevant and his lack of knowledge of the matter or presence of the obscene matter is not a defence. However, he cannot be convicted if he can establish that some public good was served by the acts alleged to constitute the offence, and that they did not extend beyond what served the public good.

● *Hate Propaganda and Hate Literature (Sections 281.1, 282.2 and 281.3 of the Criminal Code.)* These sections prohibit anyone from advocating or promoting genocide, and from inciting hatred of any identifiable group by any public statement where such incitement is likely to lead to a breach of the peace. The section also prohibits any statements, other than in private conversation, which wilfully promote hatred against any identifiable group.

● *Defamatory Libel. (Sections 262 and 280 of the Criminal Code.)* In addition to seditious libel, mentioned above, the Criminal Code makes defamatory libel subject to penal sanctions. Defamatory libel is published matter that is likely to injure the reputation of any person by exposing him to hatred, contempt or ridicule, or that is designed to insult him. A defamatory libel may be expressed directly or by insinuation or irony. It may consist of words or objects.

It is also an offence to extort money or induce someone to confer on someone or procure for someone "an appointment or office or profit or trust" by publishing, threatening to publish or offering to abstain from publishing a defamatory libel.

A newspaper publisher is responsible for any defamatory matter contained in his publication, unless he can prove that it was inserted without his knowledge and without negligence on his part. But no one is legally responsible for defamatory matter in a newspaper merely because he sells the paper, unless he knows it contains that particular defamatory matter or knows that defamatory matter is habitually contained in that newspaper.

● *Counselling. (Section 422 of the Criminal Code.)*

(a) Everyone who counsels, procures or incites a person to commit an indictable offence is, if the offence is not committed, guilty of an indictable offence and is liable to the same punishment to which a person who attempts to commit that offence is liable; and

(b) everyone who counsels, procures or incites another person to commit an offence punishable on summary conviction, is, if the offence is not committed, guilty of an offence punishable on summary conviction.

If the offence *is* committed, the person who counselled it may be part of a punishable conspiracy.

In addition to these offences, it is an offence to encourage someone to commit a crime or to assist him or conspire with him.

● *Conspiracy. (Section 424 of the Criminal Code.)* This section provides in part that:

Everyone who conspires with anyone

(a) to effect an unlawful purpose, or

(b) to effect a lawful purpose by an unlawful means, is guilty of an offence and is liable to imprisonment for two years.

Although this section has been little used against demonstrators, it is a potentially powerful weapon in the hands of the police. For example, planning to occupy the site of a future nuclear plant may be a criminal conspiracy.

● *Attempt and Accessory to the Fact. (Section 421 of the Criminal Code.)* Even attempting unsuccessfully to commit an offence or assisting someone after the fact is an offence.

● *Civil Wrongs.* The main civil restrictions on freedom of the press and freedom of speech are civil defamation, consisting of libel and slander (see chapter 10), and contempt of court (see chapter 5).

Freedom of assembly

Freedom of assembly refers to the right of people to congregate physically in one place. The location and manner of congregation may be restricted by criminal and civil laws designed to keep public order and to protect public and private property and promote public safety. Freedom of assembly is subject to the following restrictions.

● *Unlawful assembly. (Section 64 of the Criminal Code.)* An assembly of three or more people may be unlawful if it needlessly and without reasonable cause provokes others to disturb the peace tumultuously, or if it gives others in the neighbourhood reasonable grounds to fear that the people assembled will do so. Walter Tarnopolsky, an expert on civil liberties, suggests that "obviously a line must be drawn between a situation where the fault for the ensuing disturbance lies with those in the assembly, and the situation where the fault lies with those who oppose it or create the disturbance without any action on the part of those in the assembly which could be reasonably taken to be undue provocation."[9]

● *Riot. (Section 65 of the Criminal Code.)* The Criminal Code defines riot as an unlawful assembly that has begun to disturb the peace tumultuously. When this happens, the authorities may "read the Riot Act." That is, they may go to the scene of the riot and demand that everyone assembled disperse. It is not only a criminal offence to take part in a riot but also to refuse to leave the scene of a riot when ordered to by someone in authority.

● *Obstructing Police.* This offence has been described above. Tarnopolsky adds an observation that is useful in the context of freedom of assembly: "Where the police reasonably believe that an assembly is obstructing a public thoroughfare or threatens to become an unlawful assembly, resistance to their orders to move away or disperse may result in a charge of obstructing police officers."[10]

● *Watching and Besetting. (Section 381 of the Criminal Code.)* This section states that:

> Everyone who, wrongly and without lawful authority, for purpose of compelling another person to abstain from doing anything that he has a lawful right to do, or to do anything that he has a lawful right to abstain from doing,
>
> (a) uses violence or threats of violence to that person or to his wife or children, or injures his property,
>
> (b) intimidates or attempts to intimidate a person or a relative of that person by threats . . .
>
> (c) persistently follows that person about from place to place . . .
>
> (e) with one or more other persons follows that person, in a disorderly manner, on a highway,
>
> (f) besets or watches a dwelling house or place where that person resides, works, carries on business or happens to be, or
>
> (g) blocks or obstructs a highway,
>
> is guilty of an offence punishable on summary conviction.

However, subsection 2 provides that being at a dwelling house or other place only for the purpose of obtaining or communicating information does not constitute watching or besetting.

Thus the difference between lawful picketing and watching and besetting seems to be the element of intimidation, physical interference with a person or property, or threat. Protesters who obstructed a highway in British Columbia to prevent nearby exploration of uranium which they believed endangered their health and that of their families were convicted of an offence under this section in 1979. However, the court took into account evidence that the regulatory safeguards to protect health during uranium exploration were "inadequate almost to the point of being nonexistent," that the accused were upstanding members of the community who were unlikely to commit further offences, and that "a free society places a high value on dissent and other peaceful challenge of the rule of law." The judge granted each of the accused an absolute discharge.[11]

In addition to this offence, blocking a roadway has been considered unlawful assembly, and it would appear from Professor Tarnopolsky's comment above that it might also be considered obstruction of a police officer in certain circumstances.

● *Trespass*. This is a civil wrong for which the owner or occupant can sue anyone intentionally entering his property without permission. The court can award an injunction against any further illegal entry and monetary damages for any harm done to the property as a result of the trespass. The owner or occupant can succeed in obtaining an injunction or perhaps a small award of damages to "punish" the offender or set an example even if no harm is done or if any harm done is unintentional.

However, such suits are costly. The provincial governments have, therefore, created a faster, easier and cheaper remedy for trespass by passing statutes that allow the police or the owner occupant to lay charges against trespassers. These statutes place penal sanctions (usually a fine) on the same behaviour that formerly could only result in damages or an injunction.

Although the civil law of trespass is fairly uniform throughout Canada, the statutory remedies may vary from province to province. In Ontario, the Petty Trespass Act was relatively toothless until recently. Unless the land was enclosed by a fence and well posted with "No Trespassing" signs, it was not an offence to go on the land, but only to stay on the land for an unreasonable length of time after one was asked to leave. The fines ranged from a minimum of $10 to a maximum of $100. Since judges seldom give a maximum sentence and for a first offence they usually give a minimum sentence, and since trespassing was a provincial summary conviction offence that did not lead to a criminal record, the Petty Trespass Act provided little deterrence to demonstrators.

In Ontario, a new Trespass to Property Act has recently been passed that replaces the Petty Trespass Act. The new Act makes it an offence to be on any land that is marked with red paint (the symbol that no entry is allowed without permission), and raises the maximum fine to $1000. The judge can also award damages of up to $1000 in the same proceedings, without the need for the landowner or occupant to launch a separate civil action. These damages are payable to the landowner or occupant.

● *Common Nuisance. (Section 176 of the Criminal Code.)* As a criminal offence, a common nuisance consists of doing an unlawful act or failing to discharge a legal duty that:

(a)   endangers the lives, safety, health, property or comfort of the public, or

(b)   obstructs the public in the exercise or enjoyment of any right that is common to all the subjects of Her Majesty in Canada.

A common nuisance must be directed to the public generally, rather than to a few individuals. For example, a demonstration that impedes public access to private property or obstructs a roadway might be considered a common nuisance, provided that the interference is the result of an illegal act. This illegal act could be a breach of another statute or municipal bylaw, or an act or omission that is a breach of the common law.

● *Civil Nuisance.* Civil nuisance consists of both private nuisance and public nuisance. Private nuisance is the use of one's property in a manner that unreasonably interferes with another's use and enjoyment of his property. Public nuisance, which is more likely to happen at a demonstration, is an outgrowth of the criminal law. Public nuisance refers to wrongs against the public at large or against public property (such as highways). This doctrine provides the civil remedy of an injunction or damages to anyone who sues for harm that may result from a blockage of his access to public property or for harm to public property itself. However, in the case of harm to public property and public rights, usually only the Attorney General has "standing" to sue. The British Court of Appeal has suggested that demonstrators picketing an office may be committing a civil nuisance.[12]

WHAT ABOUT OTHER RESTRICTIONS ON FREEDOM OF SPEECH AND THE RIGHT OF ASSEMBLY?

Noted above are some of the main laws that restrict the right of assembly and the right of free speech; however, they are by no means the only ones. There are several provisions in the Criminal Code restricting the carrying and use of weapons (any article made or adapted for use to cause injury to humans, or intended by the person having it with him for such use), civil conspiracy and inducements to breach of contract, which are discussed in another chapter, criminal conspiracy, civil and criminal assault, the criminal offence of assault to resist arrest (Criminal Code, Section 426(2)(b)), and resisting arrest (Criminal Code, Section 228).

WHAT ARE THE "DO'S AND DON'TS" ON PICKET LINES?

Each demonstration takes on its own character, so it is impossible to draw up a set of hard and fast rules that will apply to every protest march, picket line or demonstration. However, there is some general advice the lawyer can give his clients that may have both practical and legal implications. Here is a checklist of do's and don'ts that should be helpful in avoiding legal entanglements.

DO *carry sufficient identification to satisfy a police officer as to your identity, so that he will have no excuse to hold you because of doubt as to your identity. A driver's licence or birth certificate should suffice.*

DON'T *carry any more identification than necessary. It is no one else's business where you work or what clubs you belong to. That includes the police.*

DON'T *carry anything that can be construed as a weapon.*

DO *use the buddy system. If you are provoked, attacked, arrested or charged with an offence, you will want to have witnesses.*

DO *carry with you the name, address and phone number of a lawyer.*

DO *carry a pen and paper to take notes of the badge number of a police officer, licence plate numbers, descriptions of police officers or others involved in lawbreaking or violence, significant conversations, etc.*

DO *carry a reasonable, but not an excessive, amount of money with you in case of emergency.*

DO *appoint one or more persons as "monitors" to have responsibility for putting down licence numbers of police cars that stop or appear to be observing the demonstration, other cars that appear to be observing the demonstration and any other unusual events.*

DO *instruct each person to note the badge number of any police officer with whom they speak or who speaks to them, and write down the conversation.*

DON'T *block traffic, block the entry to any building, shout, provoke or menace the police, the property owners or passersby in any way.*

DON'T *give your name to any passerby, or indeed to anyone but the police.*

DO *appoint someone as a media spokesperson and advise everyone in the group who that person is. Advise people to send the press to these spokespersons for comments if they are approached to make statements.*

DO *wear appropriate clothes, that is, clothes that will not impair your movement or endanger you in the event of violence; clothes that convey the message you want to convey about you and your cause; clothes that are either very conspicuous or very inconspicuous, depending upon the circumstances and what you hope to accomplish.* The Bust Book *and* Offence/Defence, *mentioned in the Further Reading section, go into this in greater detail.*

DO *be careful of what you say to strangers. They may be undercover police officers.*

DO *have some members of the group carry cameras and tape recorders to make a record of any untoward events. There are special rules for making photographic and tape-recorded evidence admissible in court. These are explained in* Offence/Defence.

DO *make extensive notes of any event you witness that may end up in court, including descriptions of the appearance and dress of the people involved and the names and addresses of other witnesses.*

DON'T *carry any illegal drugs during a demonstration.*

Other helpful advice can be found in *The Bust Book* and in *Offence/ Defence*. In addition, both these works contain much useful information about what to do if you are arrested, including the rights of the police, the rights of the person arrested, the kind of things that will happen at the police station, obtaining bail, and what may happen in jail.

WHAT'S THE BEST WAY TO RESPOND TO THE POLICE?

Here is one approach that the Canadian Environmental Law Association has suggested that its clients use (if accosted by the police) at the site of a demonstration.

If a police officer asks you to get into a police car for any reason, you may reply: "I would prefer to talk with you on the sidewalk." If he insists, you may ask him whether you are under arrest. If he says yes, you may say, "I consider this to be a false arrest, but I will get into the car under protest."

It would be unwise to refuse to get in the car if the police officer informs you that you are under arrest or gives you the reason for the arrest. This might leave you open to a charge of obstructing the police. Even if this charge cannot ultimately be supported, fighting it will be a lengthy, costly matter.

If the officer says you are not under arrest, then you should insist on your right to talk with him on the sidewalk or not to talk with him at all. If he still insists that you get in the car, you should ask someone to accompany you or to stand outside the car window and listen to all discussion. Do so as politely and firmly as possible without provoking the police officer's anger.

If it is necessary, ask the officer what he will do if you refuse to get in the car. If he says he will arrest you for obstructing police or on some other charge, tell him that you will get in the car under protest after you are arrested. If he says he will use force, say: "I will get in the car under protest to avoid the use of force."

In any event, before getting into a police car, you may say: "Unless you are arresting me, I am legally able to continue to walk on this sidewalk and I will not voluntarily enter the car." Remember that the back seat of a police car has no inside door handle. Once inside, you cannot get out unless someone opens the door from the outside.

If you are asked to go to a police station, again, ask, "Are you arresting me?" and if the answer is, "Yes," say, "What for?" After this, record in your notebook everything that happens or is said. Insist on being told the nature of the charge. If you are not told the nature of the charge, it is illegal for the police officer to arrest you, and it is legal for you to use reasonable force to resist arrest. However, although legal, it is unwise to physically resist arrest, even an illegal arrest, unless you have very strong reason to believe that you are in danger of being subjected to police brutality if you do.

If you and other demonstrators are taken to the police station, try to insist on going in twos and threes, rather than individually.

If the answer to the question, "Are you arresting me?" is, "No," refuse to go to the station until or unless you are arrested.

If you are taken to a police station without getting an answer to the question of what offence you are charged with or what conduct is the ground for the arrest, refuse to answer any questions beyond giving your name and address until you are charged with a specific offence.

If you are imprisoned in a police car or a police station on the grounds that you have been arrested for an offence and then released, when you are released ask whether you are still charged with any offence. A police officer who arrests or imprisons you without reasonable and probable grounds for doing so is subject to a civil suit for false imprisonment or false arrest. The fact that he has arrested you, charged you with an offence, then released you and dropped all charges, without obtaining any further information that would change the situation, may in itself be very strong evidence that he had no reasonable grounds for arrest in the first place.

It cannot be stressed too strongly that in any dealings with the police, if you can possibly arrange to do so, you should have a witness or a lawyer present.

WHAT IS THE ROLE OF THE LAWYER AT DEMONSTRATIONS?

Lawyers have the same civil liberties as anyone else: no more, or less. A lawyer may attend a demonstration as a participant, as an advisor, or both. However, in a rapidly changing situation — when a peaceful demonstration turns into a violent one — it may be psychologically and physically difficult for a lawyer to switch roles, or to play both roles at the same time.

The same laws apply to lawyers as to non-lawyers, but the consequences of breaking the law are more severe for the lawyer. The non-lawyer is subject to civil and criminal sanctions if he breaks the law. The lawyer is also subject to disciplinary action by the Law Society and possibly even loss of his licence to practise law.

In certain circumstances, such as a riot, the mere physical presence of a person at the site of the demonstration may be strong evidence of a breach of the law. In such a highly charged situation, unless he has made a conscious decision to break the law, the lawyer may want to clarify the nature of his participation to minimize his jeopardy. If the lawyer does want to draw a clear line between his role as a participant and his role as legal advisor, he should ensure that he is not a member of the group he is advising, or a public speaker at a protest in which he is also acting as legal advisor. It may be advisable for him to stay at the edge of the group, or stand apart from it.

The lawyer will want to be in as good a position as possible to show that he is at a demonstration for the purpose of assisting his client to avoid breaking the law, rather than to aid or abet any breach of the law. The lawyer may not counsel anyone to break the law. However, if the law is unclear or ambiguous, he may certainly advise his clients as to his interpretation of the meaning of the law and its application to them under the circumstances. Like any other participant at a demonstration, lawyers may want to work in pairs to ensure there are witnesses to their activity. Without such collaboration, it may be his word against a police officer's as to whether he was advising a client or obstructing justice.

9.

CONSPIRACY

Public interest advocacy is now recognized as a respectable and valuable aspect of the democratic process. It is important for everyone in society to have the right to protect his or her interests, both in the courts and on the streets. When both sides lobby hard for what they want, or use the laws to advance their own interests, that is fair play. But when vested and powerful interests resort to harassment and intimidation, that is unfair and improper.

Civil conspiracy is a combination or confederacy between two or more persons, formed to cause legal damage or injury (for example, loss of business) to a third party. It is a legitimate legal doctrine that can be distorted and used as a harassment technique. In recent years, members of Canadian public interest groups have been sued, under the law of conspiracy, for picketing in front of a retail store and for submitting briefs to their municipal council. In one case, a lawyer and other staff of a community legal clinic were sued by a landlord for conspiracy to harm his reputation and his business, and for libel, as a result of their assistance to a tenant.

In recent years it has become apparent that exercising one's right to protest can result in being sued for conspiracy. It is questionable whether such a lawsuit can succeed, but in many cases the lawsuit serves its purpose without ever going to court: it intimidates and "punishes" the outspoken.

WHAT IS THE LAW OF CONSPIRACY?

Conspiracy is another one of those legal doctrines, like obstructing police and obscenity, that are so vague they are open to abuse. Because such doctrines are so ill-defined and malleable, they may be useful to keep the peace and to redress new kinds of social injustices in a tolerant and well-meaning society. But, in the hands of powerful vested in-

101

terests such fuzzy doctrines can be used to bludgeon public interest groups and their legal advisors into silence.

Is organizing a tenants' union, boycott or protest march a conspiracy? No one knows the answer. Until the courts rule on specific cases, it would appear that the best answer is that it depends upon the circumstances of each case. Public interest groups should be reasonably safe in such activities, provided that they do not do anything illegal in the course of otherwise legal activities, and provided that they do not urge anyone to break a contract that they know is in existence.

HOW CAN CONSPIRACY BE USED AGAINST CITIZEN ADVOCACY GROUPS?

What follows is a case study that illustrates how a developer, using conspiracy charges, effectively hamstrung the efforts of a community conservation group in its fight to preserve the quality of their neighbourhood environment.

The Mississauga group found out just how costly freedom of speech can be. The Save Our Trees and Streams Society was formed in 1973 to bring together citizens in Mississauga, Ontario, who were concerned about the impact of urbanization on the natural landscape. The citizens wanted to retain as much as possible of the existing quality and features of the environment, and still allow rational development that was in the interest of their community. SOTAS could hardly be called a rabble-rousing group. The members of its executive committee included a professional forester and an architect. Its *modus operandi* consisted of preparing planning reports and presenting well-researched briefs to the municipal council. If ever a group could be said to work within the system rather than against it, it was SOTAS.

In July of 1973 SOTAS delivered a brief to the Council of the City of Mississauga, urging the municipality to protect the slopes of the Credit River Valley by zoning them as "hazard lands." (Hazard lands are areas that should not be developed because of unstable or steep slopes, occasional flooding or other environmental constraints.) SOTAS advised the Council to freeze development on lands adjacent to the Credit River and maintain the area as a greenbelt.

In the early fall of 1973, the members of SOTAS learned of a proposal to build a housing subdivision on lands on the rim of the Credit River Valley. SOTAS wanted to ensure that the development would not endanger the natural beauty of the ravine and that the public would continue to have access to the Credit River along a natural path on the cliff above the floodplain. Upon discovering that the municipal council had not yet approved the developer's draft plan of subdivision, SOTAS asked the council to reconsider the development and to ensure that public access to the River Valley was preserved.

When an election in late 1973 led to a change in the municipal council, SOTAS decided to make a submission to the new council about the proposed development. Again SOTAS asked the municipal council to preserve public access to the river and to protect the existing trail and the natural scenery of the valley. According to members of the group, they never had any intention of harming the developer. Their only motivation was to try to persuade the municipality to act in what they believed to be the community's interest and protect the Credit River Valley.

Although the members of SOTAS claim they had no knowledge of this, the Ontario government in December of 1972 had approved the developer's draft subdivision plan, subject to twelve conditions. One of these conditions required the developer to assure the Minister that the municipal council was satisfied that the other eleven conditions had been carried out to the municipality's satisfaction. Following the SOTAS brief recommending that the council not approve the developer's draft plan, the council passed a resolution "that the River Heights development be released for final registration on the understanding that the conditions set out in the attached letter being [sic] carried out." One of the new conditions in the letter was that the developer give 44 percent of its land to the local Conservation Authority.

The developer claimed that once the provincial government had given approval subject to the original twelve conditions, the municipality had no power to impose more conditions.

Alleging that this new condition was illegal, the developer sued the five members of the executive of SOTAS for $500,000 in damages and the municipal council for the same amount. The developer alleged that SOTAS and the municipal council conspired to breach a contract between the developer and the municipality, and conspired to impose an illegal condition that the developer had to satisfy before the draft plan of subdivision would be released for approval.

Four and a half years of legal manoeuvring began. Lawyers for SOTAS and the City of Mississauga moved to dismiss the developer's action on the grounds that there was no legal basis for it. In the first hearing, the judge agreed that there was no evidence of any agreement or contract between Mississauga and the developer that could have been breached. He ordered the developer to strike out of its statement of claim any references to breach of contract. However, he allowed the other aspect of the case to continue: "If the [municipality] refused to advise the Minister that the plaintiff had satisfied the conditions unless the plaintiff conveyed 44 percent of the land to the Conservation Authority there is no doubt such conduct was illegal, and if the plaintiff suffered damages as alleged as a result of that illegal conduct, the [municipality] should be responsible for it." He allowed the lawsuit to continue and ordered the municipality and SOTAS to pay the costs of their application to dismiss the action.

SOTAS and the municipality then asked the court's permission to appeal the judge's order to a higher court. The judge in the appeal agreed with the defendants that the issues involved were important enough to send it to a higher court:

> I strongly doubt if what it is alleged and admitted the defendants here did is in any sense illegal as a conspiracy. The whole process of approval of subdivision is to make sure that the public interest is protected, and the consideration of all alternatives and conditions in the public interest is the proper concern of municipalities and concerned and interested citizens. . . . Concerned citizens have no more rights than others, but they do not have less rights because they act in concert. I think that it is of basic importance to determine at this stage of the action whether municipal corporations and groups of citizens who oppose or try to regulate the granting of privileges under provincial legislation should thereby become subject to actions for conspiracy for making suggestions of which it may be argued that they are contrary to one view of some law involved.

The three judges who then heard the appeal did not dismiss the case against SOTAS and Mississauga. But the citizens had some success on their appeal. The judges did rule that the developer's statement of claim (the document in which the plaintiff sets out what he alleges to be illegal about the defendant's conduct) was unclear and must be revised. They reversed the order of costs against Mississauga and the citizens' group, and awarded them the costs of the applications before the two earlier judges and on the appeal.

Although the developer claimed that it had suffered one million dollars in damages as a result of the actions of the citizens and their municipal council, it appeared to be in no hurry to have a court decide its claim. Before a trial is held, a process known as examinations for discovery takes place, in which each side cross-examines the other party's witnesses. The process is useful for evaluating the strength of your case, to clarify and resolve as many issues as possible prior to trial and to decide whether to proceed or settle. It often leads to negotiations for settlement. By January of 1977, the developer's lawyer had only completed his examination of one of the five SOTAS members. In September of that year, the SOTAS members' lawyer, John McDougall, asked the court to order the plaintiff to get on with its case. In an affidavit in support of his motion, Mr. McDougall said he believed that the lawsuit had caused his clients embarrassment and personal anguish, and had exposed them to liability for heavy legal costs. He suggested that it was unreasonable to have this state of affairs unduly prolonged.

The court apparently agreed. It ordered the developer to complete its discoveries by the end of November, 1977. November came and went and the plaintiff's lawyers initiated no further discoveries. Instead, they asked the court for more time to examine the SOTAS members.

The case finally came to court four and a half years after the writ had been issued. On the day the trial was to begin, the developer announced that it was abandoning its case against the SOTAS members, but would continue against the municipal council. The judge granted costs for the day in court and costs of preparing the case to SOTAS on a party-and-party basis. This means that the developer had to pay about two-thirds of the SOTAS members' legal fees, leaving the individual SOTAS members to bear the remaining one-third of their lawyer's fees and disbursements, if he chose to collect them. Costs of preparing the case were estimated at somewhere between $10,000 and $40,000.

Although the SOTAS members were relieved, they were not yet out of the woods. Because the conspiracy suit was continuing against the city, the SOTAS members could be called upon as witnesses by either party at any time. The judge decided not to rule on whether the SOTAS members should be awarded the remaining one-third of their legal costs until the end of the trial against Mississauga. At the time of writing, more than two years later, that suit has never come to court.

The lawsuit effectively finished SOTAS as a conservation group. Time and energy that would otherwise have been spent in researching and developing briefs on long-range planning policies was devoted to raising money for a defence fund to pay legal bills. The case not only sapped SOTAS' energy, but it frightened many other citizens' groups from speaking out on issues.

Because the case against SOTAS never came to trial, the court had no opportunity to rule on the scope of freedom of speech between a municipal council and its ratepayers, and the threat of conspiracy action against public interest groups is no closer to being removed.

Therefore, perhaps the only useful lesson to come out of the SOTAS case is that ratepayers and other public interest groups may be wise to incorporate. Incorporation greatly increases red tape, costs of operation and paperwork and is completely unnecessary for most activities community groups carry on. But incorporation limits the liability of individual officers of an association. Plaintiffs must sue the corporation rather than its individual members and the damages they can collect are limited to the assets of the corporation. They cannot touch the assets of the individual members.

ARE PUBLIC INTEREST GROUPS LIABLE TO CRIMINAL CONSPIRACY CHARGES?

Civil conspiracy grew out of the historic offence of criminal conspiracy. Criminal conspiracy in Canada has been codified as section 423 of the Canadian Criminal Code: "Everyone who conspires with anyone (a) to effect an unlawful purpose, or (b) to effect a lawful purpose by an unlawful means, is guilty of an indictable offence and is liable to imprisonment for two years."

The "unlawful" or "unlawful means" are not restricted to criminal acts, but may include breaches of certain provincial legislation or municipal bylaws. For example, an agreement to demolish buildings without obtaining a permit required under a municipal bylaw or forming a company to sell securities without a prospectus and employing unregistered salesmen contrary to provincial laws may be subject to prosecution for criminal conspiracy.

There is little danger that most legitimate public interest activities could be construed as criminal conspiracy without the participants being aware that they are breaking the law. Nevertheless, until the law is clarified, this is always a possibility that should be kept in mind. A lawsuit for civil conspiracy, on the other hand, is somewhat more likely.

WHAT IS CIVIL CONSPIRACY?

The most common form of civil conspiracy is a conspiracy to induce a breach of contract. If an individual or a group induced some other individual or group to break a contract with a third party, and if as a result the contract is broken and the third party suffers some damage, the third party can sue for damages both the person with whom he had the contract and the person or persons who induced him to break the contract. The suit against the person who broke the contract may be for both breach of contract and for his or their participation in the conspiracy. The suit against the person who induced the other to break his contract will be for conspiracy. He will succeed against the person or group who induced the breach of contract unless they can show that they had sufficient justification to encourage the other person to break the contract.

On the other hand, you cannot be liable for inducing or procuring a breach of contract unless you know that there is a contract to be broken. A group that encourages someone not to do business with a certain firm, without knowing that he already has a contract with the firm, is not liable for any damages that the firm may suffer as a result of the group's activities. However, once the group becomes aware of a contract, the group may be liable for damages unless it can show sufficient justification for continuing its activities. Thus, where a contract is in existence, whether an individual or group is engaging in a conspiracy is to some extent merely a question of the state of their knowledge. It would be up to the plaintiff to prove that the defendant knew about the contract at the time the representations were made.

An inducement to break a contract may consist of directly requesting or persuading one of the parties to a contract to break it, or it may involve physically detaining someone or otherwise making it impossible for him to perform his contract. It may also consist of dealing with a party to a contract in a manner that one knows to be inconsistent with the contract. For example, if you know that someone has a contract with another person to sell his entire stock of goods at a certain price, you might be sued if you offered him a much higher price for the same goods.

Thus, you may be engaging in a conspiracy to breach a contract if you know of the existence of the contract and:

(1)   you persuade someone to do something inconsistent with performing his duties under the contract; or

(2)   you arrange for another person to do something that would render it impossible for him to fulfill the contract; and

(3)   your words or actions are intended to procure the breach of contract rather than to further some legitimate interest.

In order to be sued, your actions must result in some *actual* loss or damage to the third party.

It is not unlawful to induce a breach of contract if you have sufficient justification for doing so. But as Salmond, an authority on the law of torts, states: "What amounts to a justification is a question of law to which, as the authorities stand, no precise answer can be given." Whether inducing a breach of contract is justified depends on the nature of the contract broken, the position of the parties to the contract, the grounds for the breach, the means used to procure the breach, the relation of the person procuring the breach to the person who breaks the contract and the person's reasons for procuring the breach.

The main justification for inducing someone to break a contract is the advancement of one's own economic self-interest. The court will attempt to ascertain whether the primary purpose of an inducement is to hurt the third party's business or advance one's own business. Since there is often more than one way to look at such activity, and since motives may be mixed, it is often difficult to predict the outcome of any case.

Motives that are partially selfish and partially unselfish sometimes also provide a justification for inducing a breach of contract. Salmond suggests that urging a breach of contract may be justified "under the pressure of moral duties." An example would be a father persuading his daughter to break off her engagement to marry a scoundrel,[1] "where the claims of relationship or guardianship demand an interference amounting to protection."[2] In another case, the court held that members of a theatrical "joint protection committee" were justified in inducing a theatre manager to break off his contract with a theatrical agent because the agent paid his chorus girls such low wages that they had to resort to prostitution.[3] In these cases, however, there was an element of self-interest. The joint protection committee, for example, appears to have been a kind of informal "union," formed to protect the interests of entertainers.

In the pure public interest case, where neither the persons inducing the breach nor their members stand to gain anything from the inducement, it is not clear that altruism and concern for justice would justify an inducement to breach a contract. Several years ago Canadian union officials supported the widespread public boycott of California grapes, in support of an attempt to obtain better working conditions, legal recognition and higher wages for a grapeworkers' union in that state. They were held to have engaged in a conspiracy when the union members' boycott of the supermarket in which they were employed caused the supermarket to be unable to carry out its contract to buy these grapes.[4] The court held that the union had engaged in a conspiracy.

The mere fact that one is acting in the public interest certainly does not in itself justify inducing a breach of contract. In a case where a society (union) of stonemasons pressured an employer to break his contract to provide training as a mason to an apprentice, the court said it was not a justification that they acted *bona fide* in the best interests of the society of masons (i.e., in their own interests), adding that they would be liable even if they were acting "as an altruist, seeking only the good of another and careless of [their] own advantage."[5] Similarly, when leaders of a tenants' association advised members to withhold their rent until the landlord fulfilled his obligations to adequately heat and clean the building, the court held that even if they claimed to be performing a public service this did not justify interference with a contract.[6] It has also been held that the fact that an association has a duty to protect the interests of its members and has acted in pursuance of that duty is no justification.[7]

A few other principles are worthy of note. The "contracts" that are protected are not just business or written contracts. As mentioned above, a contract to marry has been protected (although recent law reforms in many jurisdictions abolishing torts such as breach of contract to marry would presumably also eliminate any suit for inducing a breach of this kind of contract). In addition, there appears to be nothing wrong with dissuading someone from entering a contract before he has committed himself and while he is still free to change his mind.

WHAT IS CONSPIRACY TO INJURE?

Although inducing a breach of contract may be actionable whether it is done by one person or by a thousand, there are other inducements that appear to be lawful if they are done by one person, but unlawful if done by more than one. These are called "conspiracies to injure." Salmond describes civil conspiracy to injure as "a combination wilfully to do an act causing damage to a man in his trade or other interests." If this agreement or combination results in actual economic loss, it is actionable as a conspiracy. However, where the element of combination is absent, the motive of the defendant is immaterial, and damage done intentionally or even malevolently to another gives no cause of action as long as no legal right of the other is infringed. To succeed, the plaintiff must prove: an agreement to do some act that would injure his economic interest, actual injury *and* intent to cause that injury. The plaintiff cannot succeed if the defendant can show that the primary purpose was not to injure the plaintiff but to promote some legitimate purpose. Just what constitutes a "legitimate interest" that gives justification to combine to injure someone's economic interest is unclear. It obviously includes the advancement of one's own economic interests, but like inducement to breach a contract, it is not clear whether it includes altruistic or "public interest" considerations. Because most of the cases involve disputes between labour unions and employers, or between trade competitors, the "public interest" question has seldom arisen. The courts have usually been asked to consider motives that involve some self-interest.

For example, in one case in England in 1941, union officials instructed dock workers who were members of the union not to handle yarn spun by the Crofter Handwoven Harris Tweed Company or cloth woven from it.[8] The workers complied with this instruction, jeopardizing Crofter's business, and the company sued. The union hoped to eliminate competition from Crofter with other manufacturers who employed members of the same union as spinners. This would strengthen the economic position of these other manufacturers. The union believed that if there was less cut-throat competition between milling companies, the remaining companies would be in a better position to increase the prices they paid to the spinners of yarn in the unionized mills. The House of Lords held that there was no conspiracy because the combination was intended to achieve the union's lawful purpose of protecting the interests of its members and to improve industrial conditions for its members by eliminating unregulated competition.

The proposition that the pursuit of economic self-interest is a legitimate justification for causing someone economic injury appears to be so well settled that by 1965 the author of the fourteenth edition of *Salmond on Torts* felt safe in asserting that:

> The pursuit of selfish ends provides in law, whatever may be the case in morals, its own justification. Even the fact that the damage inflicted to secure such a legitimate selfish purpose is disproportionately severe, though it may throw doubts in the *bona fides* of the avowed purpose, does not necessarily involve liability.

However, it is not clear whether self-interest includes one's nobler instincts. Is advancement of the public interest a legitimate extension of one's narrow self-interest or a legitimate alternative to that self-interest? Or is a person attempting to protect his financial or property interests considered justified in interfering with those of another, while the altruistic person is considered a meddler? The English Court of Appeal has said that the interests which a defendant is justified in protecting are not confined to "those which can be exchanged for cash." The court found that union officials did not engage in a conspiracy by organizing a boycott of a dance hall that barred coloured people.[9] In the Canadian grape boycott case, however, similar activities were held to be a conspiracy. Perhaps if the Canadian case had not involved a breach of contract, the result would have been different.

The independent existence of a tort of conspiracy to injure in the absence of a contract being breached was doubtful until as recently as 1942. Before the Crofter case, it had been thought by some to exist only if the activity was inspired by malice, and its application appeared to be limited to trade competition and labour disputes. Is it possible that such a questionable tort can be extended to otherwise legitimate public interest advocacy?

It would be perverse for the courts to protect harmful activities done to advance one's narrow self-interest, yet subject those whose motives are entirely altruistic, and who have nothing personal to gain from their activities, to the threat of being liable for all financial losses caused by their activities. The result of such a doctrine would be to suppress freedom of speech and elevate private interests over the public interest. Any form of advocacy of the public interest against private interests, or of the interests of the poor and weak against the rich and powerful, would be surrounded with uncertainty.

Nevertheless, conspiracy to injure suits other than the SOTAS suit have recently been initiated. In 1975, the owner of a Toronto fur store sued for conspiracy a woman who participated in a demonstration in front of his store. The demonstrators alleged that the store owner was offering the skins of endangered species of animals for sale. After issuing his writ, the store owner never proceeded any further with his lawsuit, even though a second demonstration took place after he had launched his action. A year later, members of the staff of a Toronto community legal clinic were sued by a Toronto landlord for conspiracy to injure his business and his reputation by opposing the landlord's attempts to remove a handicapped roomer from his rented premises. This case has never gone to trial either.

CONCLUSION

Until the Canadian courts decide the legitimate scope of public interest advocacy, individuals and groups cannot be certain of being free from harassment. Meanwhile, the following steps may provide some protection against conspiracy suits and other legal actions:

● Incorporate. This limits the financial liability of members of a group for actions of the corporation.

● Try to avoid any activity that could otherwise be construed as illegal. Conspiracy may consist either of illegal means, illegal ends, or both.

● Accentuate the positive and eliminate the negative. At all times, make it clear that you are *for* some legitimate goal rather than *against* any particular person or corporation. Frame all submissions and statements in terms of your goals and make it clear that you are "against" someone only to the extent that his activities impede the accomplishment of your legitimate social goals.

● If at any time you become aware of the existence of a contract or agreement that may be breached as a result of your activities, proceed with caution. Seek legal advice before taking further action.

10.

DEFAMATION, LIBEL AND SLANDER

Defamation is the offence of injuring a person's character or reputation by false or malicious statements. This includes libel and slander. Members of public interest groups and the lawyers who represent them find that they have more and more reason to believe they may be sued for libel by those who wish to silence them.

Libel and slander are also important defences for public interest advocates when opponents try to destroy their credibility by making false or malicious statements about them.

DEFAMATION AND THE DISTINCTION BETWEEN LIBEL AND SLANDER

A person defames someone's character if he makes a false statement damaging to that person's reputation. A statement is defamatory if it subjects the person to hatred, ridicule or contempt of the community because it alleges or implies some moral discredit on his or her part. A statement may also be defamatory if it tends to make ordinary members of the community shun or avoid the person about whom the statement is made, even though the statement is about something that would not constitute any moral discredit on his or her part, if it were true. For example, people who are alleged to be insane or to have certain diseases may be entitled to bring an action to protect their reputation and their honour, even though they would have no direct moral responsibility for these disabilities, had they suffered them.[1]

Professor Heuston, editor of the sixteenth edition of *Salmond on Torts*, states that:

> The typical form of defamation is an attack upon the moral character of the plaintiff, attributing to him any form of disgraceful conduct, such as crime, dishonesty, untruthfulness, ingratitude or cruelty. But a state-

113

ment may be defamatory if it tends to bring the plaintiff into ridicule or contempt even though there is no suggestion of any form of misconduct.[2]

On the other hand, words that merely hurt someone's feelings or cause him annoyance, without reflecting on his character or reputation or tending to cause him to be shunned or avoided, are not defamatory.

The test of whether a statement is defamatory is whether it would make reasonable people think less of that person. This is a "man on the street" test. As Lord Atkins, a member of the Judicial Committee of the British House of Lords, put it: "Would the words tend to lower the plaintiff in the estimation of right-thinking members of society generally?"[3] Whether a statement is defamatory would depend to some extent upon the social climate and the predominant values in the community at the time it is made. For example, in the minds of many people there is nothing wrong with being an "activist" or a "communist." In some circles such attributes may be a source of pride and a reason for acceptance. However, if many "right-thinking" people are hostile towards "communists" or "activists," attaching these labels to someone might be considered defamatory.[4]

To take another example of how changing social values might affect whether a statement is defamatory, in the 1940s it was suggested that to portray a woman as having been raped or seduced by an evil man would destroy her reputation. This was based on attitudes towards women and sex that may not reflect society's current views. Defamation is more commonly known by the term "libel" or "slander." The simplest distinction between these two kinds of defamation is given by Williams, the author of a recent textbook on the law of defamation: "Any comment communicated in a form which is permanent and visible to the eye is libel. Any communication which is temporary and only audible is slander."[5] In other words, libel is usually written and slander is usually spoken.

There are many difficulties with the rather arbitrary division between libel and slander and with the attempt to distinguish between them. To begin with, to distinguish between libel as permanent and written, and slander as temporary and spoken, is an over-simplification that does not take into account modern forms of communication such as television, radio broadcasts and computer printouts. The division also causes problems because the liability flowing from libel is sometimes different from that of slander. To simplify the law some provinces have passed legislation reuniting libel and slander as a single tort of defamation. In other provinces, the distinction is still made. This will be discussed further.

ARE LIBEL AND SLANDER THREATS TO PUBLIC INTEREST GROUPS?

There are three reasons for our concern about libel and slander in a guide on public interest advocacy. First, we are concerned because public interest advocates are particularly vulnerable to scurrilous attacks on their character made by the powerful interests they criticize or challenge. Lying about them is one way to undermine their credibility and reduce their effectiveness. Advocates should therefore be aware that they can use this remedy. Secondly, it is not difficult for public interest advocates inadvertently to cross over the fine line between fair comment and defamation in their newsletters, speeches, media interviews and other public statements. Thirdly, the people and institutions whose activities public interest groups are challenging are beginning to learn that bringing libel suits against their critics may be cheap insurance against further criticism. They know that no matter how unfounded, a libel suit tends to intimidate public interest advocates and deflect their efforts from constructive criticism to self-defence.

Defamation serves a useful purpose in protecting people's reputations from unfair and untrue attacks. However, this goal must be balanced against the need to protect freedom of speech. The courts have recognized for years that libel and slander may be abused by "gold-diggers" who launch suits to make a fast buck. They are now gradually recognizing that libel is also being abused increasingly by plaintiffs about whom nothing has been said that isn't true or whose reputations haven't suffered any harm they didn't deserve, who have no desire to protect their reputations, and whose real purpose is to "gag" their critics.

HOW EFFECTIVE ARE DEFAMATION SUITS LAUNCHED BY PUBLIC INTEREST GROUPS?

Defamation suits have been launched by public interest advocates and against them. Simon Hoad, who ran a youth hostel program in Thunder Bay, sued when the mayor of the city claimed the program cost too much because it was mismanaged. Simon and the mayor settled out of court, the mayor apologizing publicly to Simon and paying him an undisclosed sum of money. On the other hand, a landlord sued the staff of a Toronto community legal clinic for defamation after they allegedly informed the press about his attempts to remove a tenant from his apartment (the case is still technically before the courts although the landlord has taken no steps in more than three years), and the makers of Marlboro cigarettes sued the producers of a television program that showed its commercials juxtaposed with real cowboys dying of cancer and suffering from emphysema from smoking cigarettes. As a result of the suit the film has never been shown in the United States.

Unfortunately, defamation is a more useful tool for wealthy individuals or corporations who want to silence their critics than for public interest advocates who want to protect their reputations. There are several reasons for this. First, in general the reputations of activists are likely to be "worth" less than the reputations of powerful individuals or corporations they criticize. (An exception: if the activist is a member of a profession, his professional reputation is deemed to be valuable in itself, and he can recover for slurs against this "professional reputation" without showing any financial loss.)

When an activist sues someone for defamation, he puts his own reputation on trial as well as that of the defendant. A nonconformist in any community is likely to obtain a bad reputation with some "right-thinking" members of the community, who may be all too happy to testify in favour of the defendant.

It is frequently counter-productive for an activist to launch a libel action. All litigation is expensive, nerve-wracking and time-consuming. This is particularly true of libel suits because of the issues and the technicalities involved. Therefore most activists, after they get over their initial upset, will usually decide it is more important to get on with the job than to become enmeshed in a libel suit.

Finally, legal aid legislation frequently will not permit financial assistance to be given to people who sue for defamation or are sued for it. This makes it particularly unattractive to the public interest advocate who is not wealthy to sue someone who defames him. It also makes a defamation action particularly attractive to a wealthy person who wants to use a libel suit as a "gag," since the activist will be particularly ill equipped to fight back without any financial assistance.

HOW TO RECOGNIZE DEFAMATION

Generalizations are not very helpful in determining what may be defamatory. If you have any doubts, talk to a lawyer. If you are a lawyer who has little experience with this highly technical and subjective area of law, read some of the cases listed in the Further Reading section as a starting point and consider consulting with someone more experienced. It is impossible to give more than a bare outline of the law of defamation in this kind of book. However, the following thumbnail sketch should help to point you in the right direction.

Each province has its own libel and slander statute and therefore the law is slightly different in each province. In some provinces, the difference between libel and slander is extremely important for reasons that will be described below. In other provinces, the distinction between libel and slander has been abolished, and both are referred to merely as "defamation" and are subject to the same rules. There are usually very technical rules that one must follow to protect one's right to sue for defamation. The requirements for notifying the defendant and the period within which notification must be made and a defamation action can be brought vary from province to province.

Although we have described defamation as a "statement," it may be any form of communication. As well as written and oral statements, such forms of communication as a cartoon, a statute or a song can be defamatory.

Words may be defamatory in their natural and ordinary meaning. However, if the words or other forms of communication are unclear or may have more than one meaning, the court will have to determine what was meant and what the ordinary member of society would have thought was meant. Words that are otherwise innocent may be defamatory if they were uttered in a context that would make them harmful to a person's reputation. In such cases, the libel or slander involves "innuendo." An innuendo exists when the spoken or written words themselves are not defamatory, but surrounding circumstances or additional facts that are likely to be within the knowledge of people who received the communication give the words an extended meaning that is defamatory. For example, the mere inclusion of an article in a series may be libellous. Williams gives the example of a weekly publication that prints a series of articles exposing chicanery and dishonesty, and includes in the series an article about an individual. The publication does not directly say anything negative about the person's character, but the inclusion of the article about him in such a series might lead readers to draw the inference that he indulges in the kind of conduct the series exposes.[6]

If the defamation is by innuendo, it is not necessary for the plaintiff to prove that someone actually understood the words in the defamatory sense. It is only necessary for the plaintiff to prove the existence of the special circumstances that give the innocent statement a defamatory implication and that there are people who might understand the words in the defamatory context. The onus is on the person who alleges he has been defamed to show all of the following matters: that there are extrinsic circumstances that might render an innocent-sounding statement defamatory; that there are people who know these facts or circumstances; and that these people might reasonably understand the words in a defamatory sense. It is not necessary to prove that the statement actually came to the attention of such people.

For example, if a businessman issued a notice saying he would no longer accept cheques drawn on a particular bank, the mere statement might not be considered to say anything negative about the character or conduct of the bank. But the statement might be considered defamatory in the context that most such notices are issued as a result of bankruptcy or insolvency. Therefore, recipients of such a notice might reasonably think that the bank was in dire financial straits.[7]

To be defamatory, a statement must be "published." Publication does not consist only of trumpetting one's message to the world through the print or electronic media. Making an untrue statement about someone to only one other person may be defamatory in some circumstances. Sending a letter that defames a person to his spouse has been held to be grounds for a defamation action.[8]

Publication also consists of repeating a defamatory statement. Therefore, if someone is defamed in an interview or a letter to the editor, the editor and the publisher of the newspaper that prints the statement will be liable, as well as the person who made the statement. In the case of an interview, the reporter or broadcaster would also be liable.

A communication that is neither intentional nor careless is not a publication. If a statement is made with the intention that others may hear or read it, this will amount to publication. If the statement is communicated unintentionally, this may still amount to publication if the person who said it was careless or negligent about who might hear it. If someone makes a slanderous statement to another person, having no reason to know or suspect the presence of a third person who overhears it, the speaker will not be considered to have "published" the statement to a third party. On the other hand, if the speaker should have known that the third person might be listening in, the statement might constitute publication.

Obviously, one must watch what one says in the vicinity of a microphone. More than one person has made a "private" statement in the presence of an open mike. Whether such a person would be considered to have "published" a statement that goes out on nationwide television accidentally might depend upon whether a reasonable person would have realized that the microphone was inadvertently left on. If someone denies any intention to "publish" a statement, the burden of proving publication is on the plaintiff.

HOW FINE IS THE DISTINCTION BETWEEN LIBEL AND SLANDER?

The distinction between libel and slander has been briefly described above. There is a great grey area in which it is difficult to determine whether or not a matter is libellous or slanderous. As a rough rule of thumb, to be on the safe side, consider any statement that will appear in writing, on radio, on television or in a motion picture to be within the "libel" category. Restrict the "slander" category to speeches.

Libel is considered a more serious offence than slander. The major difference is that a slander is generally not actionable without proof of "special" damage (out-of-pocket loss), but libel is. In the provinces and territories where the distinction between libel and slander has been eliminated, the trend has been to treat all defamation as libellous: that is, not to require any proof of actual monetary loss.

In certain cases, both libel and slander are actionable without proof of special damage. Slander is treated as being as serious as libel when it involves an imputation of a serious crime, an imputation of unchastity to a woman (the inequality of treatment of the sexes in this case has interesting implications under modern human rights codes) or an imputation that someone has a contagious or infectious disease. From the viewpoint of public interest advocates, the most important situation in which libel and slander are actionable without proof of special damages is the discrediting of someone's performance or capacity to perform the duties of his business, trade, profession or calling. A person's "professional reputation" is considered deserving of special protection. If a doctor is called a "quack" or a car manufacturer is accused of producing "death-traps," without justification, that person could sue for damages even without showing any loss of business.

WHAT HAPPENS WHEN GROUPS ARE DEFAMED?

As a general rule, if a group or association is defamed, there is a limited right to sue. Whether the members of the group can sue in the group's name or whether they must sue as individuals will depend upon a variety of factors. To begin with, only legal entities recognized as "persons" can sue. An individual is a person. A corporation is a person. However, in many jurisdictions an unincorporated association is not a person.

Of particular concern to small, unincorporated and sometimes temporary public interest groups or community groups is the question of whether to sue if something untrue is said about the group, without mentioning its individual members by name. Williams states:

> A defamatory comment may be made about a corporation, association or other cohesive group. To be defamatory of such an entity, the statement must reflect adversely upon an aspect of the esteem in which the entity is held. It must reflect upon the management of the corporation's business and must affect the corporation rather than the individuals associated with it.[9]

Williams points out that such entities have a limited reputation. For an action to be maintained by the entity itself rather than by the individual involved with it, the entity must show "that the defamation injures it in its own sphere of activities and does not merely reflect upon its agents, officers or servants."[10] Generally, corporations may sue only if their property or financial position has been affected. Trade unions, professional associations and municipalities have launched defamation actions in their own names. Smaller, perhaps less cohesive, unincorporated citizens' groups also have a limited reputation and perhaps a mixed reputation. In many cases, it may be arguable that the reputation of the group is that they are "radicals" or "troublemakers."

It may be difficult to determine whether the individual members of a group should sue. Whether the individual members can sue will depend upon whether reasonable people would believe a defamatory statement about the group refers to that individual. Thus, if an individual feels that his personal reputation has been damaged by defamatory statements about a group to which he belongs, it may be necessary for him to show that the group is so small that a person hearing the statements would reasonably believe that they point to each member of the group. Or it might be necessary for him to show that he is so closely identified with this group in the public eye, perhaps as a spokesperson, or the group is so closely identified with him, that people would believe that the statements referred to him. Obviously, defamation suits by small groups and their members should be approached with caution.

WHAT DEFENCES ARE THERE TO A DEFAMATION SUIT?

Generally, saying that one did not intend to hurt someone's reputation is no defence to a defamation suit. The test is not the motives of the person who made the statement, but the effect the statement would have in the eyes of the community. However, making a statement that is harmful to someone's reputation is not always defamation. The most important matter to consider is the truth of the statement and whether one can prove it. If the statement is true, the speaker should have nothing to fear. However, once a speaker says something, the burden is on him to prove that it is true. This can be difficult.

For example, a reporter or broadcaster may quote someone as having said something that makes the person quoted seem ridiculous. If the person quoted actually made that statement, however stupid, the reporter or broadcaster is not liable for repeating it. (Of course, the reporter or broadcaster would be acting unethically if he reported something said "off the record.") However, if the person quoted later denies that he ever made the statement attributed to him, the burden of proving in court that the statement was made would be on the reporter or broadcaster. This is why reporters often want a witness to any statement that may be defamatory or want to confirm the truth of the statement before reporting it.

In this kind of situation, consent would also be a defence. If someone consents to his statement being reported, he cannot later sue. Similarly, if someone consents to the publication of a statement made about him by some other person, he cannot sue. Williams states that:

> The defence of consent will be available where the plaintiff has actively encouraged, solicited or induced the publication of the defamatory statements. The consent must be expressed or implied, but it cannot be passive.[11]

WHAT IS FAIR COMMENT?

Fair comment is another important defence for the public interest advocate. Even if what you say is untrue, your opinion may be protected in some circumstances. If it is important to the community that some matter or conduct be widely discussed, or if the facts are a matter of public record, such as births, marriages, deaths, convictions and changes of name, anyone can comment on them. However, to rely upon the defence of fair comment, you must "get your facts right"; that is, you must ensure that the facts upon which you base your comment are true. You must also establish that the comment is in fact fair and not distorted, and that you acted without malice. This defence applies only to comments about matters of genuine public interest. For example, it may be fair comment to say that a politician is unfit to hold public office because of activities he engages in or statements he has made.

WHAT IS THE DOCTRINE OF PRIVILEGE?

The doctrine of "privilege" provides a defence against defamatory statements made in situations where it is in the public interest to allow freedom of speech, even at the risk of harming someone's reputation. Ironically, most public interest advocates will not be able to take advantage of this defence. It is generally available only to people in authority. Communications between a lawyer and his client, many statements by Cabinet ministers and deputy ministers, reports by very senior military officers to their superiors and virtually all statements made by judges and members of quasi-judicial tribunals, as well as lawyers, witnesses, parties and jurors taking part in judicial or quasi-judicial proceedings, are absolutely privileged. Members of Parliament and of the Provincial Legislatures are also absolutely safe from defamation suits for anything they say within the legislative chamber.

Statements made by others in certain circumstances are subject to a *qualified* privilege if made without malice. If the speaker has a legal, moral or social duty to give information to the general public, or to some segment of it, he cannot be sued for defamation provided that there is a public interest in the matter being commented on. However, this defence requires both that the speaker have a duty to communicate and that there be a public interest in receiving the communication. The list of people who have such a duty is short, and is unlikely to include most public interest advocates. It consists primarily of elected officials and civil servants carrying out duties imposed upon them by statutes. It does not include newspapers.

Statements made in self-defence in response to an attack on some personal interest are also privileged. In general, someone may respond to an attack on his property or reputation even if the response crosses the border between fair comment and libel, provided that the response is disseminated to roughly the same audience to whom the original attack was communicated.

Although the media have no greater privilege to state or repeat a libel than anyone else, they are protected if they report potentially libellous statements made by participants in judicial or quasi-judicial proceedings during the course of those proceedings. The absolute and qualified privileges that relate to judicial and quasi-judicial proceedings, however, may not apply to administrative proceedings. (The distinction between the two types of tribunal is fuzzy. In general, the difference between a quasi-judicial tribunal and an administrative tribunal is that the proceedings of the former directly affect a person's financial or property interests, while the proceedings of the latter do not. An important clue as to whether a tribunal is quasi-judicial or administrative is that the former makes a decision, but the latter merely makes recommendation. Anyone who intends to make a statement that he fears may be defamatory, within the confines of a tribunal, or wants to report such a statement, would be well advised to get a lawyer's opinion as to the kind of tribunal it is.)

WHAT WILL AN APOLOGY DO?

Finally, an apology or retraction, while not providing a complete defence to the defamation action, reduces the damages available, provided that it is timely. For example, there are two doctors in the same city named John Jones. A newspaper writes a story saying that "John J. Jones, a prominent doctor, was convicted of arson yesterday," when the arsonist was John K. Jones. The following day, the newspaper prints a correction and apologizes to John J. for any embarrassment it has caused him. The retraction and apology go a long way towards rectifying any damage to John J.'s reputation, and therefore greatly reduce the damages a court would award John J. if he were to sue.

HOW CAN DEFAMATION BE AVOIDED?

Public interest groups are frequently the last line of defence against injustice. Without them, democracy would not work nearly as well as it does. It is important that they be encouraged to continue to speak out, but their right to freedom of speech is tenuous as they are vulnerable to defamation suits. Like many of the issues dealt with in this book, the law of defamation is a minefield, and it may be impossible for you to determine whether a statement is defamatory on the basis of this chapter alone.

If you feel you have something to say that is of great public importance, but you are afraid you might leave yourself open to a defamation suit, one approach would be to discuss the matter with an elected representative. He may have an absolute or qualified privilege, and you could leave it to his discretion whether to raise the matter.

It is not unreasonable to expect that our elected representatives will exercise their judgment in such a way as to balance the interests of fairness to individuals' reputations against their duty to raise matters of great importance.

As a general rule, you will be on safe ground if you attack the issue rather than the person. This is frequently a much better strategy in any event. If you must attack the person, you will generally be on safe ground if you can prove the truth of anything you say.

There are often defamatory and non-defamatory ways of saying the same thing. If you are in doubt, by all means consult a lawyer. However, lawyers are often very cautious and will advise you not to make a statement if you ask, "Should I say this?" Therefore, one Toronto lawyer has suggested, "If you feel you have something to say that is important for the public to hear, do not ask a lawyer, 'Can I say this?' but, 'How can I say this without being subject to a libel suit?'[12] Putting the question in this way will encourage the lawyer to assist you to achieve your goal rather than merely to keep out of trouble."

CONCLUSION

Unfortunately, libel and slander laws are often more useful to the person who wants to silence a critical public interest advocate than to a defender of the public interest who wants to sue to protect his reputation. Citizens who attack the establishment and their lawyers should be aware of the possibility of a "gag" suit. The suit will probably never be pursued, because it has little or no merit. It serves its purpose merely by intimidating the meek. Fortunately, such suits are not common in Canada, and the courts can often quickly dismiss an action brought purely out of malice. The best defence against such a suit is to check your facts carefully before making a public statement and know that you can prove the truth of what you say if you are called upon to do so.

On the other hand, it is reassuring to know that the law of defamation also protects public interest advocates from unwarranted slurs. If an opponent says something untrue about you that is harmful to your reputation, issuing a notice that you intend to sue is often all that is needed to obtain a retraction or apology. If this doesn't work, however, you will have to decide whether defending yourself against the attack on your reputation is worth a protracted legal battle.

11.

CHARITABLE STATUS AND PUBLIC INTEREST ADVOCACY

There are approximately 50,000 registered charitable non-profit organizations in Canada. In recent years, many of them have been tempted to use litigation or political lobbying to raise and resolve issues. But there is a risk that this activity might lead to revocation of a group's charitable status, and this would cripple their fund-raising efforts. Deprivation of charitable status is one of the most terrible threats to the financial survival of a public interest group.

Many groups are asking community legal clinics and public interest lawyers for legal opinions on which of their activities might jeopardize their charitable status. Lawyers who are employees of such charitable organizations must be in a position to advise their boards of directors on this contentious issue.

WHAT IS CHARITABLE STATUS?

Under the Income Tax Act, public interest groups that are recognized by the federal government as "charitable organizations" and "charitable foundations" are exempt from paying tax on their income. More importantly, such groups can issue a receipt that allows donors a deduction from their income tax. This "charitable status" is crucial to organizations promoting social change; without it they could not attract the donations that finance their activities. Only a handful of public interest groups in Canada have memberships large enough to sustain them; most depend on grants and donations from individuals, corporations and foundations. It is not surprising, therefore, that public interest groups often ask their lawyers, "If we engage in litigation or law reform, will we lose our charitable status?" The answer is far from clear.

HOW CAN CHARITABLE STATUS BE REVOKED?

Recognition as a charity is granted by the federal Department of National Revenue. But the government has the power to revoke the charitable status at any time if it decides the group is no longer a charity. This revocation is subject to an appeal to the Federal Court. Unfortunately, the Income Tax Act does not explain what it means by "charity" or "charitable." The definition comes from a court's 1891 categorization[1] of a long list of worthy causes in the preamble to an English law passéd in 1601, the Statute of Charitable Uses. This statute was repealed in 1888, but its preamble was retained in later statutes.

According to the judicial decisions interpreting the preamble over the years, a "charity" is a trust for the relief of poverty, a trust for the advancement of education, a trust for the advancement of religion or a trust *for other purposes beneficial to the community*. The Canadian and British courts still use this definition when interpreting the term "charity" in statutes like the Income Tax Act. In determining whether the "objects" or "purposes" for which a group is formed are "charitable," the Saskatchewan Court of Appeal ruled in 1951 that, "Trusts for the attainment of political objects have always been held not to be valid charitable trusts."[2] This statement of the law has been adopted several times by Canadian courts, and, unless and until the Supreme Court of Canada rules otherwise, this would seem to be the law in Canada.

Thus, while we do not have a comprehensive legal definition of charity, we do know that the definition excludes groups whose purposes are "political." What "political" means, however, is even more unclear. It is not defined in the Income Tax Act. To clarify its meaning, Revenue Canada drafted an "Information Circular" in 1977 explaining what activities it considered to be "political."[3] The circular restricted the activities of public interest groups so severely that it created an uproar. Public interest groups (even traditional charities like the United Way and the churches), civil libertarians and the press claimed that the government's definition of "political" was an attempt to muzzle free speech and handcuff public interest groups. According to the circular, writing letters to the editor could be "political" and, if a group published a newsletter containing political comment or held a conference on political issues, it must give equal space or time to all viewpoints.

HOW DO THE COURTS INTERPRET THE LAW IN REGARD TO CHARITABLE STATUS?

The government claimed the circular did nothing more than set out the state of the law as interpreted over the years by the courts. (In fact, in some respects, the government's interpretation may have been less restrictive than some of the courts' decisions.) Nevertheless, to quiet the backlash, the government "withdrew" the circular.

Perhaps the clearest and most complete description of the meaning of "political" is in the Saskatchewan decision mentioned earlier: "The word 'political' includes activities for the purposes of influencing Legislature or Parliament to change existing laws or to enact new laws in accordance with the view or the views of the interested parties."[4] Opposing or resisting proposed changes in the law appear to be equally "political."[5] According to this definition, all law reform activities would seem to be "political." Chief Justice Martin's statement alone would lead one to believe that the preparation of law reform proposals, briefs and submissions to government can lead to loss of charitable status; but, in fact, there are no cases stating whether preparing law reform proposals is "political" activity.

In its Information Circular, Revenue Canada gave the opinion that the presentation of briefs, whether spontaneously or at the request of a public body, and representations to legislators are not "political" as long as a group does not undertake a program to promote its recommendations, otherwise attempt to influence legislation, or engage in a "campaign" to influence intended or specific legislation.

But in reality, the decision of a court as to whether an activity is "political" or "charitable" often seems to depend on the time, the place and the cause being promoted. Ontario courts have considered the promotion of civil rights[6] and the promotion of legislation prohibiting the consumption of alcohol to be charitable.[7] British courts have held that campaigns for free milk for pupils in public schools[8] and for anti-vivisection legislation are uncharitable.[9] A fund to be used to persuade people to free slaves or not to acquire slaves was held to be charitable in Massachusetts in 1867,[10] but in the same year, a Massachusetts court held that securing the passage of legislation granting women equal political rights with men was not charitable.[11] Promoting the enjoyment of civil rights is charitable in Illinois[12] and California,[13] but not in Massachusetts.[14] Advocating prohibition is uncharitable in New York,[15] but charitable in Ontario.[16]

Courts and commentators have often suggested that as long as the *main* objects of an organization (it no longer need be a "trust") are charitable, the fact that it has some *ancillary* objects that are not will not deprive it of charitable status. Whether that is still true in Canada, however, is questionable. The Income Tax Act says that a charitable organization must devote *all* its resources to charitable activities, and a charitable foundation (a charitable organization that gives money to other charitable organizations) must be operated *exclusively* for charitable purposes. Perhaps one way around this narrow definition is the approach taken by some courts which have said that certain objects of an organization were exclusively charitable and others were not.[17] Money spent on these "exclusively charitable" objects is not subject to income tax, while money spent to advance its other objects would be taxable.

A major source of confusion in this issue is the fact that the cases talk about charitable "purposes" and "objects," while groups really want to know about specific *activities*. The activities or operations of a group can be used by the government to interpret what the group's real objects (objectives) are, regardless of what the constitutional objects say. No group is likely to state its objects as being "the violent overthrow of the Canadian government" when applying for charitable status. It is much more likely to couch them in terms of "educating the public about alternative public policies" or some other such thing.

Regardless of what a group *says* its objects are, the government can look at what it actually *does*. By the same token, however, the government must interpret the reasons for a group's activities in light of its stated objects. For instance, if an environmental group submits a brief to Parliament asking for new environmental protection legislation, or if it takes a test case to court, is the primary purpose of this action to achieve political change or to enhance the quality of the environment? In the case of litigation, under our corporate laws, any corporation can engage in litigation for the purposes of obtaining any end that is within its objects. This should also be true of any incorporated charitable trust. There are no cases saying that litigation itself is uncharitable. Whether the use of litigation as a tool to achieve social change can be considered "political" will probably depend on the circumstances of the individual case.

The distinction between activities and objects is important because isolated activities should not be sufficient justification for refusing or revoking charitable status if the group's overall objects are the test of whether it is a charity. To prove that a group is not a charity the government should have to show that its activities are overwhelmingly "political." If a group publishes a newsletter or magazine, for example, using the "objects" test, a single editorial or article criticizing the government should provide very little evidence that the group's overall purpose is political. But how many critical articles will it take before a "charitable" group becomes a "political" one? With such ambiguity, the potential for government harassment and intimidation of public interest groups is obvious.

CAN A PUBLIC INTEREST GROUP LOSE ITS CHARITABLE STATUS?

Until now, no public interest group has ever had its charitable status revoked, although over the past three years there have been persistent rumours about the government threatening to revoke the charitable status of one group or another because of involvement in protest marches or demonstrations. The cases interpreting whether a group's objects were charitable have always arisen in a different context — usually arguments over how a charity is entitled to spend its money and who is eligible to receive it, and the question of whether the recipient of a grant or donation has to pay tax on it.

However, Canada is now facing its first test case. Recently Revenue Canada decided to revoke the charitable status of the Manitoba Foundation for Canadian Studies, which publishes the left-leaning magazine *Canadian Dimension*.

The magazine claims to be educational, and therefore qualified to have charitable status, but the government department claims that to be educational a magazine must canvass all sides of an issue. It says that *Canadian Dimension* is political because its political articles always take a socialist position. But the magazine also features many non-political articles. In the letter announcing the deregistration, Revenue Canada explained that "it would appear that [*Canadian Dimension*'s] goal is not to educate the reader in the sense of training the mind in matters of political science, but to promote a particular ideology." The magazine's editor responded that this is a "crude attempt at political censorship." The foundation has appealed the deregistration to the Federal Court. The *Canadian Dimension* case may be merely the beginning of a widespread deregistration of controversial public interest groups. As the Ottawa tax lawyer Arthur Drache has been quoted as saying, "*Canadian Dimension* is clearly an easy target because it does not command widespread popular support. If *Canadian Dimension* is hit, there is no telling how far Revenue Canada will go."[18]

CONCLUSION

There are about 50,000 registered charities in Canada. The state of uncertainty about what constitutes "politicking" is detrimental not only to their freedom of expression but to the development of social policy, which has been assisted by the advice of such groups in the past. The outcome of the *Canadian Dimension* case may help to clarify the rights of public interest groups, although it would be better to have the government enunciate clear policy and invite public discussion of the appropriate role for charities in modern society than to ask the courts to make social policy on the basis of 300-year-old laws.

In the meantime, groups may obtain some protection through the traditional approach of establishing two separate organizations: a charitable foundation that raises money and a separate association that engages in the activities that may prove controversial. In the past these foundations have donated some or all of the money they raised to the "activist" organizations. This worked as long as the government was liberally minded, but it is questionable whether it can withstand close scrutiny. To enhance the separation between such bodies, it might be advisable for them each to have boards of directors consisting largely of different individuals, and for the bulk of the activist group's activities to be clearly non-political.

It is also wise for a controversial group to diversify its sources of revenue as much as possible so that its survival does not depend on charitable donations. Membership drives, sales of publications and development of marketable services and products can help.

CONCLUSION

We've now explored the various strategies available to public advocates and their lawyers in getting an issue into the courts, what to do in the courts and how to avoid the courts. Clearly the situation is weighted against the citizen advocate. But, as this book has shown, public advocates can win in the face of very stiff opposition.

But the fact remains that the challenges facing public interest groups and their lawyers are difficult ones. In many instances, the full weight of big business or big government can shatter the financial and organizational capabilities of citizen groups before such groups have had the opportunity to effectively present their cases. The opposition is very powerful and benefits from close association with legislators and bureaucrats. Citizen groups are denied the kind of access that business has always had — access through their lobbyists to government cabinet ministers and senior bureaucrats. The data flow between government and big business means that decisions affecting all of us are based on information that few of us have access to. Frequently, government relies on statistics and figures that are supplied by business to make major policy decisions. If government does undertake policies that will affect the property and financial interests of business, lengthy court cases can occur and all too frequently government backs down.

Citizens can and do fight back. But getting a case into the courts is only the beginning of what can prove to be a lengthy, frustrating and very expensive lesson in how the law works. The question of costs looms very large for individuals or groups who can overcome the standing barrier. Because of the costs involved if a case is lost, few citizens are willing to use the courts to seek redress. A wealthy corporation that stands to lose millions of dollars because of a consumer protection policy will challenge the policy in the courts. But thousands of consumers who individually lose a few hundred dollars because they have had to repair a defective product will never sue the manufacturer as long as each of them is liable for what may amount to several thousands of dollars in costs. The law needs to be reformed. There should be a special costs rule in cases where the plaintiff has little to gain financially if he wins, but much to lose if he doesn't. In an issue where it's a matter of principle rather than financial gain, the plaintiff should be protected against costs. But that hasn't happened yet.

Because of the costs involved and the intimidating strength of the opposition, citizen groups feel isolated and vulnerable. In the past the legal profession has not gone out of its way to fight for citizen activists. Consumers, ethnic minorities, victims of pollution, the poor, denied the kind of access that their opponents enjoy, have taken to the streets to protest. Frequently their actions have gotten them into court, but on the wrong side of the law. Recently, a new breed of lawyer has emerged, running storefront offices and community legal clinics. The tide is turning slowly in the fight to redress grievances and speed social change, but it is an uphill battle.

Advocates have challenged the barriers the courts put in their way. They have explored ways of getting the courts to give the same consideration to arguments based on principle and the public good as they give to private concerns. The lawyers have needed to learn how to protect themselves and their clients from harassment by the establishment. Lawyers and public interest groups have fought, with some success, for better legal aid plans. Some pressure groups that formed in the Sixties were so successful that they now can pick up the telephone and get results from government agencies without having to get the attention of bureaucrats and politicians by first demonstrating on the steps of Parliament. Some groups are now routinely consulted before changes in law or policy are made that affect their constituents. There is still a long way to go.

It's worthwhile recalling that civil conspiracy laws were originally developed by a legal system intent on supporting employers who were trying to prevent their employees from organizing unions. The courts repeatedly ruled against workers in declaring the illegality of strikes and picket lines. Only militant labour action forced a change. Gradually the courts and government have come to recognize the legitimacy of unionism — though the fight is never quite over. Today those same conspiracy laws are being used to stop boycotts and picket lines thrown up by consumer advocates and tenants. And government actions in regard to charitable status pose a frightening new threat to groups who use dissent to urge social change.

By now you have some idea how to raise social issues in the courts despite the standing barrier, how to launch a test case, how to organize or join a protest march without being arrested, and how to speak out or support public interest litigation without being sued.

But is this enough? Should the right to dissent be subject to so many restrictions in a democratic society? Does the limited right you have to raise public issues in the courts guarantee anything but a hostile reception? It should be apparent from reading this book that law reform is necessary just to ensure that people have the right to speak out about injustice without fear of harassment and to use the courts without paying crushing costs.

The need for reform of our laws is a pressing one. Social change and a fair and equitable society will only come about when the law recognizes the right to peaceful dissent, encourages the formation of public interest groups and gives the weak the same rights and resources as the strong.

NOTES

PART I: GETTING INTO COURT

Chapter 1: Standing

1. Boyce v. Paddington Council, 1 Ch. 109 (1903).

2. Re Save Our Parkland Association *et al*, 50 WWR 92 (1964).

3. Thorson v. Attorney General of Canada, 43 DLR 1 (1974).

4. Nova Scotia Board of Censors v. McNeil, 55 DLR (3d) 632 (1975).

5. Rosenberg *et al* v. Grand River Conservation Authority, 69 DLR (3d) 384 (1975).

6. Re Pim and Minister of the Environment, 23 OR (2d) 45; 94 DLR (3d) 254 (1978).

7. Re Brown *et al* and Patterson, 21 CCC (2d) 373 (1974).

8. Re Royal Commission on Conduct of Waste Management Inc. *et al*, 17 OR (2d) 207 (1977).

9. See for example Re Canadian Broadcasting League and CRTC and Rogers *et al*, 101 DLR (3d) 669 (1980).

Chapter 2: *Amicus Curiae*

1. For a detailed discussion of the background and practice of the *amicus curiae*, see "The *Amicus Curiae*," 20 *Chitty's Law Journal* 94 (1972), and *Gazette of the Law Society of Upper Canada*, Vol. V, No. 2, p. 110 (1971).

2. United States v. Spock, 416 F. (2d) 165 at 169, note 5 (1969).

3. Beaty & Co. v. McCarty, 52 OLR 203.

4. Reference re Sections 222, 224 and 224A of the Criminal Code, 3 CCC (2d) 243.

5. Re MacMichael (1969), *Times*, January 14 and January 17, cited in G.J. Borrie and N.V. Lowe, *The Law of Contempt* (London, Butterworths, 1973) at p. 18.

6. Re Drummond Wren, 4 DLR 674 (1945).

7. R. v. ex rel. Rose v. Marshal, 48 MPR 64, at 66-7.

8. Re Château-Gai Wines Ltd. and Attorney General of Canada, 14 DLR (3d) 411, at p. 413 (1970).

9. Regina v. Wiebe, Provincial Court (Criminal Division) of Alberta, Three Hills, January 12, 1978, His Honour Judge Oliver. The decision is reported at 3 WWR 36 (1978), but the judge's reasons for appointing an *amicus* are unreported.

10. Copithorne v. Copithorne, Supreme Court of Alberta, Trial Division, Calgary, December 23, 1976, decision of the Honourable Chief Justice Milvain.

11. "The *Amicus Curiae*," supra, note 1, *Chitty's* at p. 136, *Gazette* at p. 125.

12. Saumur v. City of Quebec, 2 SCR 299, at 325 (1953).

13. Re Clark *et al* and Attorney General of Canada, 17 OR (2d) 593 at 598 (1977).

14. Re Ronark Developments and City of Hamilton *et al*, 4 OR 195 (1974). Upheld in the Court of Appeal: 5 OR (2d) 136.

15. McDonald's Restaurants of Canada v. Corporation of the Borough of Etobicoke, 5 CPC 55 at 57 (1977).

16. R. v. Lake Ontario Cement Ltd. 2 OR 247, 11 CCC (2d) 1 (1973). The reported case makes no mention of *amicus curiae,* describing counsel merely as solicitors for the complainant. However, see the comment on this case in Volume 11, Number 2 of the *Canadian Environmental Law News*, April 1973, at p. 25.

17. However, the recent practice of the Supreme Court of Canada has been to award no costs in favour of or against an intervenor unless the intervenor has misbehaved in some way.

18. Rule 60 of the Supreme Court Rules (SOR/72-596):

    60(1) Any person interested in an appeal between other parties may, by leave of the court or judge, intervene therein upon such terms and conditions and with such rights and privileges as the court or judge may determine.
    (2) The costs of such intervention shall be paid by such party or parties as the Supreme Court shall order.

19. Nova Scotia Board of Censors and Attorney General of Nova Scotia v. McNeil, 32 CRNS 376 (1975).

20. Morgentaler v. the Queen, 20 CCC (2d) 449 (1975).

21. Working Draft of Proposed Ontario Rules of Civil Procedure, April 1978, Rule 15, Civil Procedure Revision Committee, Walter B. Williston, Chairman.

22. Rule 504a of the Rules of Practice and Rule 24a of the Rules of Respecting Criminal Proceedings of the Supreme Court of Ontario, effective September 12, 1979.

23. The Ontario Court of Appeal recently permitted twenty groups and individuals to intervene under Rule 504a in a constitutional reference concerning the validity of new landlord-tenant legislation: Reference Re Residential Tenancies Act, 26 OR (2d) 609 (1980).

24. Reference Re Regina v. Truscott, 62 DLR (2d) 547 (1967).

25. Reference Re Legislative Privilege, 83 DLR (3d) 161 (1978).

26. Reference Re Residential Tenancies Act, 26 OR (2d) 609 (1979).

27. Reference Re Proposed Legislation Concerning Leased Premises and Tenancy Agreements, 89 DLR (3d) 460 (1978).

28. Reference Re Validity of Wartime Leasehold Regulations, SCR 124 (1950).

29. Reference Re Anti-Inflation Act, 68 DLR (3d) 452 (1976).

30. Central Canada Potash Company v. Government of Saskatchewan, 88 DLR (3d) 609 (1978).

Chapter 3: Test Cases

1. Loew's Montreal Theatres Limited v. Reynolds, KBD 30 (1929).

2. R. v. McKay, 113 CCC 56 (1955).

3. R. v. Emerson, 113 CCC 69 (1955).

4. R. ex rel. Nutland v. McKay, 115 CCC 104 (1956).

5. R. v. Toronto Refiners and Smelters, 20 OR (2d) 772 (1978).

6. R. v. Watts and Gaunt, 1 DLR 610 (1953); revd on other grounds 3 DLR 152 (1953); R. v. Newsome; R. v. Browne, 54 Cr. App. R. 485 at 493 (1970).

7. Stokes v. B.C. Electric Railway Co., 12 DLR 379 (1913).

PART II: BEFORE THE COURTS AND TRIBUNALS

Chapter 4: Costs

1. Anderson v. Busse and Federation Insurance Co. of Canada, 2 OR 454 (1946); Gracie v. King, OWN 356 (1943).

2. Re McMaster, 2 WWR 1032 (1947); aff'd 1 WWR 648 (1948).

3. Re Bothwell Estate 1 WWR 1041 (1950); York Condominium Corp. No. 148 v. Singular Investments Ltd., 16 OR (2d) 31 (1977).

4. Rosenberg *et al* v. Grand River Conservation Authority, 9 OR (2d) 771; 5 CELN 156 (1976).

5. Rosenberg *et al* v. Grand River Conservation Authority, 12 OR (2d) 496 (1976).

6. Miller v. City of Winnipeg, 4 CELN 167 (Man. QB) (1975).

7. Re Pim and Minister of the Environment, 23 OR (2d) 45; 94 DLR (3d) 254 (1978).

8. Re Central Wellington Planning Area Official Plan Amendment, 80 OMBR 263 at p. 284 (1978).

9. Reference re Principles of Power Costing and Rate Making for Use by Ontario Hydro, 6 CELN 171 (1977).

10. Re Pajelle Investments Ltd. and Booth (No. 2), 7 OR (2d) 229 at 239-41; 5 CELN 163 (1975).

11. Federal Court Act, RSC 1970, c. 10 (second supplement), rule 348.

12. Scribner v. Parcells, 20 OR 554 (1890).

13. Barrie Public School Board v. Town of Barrie, PR 33 (1899).

14. Re Avery, OWN 475 (1952).

15. Fraser River Contracting Ltd. v. FWP Construction Ltd., 2 WWR 354 (1978).

16. Myers v. Elman, AC 282 (1940).

17. Re Ontario Crime Commission, 1 OR 391 (1962).

18. Re the Queen and Fisher *et al*, 76 DLR (3d) 332; aff'd 78 DLR (3d) 215 (1976).

19. Re Hawrish, 50 WWR 616 (1964).

Chapter 5: Contempt

1. R.v. Larue-Langlois, 14 CRNS 68 (1970).

2. Re Tilco Plastics Ltd. v. Skursat *et al*, 57 DLR (2d) 596 (Ont. H.C.) (1966); R. v. United Fishermen and Allied Workers *et al*, 65 DLR (2d) 220 (1967); Bassel's Lunch Ltd. v. Kick *et al*, 4 DLR 106 (1936).

3. Borrie and Lowe, *The Law of Contempt* at p. 2.

4. Tony Poje *et al* v. Attorney General of British Columbia, 2 DLR 785 (1953).

5. Borrie and Lowe, at p. 17.

6. Borrie and Lowe, at p. 17.

7. For example Re Duncan (1957), see Borrie and Lowe, at p. 20.

8. Law Reform Commission of Canada, Contempt of Court, Working Paper 20 (Ottawa, Minister of Supply and Services Canada, 1977) at p. 35.

9. Ibid at p. 30.

10. Borrie and Lowe, chapter 6.

11. Ambard v. Attorney General for Trinidad and Tobago, AC 322 at 355 per Lord Atkin (1936).

12. R. v. Metropolitan Police Commissioner, *ex parte* Blackburn (no. 2) 2 QB 150 at 155 per Salmon, L.J.(1968).

13. R. v. Gray, 2 QB 36 at 40 per Lord Russell, C.J. (1900).

14. Lord Denning, M.R. in the Blackburn case, note 12.

15. Re Regina and Carocchia, 14 CCC (2d) 354 (1972).

16. Attorney General of Ontario v. Canadian Broadcasting Corporation *et al*, 39 CCC (2d) 182 (1977).

17. Re Attorney General for Manitoba and Radio OB Ltd. *et al*, 31 CCC (2d) 1 (1976).

18. Sommers v. Sturdy, 6 DLR (2d) 642 (1956). The speech was given under certain extenuating circumstances, however, and the decision may not have much application to other circumstances.

19. R. v. Bryan *et al*, 18 CR 143. See also Fortin v. Moscarella et al, 23 WWR 91 (BCSC) (1957).

20. Re Depoe *et al* and Lamport *et al*, 1 OR 185 (1968).

21. C.J. Miller, *Contempt of Court* (London, Paul Elek, 1976).

Chapter 6: Maintenance and Champerty

1. Prosser v. Edmonds 1 Y & C Ex 481; 160 ER 196; Goodman v. the King, 4 DLR 361 (1939).

2. Alabaster v. Harness, 1 QB 339 (CA) (1895).

3. Greig v. National Union of Shop Assistants, 22 TLR 274 (1906).

4. Fleming, *The Law of Torts*, 5th ed. (Melbourne, The Law Book Co., 1977) at p. 611.

5. Fleming, p. 612.

6. Grant v. Thompson, 72 LT 264 (1895).

7. Amacher v. Eriksen, 42 WWR 348 (1963).

8. Neville v. London Express, AC 368 (1919).

9. Skelton v. Baxter, 1 KB (CA) (1916).

10. This would be a logical implication of the principle set out in Amacher, note 7. Also Goodman, note 1.

11. Greig v. National Union of Shop Assistants, note 3 at 275.

12. Martell v. Consett Iron Co., Ch. 363 (1955); cf. Plating Co. v. Farquharson, 17 Ch. D. 49 (1881).

13. Harris v. Briscoe, 17 QBD 504 (1886); Stevens v. Keogh, 72 LLR 1 (1946).

14. Fleming, at p. 615.

15. Orkin, *Legal Ethics,* (Toronto, Cartwright and Sons, 1957) at p. 160.

Chapter 7: Seeking an Adjournment

1. Re Piggott Construction Ltd. and United Brotherhood of Carpenters and Joiners of America, Local 1990, 31 DLR (3d) 758 (1972); 39 DLR (3d) 311 (1973).

2. R. v. Ontario Labour Relations Board, *ex parte* Nick Masney Hotels Ltd., 7 DLR (3d) 119 (1969); 13 DLR (3d) 289 (1970).

3. Re Crux and Leoville Union Hospital Board (No. 2), 32 DLR (3d) 373 (1972); 35 DLR (3d) 619 (1973). See also Masney, note 3.

4. Re Flamboro Downs Holdings Ltd. and Teamsters Local 79, 24 OR (2d) 400 (1979).

5. Re Ramm, 7 DLR (2d) 378 (1957); Re Sreedhar and Outlook Union Hospital Board, 32 DLR (3d) 491 (1972); Re Gasparetto and City of Sault Ste. Marie, 35 DLR (3d) 507 (1973).

6. Flamboro, note 5.

7. Piggott, note 1.

8. Re Gill Lumber and United Brotherhood of Carpenters, 42 DLR (3d) 271 (1973).

9. Re Bass, 19 DLR (2d) 485 (1959).

PART III: KEEPING OUT OF COURT AND OUT OF TROUBLE

Chapter 8: Demonstrations, Protest and the Law

1. Robertson and Rosetanni v. the Queen, SCR 651 (1963).

2. For a more complete account of the legal entanglements that organizing and participating in a demonstration have created for

Greenpeace and its lawyer, see Peter C. Ballem, "The Icemen Killeth," in *Canadian Lawyer,* April, 1980.

3. Rex v. Aldred, 22 Cox CC 1 at 4 (1909).

4. Ruby, Clayton C., "Obstructing a Police Officer," 15 *Criminal Law Quarterly* 375 at 376.

5. Hogben, v. Camber, VLR 285; (1940); R. v. Boulanger, 4 CCC 85 (1969).

6. R. v. Long, 1 CCC 313 (1970).

7. Ibid.

8. R. v. Moore, 1 SCR, 195, 90 DLR (3d) 112 (1979).

9. W.S. Tarnopolsky, *The Canadian Bill of Rights,* 2nd ed. (Toronto, McClelland and Stewart, 1975) Carleton Library edition at p. 204.

10. Ibid at 206.

11. Regina v. McGregor, Taylor and Lee, 8 CELR 127 (1979).

12. Hubbard v. Pitt, 3 WLR 201 (1975), affirming 2 WLR 254 (1975).

Chapter 9: Conspiracy

1. Crofter Hand Woven Harris Tweed Co. v. Veitch, AC 435 at 442-3 (1942).

2. South Wales Miners' Federation v. Glamorgan Coal Co., AC 239 at 249 (1905).

3. Brimelow v. Casson, 1 Ch. 302 (1924).

4. Slade and Stewart v. Haynes, 5 DLR (3d) 736 (1969).

5. Read v. Friendly Society of Stonemasons, 2 KB 88 at 97 (1902).

6. Camden Nominees Ltd. v. Forcey, 1 Ch. 352 (1940).

7. South Wales Miners' Federation v. Glamorgan Coal Co., note 2.

8. Crofter Hand Woven Harris Tweed Co. v. Veitch, note 1.

9. Scala Ballroom (Wolverhampton) Ltd. v. Ratcliffe, 1 WLR 1057 (1958).

Chapter 10: Defamation

1. Youssoupoff v. MGM Ltd., 50 TLR 581, per Slesser, L.J. (1934).

2. *Salmond on Torts*, 16th ed. (1973) at p. 143.

3. Sim v. Stretch, 52 TLR 669 (1936); 2 All ER 1237 (1936).

4. See Dennison v. Sanderson, OR 601 (1946); 4 DLR 314 (1946); Braddock v. Blevins 1 KB 580 (1948); 1 All ER 450 (1948); and Grant v. Reader's Digest Assoc. Inc. 151 F. (2d) 733 (1945).

5. J.S. Williams, *The Law of Defamation* (Toronto, Butterworths, 1976) at p. 53.

6. Williams, p. 17.

7. Capitol and Counties Bank v. Henty, 7 App. Cas. 741 (H.L.) (1882).

8. Wenman v. Ash, 13 CB 836 (1853); 138 ER 1432.

9. Williams, p. 21.

10. Williams, p. 22. See Bognor Regis Urban District Council v. Campion, 2 All ER 61 at p. 66 (QB) (1972).

11. Williams, at p. 106.

12. Lorne Slotnik, speaking to a Law Union of Ontario "Survival Seminar for Activists" in 1980.

Chapter 11: Charitable Status

1. Commissioners for the Special Purposes of the Income Tax Acts v. Pemsel, AC 531 (1891).

2. Re Patriotic Acre Fund, 2 OLR 624 at 634, per Martin, CJS (1951).

3. Registered Charities: Political Objects and Activities, Information Circular No. 78-3, Revenue Canada, February 27, 1978.

4. Op. cit. note 2.

5. See, for example, Re Hopkinson, 1 All ER 346 at 350 (1849), and Re Co-operative College of Canada and Saskatchewan Human Rights Commission, 64 DLR (3d) 531 (1975).

6. Lewis v. Doerle, 25 OAR 206 (1898).

7. Farewell v. Farewell, 22 OR 573 (1892).

8. Baldry v. Feintuck, 1 WLR 552 (1972).

9. Animal Defence and Anti-Vivisection Society v. Island Revenue Commissioners, 66 TLR (pt. 2) 1091 (1950).

10. Jackson v. Phillips, 96 Mass. 539 (1867).

11. Ibid.

12. Garrison v. Little, 75 Ill. App. 402 (1897).

13. Collier v. Lindley, 266 P. 526 (1928).

14. Op. cit. note 10.

15. Buell v. Gardner, 144 NY 5945 (1914).

16. Op. cit. note 7.

17. See Towle Estate v. MNR, 67 DTC 5003 (1966).

18. In *The Toronto Clarion,* April 16 to April 29, 1980, p. 3.

Abbreviations

Most of the works cited above are available only in the libraries of law schools and in court libraries. The public is not assured of automatic access to these libraries but if you are specific about what you are looking for, librarians will frequently take the time to help you out.

AC   Appeal Cases, Britain
All ER   *All England Law Reports*, Britain
BCSC   British Columbia Supreme Court
CA   Court of Appeal
CCC   *Canadian Criminal Cases*
CELN   *Canadian Environmental Law News*
Cox CC   *Cox's Criminal Cases*, Britain
CRNS   *Criminal Reports (New Series)*, Canada
DLR   *Dominion Law Reports*, Canada
DTC   *Dominion Tax Cases*
ER   *English Reports*, Britain
HL   House of Lords
Ill App   *Illinois Appellate Reports*
KBD   *King's Bench Division Reports*, Britain

LT   *Law Times Reports*, Britain
Mass   *Massachusetts Reports*
MPR   *Municipal and Planning Reports*, Canada
NY   *New York Reports*
OAR   *Ontario Appeal Reports*
OLR   *Ontario Law Reports*
OMBR   *Ontario Municipal Board Reports*
OR   *Ontario Reports*
OWN   *Ontario Weekly Notes*
P   *Pacific Reporter*, U.S.
PR   *Ontario Practice Reports*
SCR   *Supreme Court Reports*, Canada
SOR   *Statutory Orders and Regulations*, Canada
TLR   *Times Law Reports*, Australia
VLR   *Victoria Law Reports*, Australia
WWR   *Western Weekly Reports*, Canada
Y & C EX   *Yonge and Collier, Exchequer Cases*, Britain

GLOSSARY

Action: Proceedings taken by one person against another in a court of justice for the enforcement or protection of a right, or the redress or prevention of a wrong.

Appellant: A person who, having lost his case, has appealed it to a higher court.

Appellate court: Any court that has jurisdiction to hear appeals from other courts.

Defendant: The person against whom legal proceedings are brought in a civil court or who is charged with an offence in a criminal court. In criminal proceedings this person is sometimes called "the accused."

Disbursements: Money paid out by a lawyer in the conduct of a case, and for which he is entitled to a credit from his client on rendering his account.

Natural justice: The rules of natural justice are rules to ensure fairness and impartiality in the courts and in many administrative procedures. The rules provide that public officials such as judges, arbitrators, municipal council members and others who have a substantial interest in the outcome of any decision may not participate in making the decision. They also provide a right to a fair hearing, although what is a "fair hearing" varies according to the circumstances of each case.

Plaintiff: The person commencing an action in the civil courts.

Respondent: The person who, having won his case, is "responding" to an appeal in a higher court, brought by the loser.

Sub judice: Under consideration by a court.

Sub judice **rule:** The rule that it is a contempt of court to publicly express opinions about or publish unbalanced reports of any matter while it is before the courts.

Tort: A private or civil wrong or injury based on a general duty rather than on a contract. The most common tort is negligence, a duty to take reasonable care not to harm those around you. The torts discussed in this book are conspiracy, maintenance and champerty, and defamation.

FURTHER READING

PART I: GETTING INTO COURT

Chapter 1: Standing

S.H. Berner, *Private Prosecution and Environmental Control Legislation* (University of British Columbia Faculty of Law, commissioned by the Federal Department of the Environment, 1972).

A.R. Roman, "Is the Locus Standi Cure Worse than the Disease?" in *Environmental Rights In Canada* (Butterworths, Toronto, 1981).

L.A. Stein, ed., *Locus Standi* (Law Book Company, Sydney, 1979).

S.M. Thio, *Locus Standi and Judicial Review* (Singapore University Press, Singapore, 1971).

Chapter 2: *Amicus Curiae*

Albert S. Abel, *Laskin's Canadian Constitutional Law* (4th ed., Toronto: Carswell, 1973). See pages 84 to 91, especially regarding the use of extrinsic evidence in a constitutional reference.

Alan D. Levy, "The *Amicus Curiae*," 20 *Chitty's Law Journal* 94 (1972).

Chapter 3: Test Cases

Ross Howard, *Poisons in Public* (Toronto, James Lorimer & Company, 1980).

Clayton Ruby, *Sentencing*, 2nd ed. (Toronto, Butterworths, 1979). See pp. 172-3.

PART II: BEFORE THE COURTS AND TRIBUNALS

Chapter 4: Costs

Costs: Party and Party Updated (Toronto, Department of Continuing Education, Law Society of Upper Canada, 1979).

Costs: Solicitor and Client Updated (Department of Continuing Education, Law Society of Upper Canada, Toronto, 1979).

Jerome Carlin, *Lawyer's Ethics: A Survey of the New York City Bar* (Russell Sage Foundation, New York, 1966).

Henry Drinker, *Legal Ethics* (New York, Columbia University Press, 1965).

Mark Orkin, *The Law of Costs* (Toronto, Canada Law Book Limited, 1968).

Mark Orkin, *Legal Ethics: A Study of Professional Conduct* (Toronto, Cartwright, 1957).

Ola Orojo, *Conduct and Etiquette for Legal Practitioners* (Sweet and Maxwell, London, 1979).

Chapter 5: Contempt

G.J. Borrie and N.V. Lowe, *The Law of Contempt* (London, Butterworths, 1973).

Law Reform Commission of Canada, *Contempt of Court,* Working Paper 20 (Ottawa, Supply and Services Canada, 1977).

C.J. Miller, *Contempt of Court* (London, Paul Elek, 1976).

Chapter 6: Maintenance and Champerty

Fleming, *The Law of Torts,* 5th ed. (Melbourne, The Law Book Co., 1977). See pp. 611-615.

Halsbury's Laws of England, vol. 9. See. pp. 272-7.

R.F.V. Heuston, ed., *Salmond on Torts,* 14th ed. (London, Sweet and Maxwell, 1965). See pp. 598-601, 780-82.

Chapter 7: Seeking an Adjournment

J. Kavanagh, *A Guide to Judicial Review* (Toronto, Carswell, 1978).

D.J. Mullan, *Administrative Law* (Toronto, Carswell, 1973).

D. Mundell, *Manual of Practice; on Administrative Law and Procedure in Ontario* (Ontario Department of Justice, 1977).

R. Reid and H. David, *Administrative Law and Practice*, 2nd ed. (Toronto, Butterworths, 1978).

A.J. Roman, *Guidebook on How to Prepare Cases for Administrative Tribunals* (Ottawa, Consumers Association of Canada, 1977).

S.A. de Smith, *Judicial Review of Administrative Actions* (London, Stevens and Sons, 1973).

H.W.R. Wade, *Administrative Law*, 4th ed. (Oxford, Clarendon Press, 1977).

PART III: KEEPING OUT OF COURT AND OUT OF TROUBLE

Chapter 8: Demonstrations, Protest and the Law

David G. Barnum, "The Constitutional Status of Public Protest Activity in Britain and the United States" (1977) *Public Law* 310.

Kathy Boudin, Brian Glick, Eleanor Raskin and Gustin Reichback, *The Bust Book: What to Do Until the Lawyer Comes* (New York, Grove Press, 1970). Not everyone will appreciate the tone of this book: "In the future, as our Movement grows, it will be increasingly under attack. Leaders are no longer the only political people who are arrested. Everyone who goes to a demonstration, hands out a leaflet, smokes a joint, goes to a meeting, or runs away from home—each and all are possible targets for the cops and courts." Nevertheless, it contains a great deal of practical advice about demonstrations, arrests, incarceration, bail and trial strategy, although the law is American. Unfortunately, *The Bust Book* is out of print, but you might find it in a library.

Paul Copeland, Clayton Ruby and Greg King, *Law, Law, Law*, 4th ed. (Toronto, Anansi, 1976).

Offence/Defence: Survival Seminars for Activists, the Law Union of Ontario, 1980. These materials contain information about law and tactics relating to public meetings, demonstrations, strikes, when an object becomes a weapon, meeting the police, immigration law, the legality of postering and other useful information.

Clayton C. Ruby, "Obstructing a Police Officer" (1972-3) 15 *Criminal Law Quarterly*, 375.

W.S. Tarnopolsky, *The Canadian Bill of Rights,* 2nd ed. (Toronto, McClelland and Stewart, 1975) Carleton Library edition.

Chapter 9: Conspiracy

John G. Fleming, *The Law of Torts,* 5th ed. (Melbourne, The Law Book Co, Ltd., 1977). See pp. 676-684, 689-694.

R.F.V. Heuston, ed., *Salmond on Torts,* 17th ed. (London, Sweet and Maxwell, 1977).

Chapter 10: Defamation

Fleming, *The Law of Torts,* 5th ed. (Melbourne, The Law Book Company, 1977). See pp. 516-589.

Gatley on Libel and Slander, 7th ed. (London, Sweet and Maxwell, 1974).

R.F.V. Heuston, ed., *Salmond on Torts,* 17th ed. (London, Sweet and Maxwell, 1977). See pp. 138-192.

W.H. Kesterton, *The Law and the Press in Canada* (Toronto, Macmillan, 1976) Carleton Library edition.

Williams, *The Law of Defamation* (Toronto, Butterworths, 1976).

Chapter 11: Charitable Status

Anonymous, "The Sierra Club, Political Activity and Tax Exempt Charitable Status," 55 *Georgetown Law Journal* 1128 (1967).

J.C. Brady, "The Law of Charity and Judicial Responsiveness to Changing Social Needs," 27 *Northern Ireland Legal Quarterly* 198 (1976).

Maurice C. Cullity, "Charities—the Incidental Question," 6 *Melbourne University Law Review* 35 (1967).

Arthur B.C. Drache, "Political Activities: A Charitable Dilemma," *The Philanthropist,* vol. 2, no. 4, Fall, 1980.

William J. Lehrfeld, "How Much Politicking Can a Charitable Organization Engage In?" *The Journal of Taxation,* October, 1968 at p. 236.

L.A. Sheridan, "Charitable Causes, Political Causes and Involvement," *The Philanthropist,* vol.2, no. 4, Fall, 1980.

L.A. Sheridan, "The Charpol Family Quiz," *The Philanthropist,* vol. 2 no. 1, Spring, 1977.

Also from James Lorimer & Company
in the Citizens and the Environment Series

Poisons in Public

Ross Howard

Poisons in Public, by Toronto journalist Ross Howard, was the first title in a series of books published by James Lorimer & Company in association with the Canadian Environmental Law Research Foundation.

Ross Howard details four cases of environmental pollution in Canada, focusing on the workings of the political process and on the role of government in responding to pressures from business and environmental groups.

"Howard presents his case clearly, providing numerous examples of injustices experienced by the ordinary citizen as a result of negligence by industry and of red tape and buck-passing by provincial and federal authorities. . . . The book will be of interest to any reader concerned with keeping Canada's air, soil and water free from chemical contamination." — *The Royal Canadian Geographical Society.*

"An intelligent indictment of this country's failure to develop an environmental protection policy that actually protects anyone or anything other than the profits of polluters." — *Harrowsmith.*

"Accurate and well-researched reporting." — *The Whig-Standard.*

"A harsh but real picture of the dark side of chemicals . . . *Poisons in Public* is recommended reading for Canadians."
— *Vancouver Province.*

Pocket Rough Guide

MADRID

written and researched by

SIMON BASKETT

Contents

INTRODUCTION TO

MADRID

The sunniest, highest and liveliest capital city in Europe, Madrid has a lot to take pride in. Indeed, its inhabitants, the Madrileños, are so proud of their city that they modestly declare "desde Madrid al Cielo": that after Madrid there is only one remaining destination – Heaven. While their claim may be open to dispute, this compact, frenetic and fascinating city certainly has bags of appeal and its range of attractions is fast making it a deservedly popular short-break destination.

PALACIO REAL

Best places for tapas

There is a vast array of bars in Madrid, serving up tasty tapas: take a stroll around Huertas, La Latina, Chueca and Malasaña and you will stumble on some of the best. A few of our favourites are: *La Chata* (p.35), *El Tempranillo* (p.37), *Los Caracoles* (p.50), *La Toscana* (p.63), *Casa del Abuelo* (p.62) and *El Bocaito* (p.88).

King Felipe II plucked Madrid from provincial oblivion when he made it capital of the Spanish empire in 1561. The former garrison town enjoyed an initial Golden Age when literature and the arts flourished, but centuries of decline and political turmoil followed. However, with the death of the dictator Franco in 1975 and the return to democracy the city had a second burst of creativity, *La Movida Madrileña*, an outpouring of hedonistic, highly innovative and creative forces embodied by film director Pedro Almodóvar. In recent years Madrid has undergone a major facelift, with the opening of state-of-the-art extensions to the leading museums, the redevelopment of the river area and the pedestrianization of some of the historic streets in the centre.

The vast majority of the millions of visitors make a beeline for the Prado, the Reina Sofía and the Thyssen-Bornemisza, three magnificent galleries that give the city a weighty claim to being the "European capital of art". Of equal appeal to football fans is the presence of one of the world's most glamorous and successful clubs, Real Madrid. Aside from these heavy hitters, there's also a host of smaller museums, palaces and parks, not to mention some of the best tapas, bars and nightlife in Spain.

FLAMENCO

When to visit

Traditionally, Madrid has a typical **continental climate**, cold and dry in winter, and hot and dry in summer. There are usually two rainy periods, in October/November and any time from late March to early May. With temperatures soaring to over 40ºC in July and August, the best times to visit are generally **spring** and **autumn**, when the city is pleasantly warm. The short, sharp winter takes many visitors by surprise, but crisp, sunny days with clear blue skies compensate for the drop in temperature.

Although Madrid is increasingly falling into line with other European capitals, many places still shut down in **August** as its inhabitants head for the coast or countryside. Luckily for visitors, and those Madrileños who choose to remain, sights and museums remain open and nightlife takes on a momentum of its own.

Madrid's short but eventful history has left behind a mosaic of traditions, cultures and cuisines, and you soon realize it's the inhabitants who play a big part in the city's appeal. Hanging out in the cafés or on the summer *terrazas*, packing the lanes of the Rastro flea market, filling the restaurants or playing hard and very, very late in a thousand bars and clubs, Madrileños have an almost insatiable appetite for enjoying themselves. The nightlife for which Madrid is renowned is merely an extension of the Madrileño character and the capital's inhabitants consider other

European cities positively dull by comparison with their own. The city centre with its mix of bustling, labyrinthine streets and peaceful squares, punctuated by historic architectural reminders of the past, is in better shape now than for many years. As with many of its international counterparts, an influx of fast-food and coffee chains has challenged the once dominant local bars and restaurants, but in making the transition from provincial backwater just thirty years ago to major European capital today, Madrid has managed to preserve many key elements of its own stylish and quirky identity.

RETIRO PARK

MADRID AT A GLANCE

>> EATING

Eating out in Madrid is one of the highlights of any visit to the city. There's plenty to suit every pocket, from budget backstreet bars to high-class designer restaurants, and a bewildering range of cuisines encompassing tapas, traditional Madrileño and Spanish regional dishes. Lunch is taken late, with few Madrileños starting before 2pm, while dinner begins after 9pm. Opening hours can be flexible, with many bars and restaurants closing on Sunday evenings or Monday and for all or part of August. You should spend at least one evening sampling the tapas bars around Santa Ana/Huertas and La Latina. Chueca and Malasaña have some superb traditional bars and bright new restaurants, serving some of the most creative food in the city. The smarter district of Salamanca contains few bars of note, but some extremely good (and expensive) restaurants.

>> DRINKING

Madrid is packed with a variety of bars, cafés and *terrazas*. In fact they are a central feature of Madrileño life and hanging out in bars is one of the best, and most pleasant, ways to get the feel of the city and its people. The areas bordering Puerta del Sol, in and around Cava Baja and Plaza Chueca are some of the liveliest, but you can stumble across a great bar in almost every street in the city centre.

>> NIGHTLIFE

As you'd expect with a city whose inhabitants are known as the "gatos" (the cats), there's a huge variety of nightlife on offer in the Spanish capital. The mainstays of the Madrid scene are the *discobares*, which get going around 11pm and stay open till 3am. The flashier *discotecas* are rarely worth investigating until around 1 or 2am, although queues often build up quickly after this time. Alonso Martínez, Argüelles and Moncloa are student hangouts, Salamanca is for the wealthy and chic, while head for Malasaña and Chueca if you want to be at the cutting edge of trendiness. You'll find a more eclectic mix on offer in the streets around Sol and Santa Ana.

>> SHOPPING

Head for Gran Vía and Calle Preciados if you're looking for department and chain stores and for the streets around Plaza Mayor if you're on the hunt for traditional establishments. For fashion and designer labels, the smartest addresses are in Salamanca, but more alternative designers are in Malasaña and Chueca. Fans of street fashion will like the shops on C/Fuencarral. Most areas of the city have their own *mercados* (indoor markets) devoted mainly to food, but for the classic Madrileño shopping experience make your way to the flea market in the Rastro on a Sunday.

OUR RECOMMENDATIONS FOR WHERE TO EAT, DRINK AND SHOP ARE LISTED AT THE END OF EACH CHAPTER.

Day One in Madrid

1 The Prado > p.66–67. The Prado contains a fabulous array of masterpieces by artistic greats such as Bosch, El Greco, Titian, Rubens Velázquez and Goya.

2 The Retiro > p.72. Ward off any museum fatigue by freshening up with a stroll around beautiful Retiro park.

Lunch > p.77. Housed in the state-of-the-art CaixaForum exhibition space on Paseo del Arte, *Arturo* offers a creative €12 *menu del día* in designer surroundings.

3 The Palacio Real > p.38–39. Marvel at the magnificent, over-the-top decor in this one-time royal residence now used only for ceremonial purposes.

Coffee > p.44. Looking out over the plaza towards the royal palace, the elegant *Café Oriente* makes a great place for a relaxing drink.

4 Plaza Mayor > p.28. Built when the city became Spain's capital in the sixteenth century, Madrid's atmospheric main square retains an aura of traditional elegance.

5 Madrid de los Austrias > p.28. Take a step back in time and explore the twisting streets of ancient Madrid around La Latina.

Dinner > p.62–63. Hit the tapas trail around Huertas. Hop from bar to bar, sampling local specialities. *Vina P*, *La Trucha* and *El Abuelo* are good places to make a start.

6 Flamenco > p.51. Finish the night off with some authentic flamenco at *Casa Patas*.

Day Two in Madrid

1 The Thyssen > p.72. An outstanding art collection assembled by the Thyssen-Bornemisza dynasty and providing an unprecedented excursion through Western art.

2 The Santiago Bernabéu > p.93. Home to the all-star Real Madrid, a tour of this awesome stadium is a must for any football fan. Better still, take in a game.

Lunch > p.96. Prepare yourself for a spot of shopping in Salamanca by sampling a mouth-watering range of *pintxos* and canapés at *Estay*.

3 Shopping > p.94. The swish Salamanca district is home to some of the city's most exclusive – and expensive – designer outlets. If your wallet isn't up to it, you can enjoy some window-shopping.

4 Reina Sofia > p.70. An impressive home for Spain's collection of contemporary art, worth the visit if only to see Picasso's *Guernica*.

5 Atocha train station tropical garden > p.75. A tropical plant garden and pond provide a surreal backdrop in this elegant nineteenth-century station.

Dinner > p.34. *El Botín* is reputedly the oldest *meson* in the city and serves up superb, traditional Castillian fare.

6 Club > p.45. Work off some calories with a dance at one of Madrid's clubs. *Joy Madrid* has an eclectic mix of music, a fun atmosphere and a fantastic setting for a late-night drink.

Budget Madrid

Many of Madrid's biggest sights are free at certain times of the week, while others charge no entry free at all. Here are some suggestions on how to spend a great day without spending a penny on anything, apart from food and drink.

1 Museo de Orígenes > p.33.
Housed in a sixteenth-century mansion that was supposedly once home to the city's patron saint, this museum traces the early history of the Spanish capital.

2 Iglesia de San Andrés > p.33.
Next door to the Museo de Orígenes, this beautiful church and its adjoining chapels have been tastefully restored to their former glory.

Lunch > p.68 & p.87. With a great three-course set lunch menu for under €10, the *Gloria de Montero* and its sister restaurant *La Finca de Susana* are two of the best-value restaurants in the city.

4 Templo de Debod > p.102.
Shipped stone by stone from the banks of the River Nile, this ancient Egyptian temple is an incongruous sight in the city. The little exhibition inside is free.

5 The Prado > p.66. Head here between 6 and 8pm on Tuesdays to Saturdays (5–8pm Sun) and you'll see an unparalleled collection of art for nothing.

6 The Retiro > p.72. Take a stroll by the lake in the Retiro park to relax and unwind.

Dinner > p.106. The cheap and cheerful *Casa Mingo* serves some fantastic roast chicken and bottled cider.

3 Palacio Real > p.38. Visit the sumptuous royal palace on a Wednesday and you may have to queue, but you'll get in for nothing.

7 Río Manzanares > Finish off the evening with a stroll by the newly developed river area by the Puente de Segovia.

Off-the-beaten-track-Madrid

If you've got the time and have done the big sights, then why not take a break from the crowds and seek out some of Madrid's lesser-known, but highly rewarding attractions. Here are some of our suggestions.

1 Monasterio de las Descalzas Reales > p.42. Hidden behind an innocuous-looking door, this sixteenth-century convent is brimming full of artistic treasures.

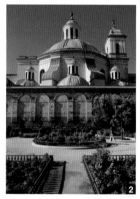

2 San Francisco el Grande > p.33. Limited opening hours mean that this magnificent church and its frescoes are often overlooked.

3 Campo de Moro > p.41. Surprisingly under-visited, this English-style park below the Palacio Real provides a verdant retreat away from the bustle of the nearby streets.

4 Casa Lope de Vega > p.53. Step back in time with a visit to this charming little museum in the house where the famous Golden Age dramatist once lived.

Lunch > p.78. Tucked away at the bottom of one of the little streets in Huertas, *La Vaca Veronica* serves an excellent *menú del día*.

5 Museo Nacional del Romanticismo > p.84. This delightful museum recreates bourgeois life in nineteenth-century Madrid.

6 Museo Sorolla > p.91. The artist's elegant former home provides the perfect setting for his luminescent paintings.

7 Lazaro Galdiano > p.93. Well off the tourist trail, this former private collection gets less than its fair share of attention and yet it houses an amazing cornucopia of art treasures.

Drink > p.99. Try out the little-known Plaza de Comendadoras and its *terrazas* for a pre-meal *aperitivo*.

Dinner > p.107. Just a handful of tables, but the tiny little *Toma* serves some tasty creative cuisine.

Big sights

1 Museo del Prado Quite simply one of the greatest art museums in the world. > **p.66**

2 **Museo Thyssen-Bornemisza** A superb collection of art put together by the Thyssen family and acting as a marvellous complement to the Prado. > **p.72**

4 **Estadio Santiago Bernabéu**
The Galacticos may have gone, but this magnificent stadium merits a visit even if you are unable to get to a game. > **p.93**

3 **Palacio Real** A sumptuous royal palace reflecting the past glories of the Spanish royal family. > **p.38**

5 **Centro de Arte de Reina Sofia** An essential stop on the art circuit, the Reina Sofia is home to Picasso's iconic masterpiece *Guernica*. > **p.70**

Eating out

1 Regional dishes Madrid offers every regional style of Spanish cooking. Try *La Barraca* for an authentic Valencian paella. **> p.86**

2 Haute cuisine Ramón Freixa's flagship restaurant *Ramón Freixa Madrid* is one of Madrid's best new celebrity chef restaurants. **> p.96**

3 Tapas For an authentic night out eating tapas, copy the locals and go bar-hopping in Huertas or La Latina. **> p.50 & p.62**

4 Eating alfresco When you start to feel the heat, head outside to eat. The summer rooftop terrace at *Gaudeamus* has great views. **> p.50**

5 Madrid specialities The meat and chickpea stew *cocido* is one of the city's traditional dishes, try it out at *Malacatín*. **> p.50**

17

After dark

1 Bar culture Bars are a central feature of Madrileño life. The *Taberna Angel Sierra* on Plaza Chueca is a classic choice. > **p.89**

2 Flamenco Andalucía may be the home of flamenco, but Madrid has some top acts. *Casa Patas* is a favourite. > **p.51**

3 Cocktails Start or finish a Madrid night out with some cocktails. The stylish *Del Diego* serves up some of the best in town. > **p.88**

4 Clubbing Madrid has a massive range of clubs, from unpretentious *discobares* to serious cutting-edge dance venues. > **p.7**

5 Terrazas As temperatures soar, life moves outside and so do the bars – head for the *terrazas* in Plaza Santa Ana. > **p.64**

Museums and galleries

1 Real Fábrica de Tapices A fascinating museum and a thriving workshop, allowing visitors the chance to view works in progress. **> p.76**

3 Museo Sorolla The life and works of artist Joaquín Sorolla is housed in his lovely former residence. **> p.91**

2 Museo Arqueológico An impressive collection of Visigothic, Roman, Greek and Egyptian finds in a beautiful building next to Plaza Colón. **> p.91**

5 Museo Lázaro Galdiano A treasure-trove of paintings, furniture and *objets d'art* in this personal collection assembled by publisher and businessman José Lázaro Galdiano. **> p.93**

4 Real Academia de Bellas Artes It may not boast the heavyweight attractions of the big three, but this gallery contains some captivating work by Goya, El Greco, José de Ribera and Zurbarán. **> p.56**

Green spaces

1 Casa de Campo Once part of the royal hunting estate, Casa de Campo is the biggest and wildest of the city's parks. > **p.103**

2 The Retiro This city-centre park has become Madrileños' favourite playground, with a boating lake and a crystal palace hosting regular exhibitions. **> p.72**

3 Campo del Moro One of the city's most beautiful, and underused, parks with shady paths and ornamental pools. **> p.41**

5 Parque del Oeste The lovely Parque del Oeste contains assorted statues, a fragrant rose garden and even a genuine Egyptian temple. **> p.102**

4 Real Jardín Botánico Dating back to the eighteenth century, the botanical gardens form an amazingly tranquil oasis in the city. **> p.73**

Kids

1 Parque de Atracciones A popular theme park situated in Casa de Campo with a vast range of rides catering for all ages. **> p.104**

3 The Retiro The Retiro park has plenty of child-friendly attractions including play areas, puppet shows, duck ponds and a boating lake. **> p.72**

2 The Teleférico For a bird's-eye view of the city, take the cable car across the Manzanares river to Casa de Campo. **> p.103**

4 Madrid's Zoo Casa de Campo is home to an attractive zoo complete with lions, bears, koalas, sharks and many reptiles. **> p.104**

5 Museo de Ferrocarril With its model railways and array of full-size locomotives, this museum will be a hit with most children and many parents too. **> p.49**

PLACES

Madrid de los Austrias

Named after the royal family and their original homeland, the district known as Madrid de los Austrias, or Habsburg Madrid, is made up of some of the oldest and most atmospheric parts of the city. Centred around grandiose Plaza Mayor, the area is a twisting grid of streets, filled with Flemish-inspired architecture of red brick and grey stone. Most visitors only make it to the Plaza Mayor and its over-priced cafés and restaurants, but there are appealing sights scattered throughout the area, especially in the barrio (district) of La Latina, which stretches south of the square. This region is also home to some of the city's best restaurants, tapas bars and flamenco tablaos, especially around calles Almendro, Cava Baja and Cava Alta.

PLAZA MAYOR

Sol. MAP P.30–31, POCKET MAP C12

The splendidly theatrical Plaza Mayor was originally the brainchild of Felipe II who, in the late sixteenth century, wished to construct a more prestigious focus for his new capital. The Casa de la Panadería on the north side of the square is the oldest building, dating from 1590, but, like much of the plaza, it was rebuilt after fires in the seventeenth and eighteenth centuries. The gaudy frescoes that adorn the facade were only added in 1992. It now houses the municipal tourist office (daily 9.30am–8.30pm).

Capable of holding up to fifty thousand people, the square was used for state occasions, autos-de-fé (public trials of heretics followed, usually, by burning of the victims), plays and bullfights. The large bronze equestrian statue in the middle is of Felipe III and dates from 1616.

PLAZA MAYOR

Today, Plaza Mayor is primarily a tourist haunt, full of expensive outdoor cafés and restaurants. However, an air of grandeur clings to the plaza and it still hosts public functions, from outdoor theatre and music to Christmas fairs and a Sunday stamp and coin market.

CALLE MAYOR

Ⓜ **Sol.** MAP P.30–31, POCKET MAP A12–D12

One of the oldest thoroughfares in the city, Calle Mayor was for centuries the route for religious processions from the Palacio Real to the Monastery of Los Jerónimos. The street is home to little shops and bars and is flanked by the facades of some of the most evocative buildings in the city. Set back from the road, near the entrance to the Plaza Mayor, is the splendid decorative ironwork of the **Mercado de San Miguel** (Sun–Wed 10am–midnight, Thurs–Sat 10am–2am; Ⓦ www .mercadodesanmiguel.es; see p.36). Built in 1916 it was formerly one of the old-style food markets scattered throughout the city, but it has now been refurbished and converted into a stylish tourist-oriented emporium complete with oyster and champagne bar.

SAN NICOLÁS DE LOS SERVITAS

Plaza de San Nicolás 1 Ⓜ Ópera. Mon 8.30am–1.30pm & 5.30–9pm, Tues–Sat 8.30–9am & 6.30–9pm, Sun 9.30am–2pm & 6.30–9pm. MAP P.30–31, POCKET MAP A12

Largely rebuilt between the fifteenth and seventeenth centuries, Madrid's oldest church still includes a twelfth-century Mudéjar tower featuring traditional Arabic horseshoe arches. Juan de Herrera, architect of El Escorial (see p.116), is buried in the crypt.

PLAZA DE LA VILLA

PLAZA DE LA VILLA

Ⓜ **Sol.** MAP P.30–31, POCKET MAP A12

This charming plaza, just off Calle Mayor, showcases three centuries of Spanish architectural development. The oldest buildings are the simple but eye-catching fifteenth-century **Torre y Casa de Los Lujanes** where Francis I of France is said to have been imprisoned by Emperor Charles V after the Battle of Pavia in 1525. On the south side of the square is the **Casa de Cisneros**, constructed for the nephew of Cardinal Cisneros (early sixteenth-century Inquisitor-General and Regent of Spain) in the intricate Plateresque style.

The remaining side of the square is taken up by the **Casa de la Villa**, one of the most important and emblematic buildings of Habsburg Madrid. The weekly tour (5pm every Mon; free; sign up in the tourist office in Plaza Mayor) is normally only in Spanish but is still worth it to get a peek inside. The Patio de Los Cristales features a stunning stained-glass roof, but the highlight is the Salón de Plenos with its lavish decor and frescoes by Antonio Palomino.

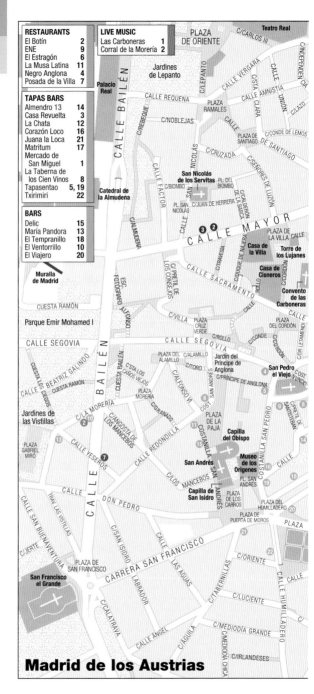

RESTAURANTS	
El Botín	2
ENE	9
El Estragón	6
La Musa Latina	11
Negro Anglona	4
Posada de la Villa	7

TAPAS BARS	
Almendro 13	14
Casa Revuelta	3
La Chata	12
Corazón Loco	16
Juana la Loca	21
Matritum	17
Mercado de San Miguel	1
La Taberna de los Cien Vinos	8
Tapasentao	5, 19
Txirimiri	22

BARS	
Delic	15
María Pandora	13
El Tempranillo	18
El Ventorrillo	10
El Viajero	20

LIVE MUSIC	
Las Carboneras	1
Corral de la Morería	2

Madrid de los Austrias

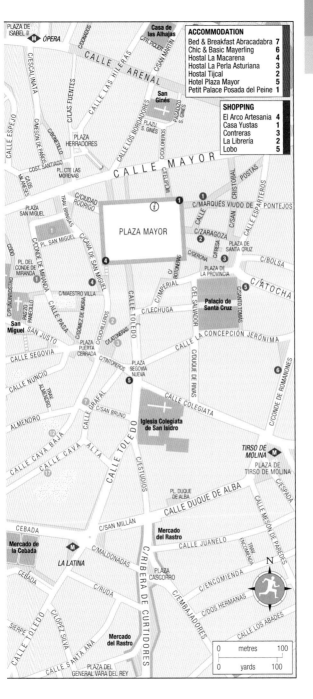

PARQUE EMIR MOHAMED I

ⓂÓpera. MAP P.30–31, POCKET MAP B6

Though little more than a scrap of parched land, Parque Emir Mohamed I is notable for its fragments of the city walls that date back to the ninth and twelfth centuries. The park stands next to the Cuesta de la Vega, former site of one of the main entrances to Muslim Madrid, while nearby, the narrow, labyrinthine streets of the former Moorish quarter, La Morería, are still clearly laid out on medieval lines.

CONVENTO DE LAS CARBONERAS

Plaza Conde de Miranda 3 ⓂSol. MAP P.30–31, POCKET MAP B13

Founded in the early seventeenth century, this convent belongs to the closed Hieronymite Order. It's famous for its home-made biscuits and cakes – a tradition in Spanish convents since the time of St Teresa of Ávila, who gave out sweetened egg yolks to the poor – which can be purchased every day (9.30am–1pm & 4–6.30pm). Ring the bell above the sign reading *venta de dulces* to be let in, then follow the signs to the *torno*; the business takes place by means of a revolving drum to preserve the closed nature of the order.

BASÍLICA DE SAN MIGUEL

C/San Justo 4 ⓂLa Latina or Sol. July to mid-Sept Mon–Sat 10.15am–1.15pm & 6–9pm, Sun 10am–1.30pm & 6.30–9.15pm; mid-Sept to June Mon–Sat 9.45am–1.30pm & 5.30–9pm, Sun 9.45am–2.15pm & 6–9.15pm. MAP P.30–31, POCKET MAP B13

Standing among a host of other graceful buildings – most of which house local government offices – San Miguel stands out as one of the few examples of a full-blown Baroque church in Madrid. Designed at the end of the seventeenth century

for Don Luis, the precocious 5-year-old Archbishop of Toledo and youngest son of Felipe V, its features include an unconventional convex facade with four recesses, each containing a statue, variously representing Charity, Strength, Faith and Hope.

SAN PEDRO EL VIEJO

Costanilla de San Pedro ⓂLa Latina. Mon–Sat 9am–noon & 6–8pm, Sun 9am–1pm. MAP P.30–31, POCKET MAP B13

At the heart of busy La Latina is the Mudéjar tower of San Pedro El Viejo. The second-oldest church in Madrid, it's said to have been founded in the fourteenth century by Alfonso XI, and stands on the site of an old mosque, though most of the church was rebuilt in the seventeenth century.

PLAZA DE LA PAJA

ⓂLa Latina. MAP P.30–31, POCKET MAP A14

One of the real gems of old Madrid, this ancient sloping plaza was the commercial and civic hub of the city before the construction of the Plaza Mayor, and was once surrounded by a series of mansions owned by local dignitaries. With the restored houses beaming down on the former market square, this is a rare peaceful and traffic-free spot in the city. At the bottom is the pretty little Jardín

PLAZA DE LA PAJA

del Príncipe de Anglona (daily: winter 10am–6.30pm; summer 10am–10pm), a survivor of the gardens that used to be attached to the nearby mansions.

IGLESIA DE SAN ANDRÉS, CAPILLA DEL OBISPO AND CAPILLA DE SAN ISIDRO

Plaza de San Andrés ⓜ La Latina. Mon–Thurs & Sat 8am–1pm & 6–8pm, Fri 6–8pm, Sun 9am–2pm. MAP P.30–31, POCKET MAP A14

The Iglesia de San Andrés was badly damaged by an anarchist attack in 1936, and the adjoining Gothic Capilla del Obispo (guided tours Tues 9.30am–12.30pm & Thurs 4–4.45pm; reservation only on ☎915 592 874; €2), with its polychromed altarpiece and alabaster tombs, has only recently been reopened following a forty-year restoration. The main church and the Baroque Capilla de San Isidro are reached by walking round the building into Plaza de San Andrés. The chapel was built in the mid-seventeenth century to hold the remains of Madrid's patron saint, San Isidro (since moved to the Iglesia de San Isidro), and the interior is decorated with a beautifully sculpted dome.

MUSEO DE LOS ORÍGENES

Plaza de San Andrés 2 ⓜ La Latina. Aug Tues–Fri 9.30am–2.30pm, Sat & Sun 10am–2pm; Sept–July Tues–Fri 9.30am–8pm, Sat & Sun 10am–2pm. Free. MAP P.30–31, POCKET MAP A14

Housed in a reconstructed sixteenth-century mansion – supposedly home to San Isidro – this museum includes an exhibition on the history of Madrid. The city's archeological collection is in the basement, while the rest of the building is given over to the saint himself, with displays relating to his life and miraculous activities. The house also contains a well, site

IGLESIA DE SAN ANDRÉS

of one of Isidro's most famous exploits: he rescued his young son from the murky depths, by praying until the waters rose to the surface. The seventeenth-century chapel contained within the museum is built on the spot where the saint was said to have died in 1172.

SAN FRANCISCO EL GRANDE

Plaza de San Francisco 11 ⓜ La Latina. Tues–Sat 10.30am–1pm & 5–7.30pm (ticket on sale 10.30am–12.30pm & 5–7pm). €3 with guided tour. MAP P.30–31, POCKET MAP B7

Following a twenty-year restoration programme, you can appreciate this magnificent eighteenth-century domed church in something close to its original glory. Inside, each of the six chapels is designed in a distinct style ranging from Mozarab and Renaissance to Baroque and Neoclassical. Look out for the early Goya, *The Sermon of San Bernadino of Siena*, in the chapel on your immediate left as you enter, which contains a self-portrait of the 37-year-old artist (in the yellow suit on the right).

Even if your Spanish is not that good, follow the guided tour to get a glimpse of the church's other art treasures, including paintings by José de Ribera and Zurbarán.

Shops

EL ARCO ARTESANIA

Plaza Mayor 9 Ⓜ Sol. Mon–Sat 11am–8pm,
Sun 11am–2.30pm. MAP P.30–31, POCKET MAP B13

Though at the heart of tourist
Madrid, the goods for sale here
are a far cry from the swords,
lace and castanets that fill
most shops in the area. Crafts
include ceramics, leather,
wood, jewellery and textiles.

CASA YUSTAS

Plaza Mayor 30 Ⓜ Sol. Mon–Sat
9.30am–9.30pm, Sun 11am–9.30pm.
MAP P.30–31, POCKET MAP C12

Established in 1894, Madrid's
oldest hat shop sells every
conceivable model from pith
helmets and commando berets
to panamas and bowlers.
There's also a large range of
souvenir-style goods, including
Lladró porcelain figurines.

CONTRERAS

C/Mayor 80 Ⓜ Sol. Mon–Fri 10am–1.30pm
& 5–8pm, Sat 10am–1.30pm. MAP P.30–31,
POCKET MAP A12

Award-winning guitar
workshop, run on this site for
over 40 years by the Contreras
family, the perfect place for
budding flamenco artists to buy
the genuine article.

CASA YUSTAS

LA LIBRERÍA

C/Mayor 80 Ⓜ Sol. Mon–Fri 10am–2pm &
4.30–7.30pm, Sat 11am–2pm. MAP P.30–31,
POCKET MAP A12

Tiny place full of books just
about Madrid. Most are in
Spanish, but many would serve
as coffee-table souvenirs. Also a
good place to pick up old prints
of the city.

LOBO

C/Toledo 30 Ⓜ La Latina. Mon–Fri
9.45am–1.45pm & 4.30–8pm, Sat
9.45am–1.45pm. MAP P.30–31, POCKET MAP C13

Great little old-fashioned
shoe shop, selling anything
from espadrilles to Menorcan
sandals (€25) in every conceivable colour. Particularly good
for kids' shoes.

Restaurants

EL BOTÍN

C/Cuchilleros 17 Ⓜ Sol ☎ 913 664 217.
Daily 1–4pm & 8pm–midnight. MAP P.30–31,
POCKET MAP C13

Established in 1725, the
atmospheric *El Botín* is
cited in the *Guinness Book
of Records* as Europe's oldest
restaurant. Favoured by
Hemingway, it's inevitably a
tourist haunt, but not such a
bad one. Highlights are the
Castilian roasts – especially
cochinillo (suckling pig) and
cordero lechal (lamb).

ENE

C/Nuncio 19 Ⓜ La Latina ☎ 913 662 591.
Mon–Wed 11am–11.30pm, Thurs open till
2am, Fri & Sat till 3am, Sun till midnight.
MAP P.30–31, POCKET MAP A14

Fashionable bar/restaurant just
below Plaza de la Paja serving
a sophisticated, fusion-style
€11 *menú del día* and a tasty
but overpriced €20 brunch at
weekends. Cocktails and DJs
Thurs–Sun.

EL ESTRAGÓN

Plaza de la Paja 10 Ⓜ La Latina
☎ 913 658 982. Daily 1.30–4pm &
8pm–midnight. MAP P.30–31, POCKET MAP A14

With a fine setting on this
ancient plaza, this cosy
vegetarian restaurant serves
hearty food; think stuffed
peppers, lasagne and paella.
It does a varied *menú del día*
for €10 (dinner *menú* €19),
while eating à la carte is more
expensive.

LA MUSA LATINA

Costanilla San Andrés Ⓜ La Latina.
Mon–Thurs noon–1am, Fri 10am–2am,
Sat 1pm–2am, Sun 1pm–1am. MAP P.30–31,
POCKET MAP A14

Stylish place serving a great-
value €11 *menú del día*, and a
small selection of modern tapas
such as vegetable tempura,
fried green tomatoes and wok
dishes. It has a cool brick-
walled bar downstairs with DJ
sessions.

NEGRO ANGLONA

C/Segovia 13 Ⓜ La Latina ☎ 913 663 753.
Tues–Thurs & Sun 9pm–1am, Fri & Sat till
2am. MAP P.30–31, POCKET MAP A13

All-black decor in this refurbished and romantic pasta
and pizza joint, situated in
the cellars of an old palace.
A handy late-night option,
but service can be slow at
weekends. Expect to pay
around €30 a head.

POSADA DE LA VILLA

C/Cava Baja 9 Ⓜ La Latina ☎ 913 661 860.
Mon–Sat 1–4pm & 8pm–midnight,
Sun 1–4pm. Closed Aug. MAP P.30–31, POCKET
MAP B14

The most attractive restaurant
in La Latina, spread over three
floors of a seventeenth-century
coaching inn. Cooking is
Madrileño, including superb
roast lamb. Reckon on €45–50
per person for a splurge.

POSADA DE LA VILLA

Tapas bars

ALMENDRO 13

C/Almendro 13 Ⓜ La Latina. Mon–Fri 1–4pm
& 7.30pm–midnight, Sat, Sun & hols 1–5pm
& 8pm–midnight. MAP P.30–31, POCKET MAP B14

Packed at weekends, this
fashionable wood-panelled bar
serves great *fino* sherry and
house specials of *huevos rotos*
(fried eggs on a bed of crisps)
and *roscas rellenas* (rings of
bread stuffed with various
meats).

CASA REVUELTA

C/Latoneras 3 Ⓜ Sol or La Latina. Tues–Sat
1–4pm & 8pm–midnight, Sun 1–4pm. Closed
Aug. MAP P.30–31, POCKET MAP C13

A timeless, down-to-earth little
bar located in an alleyway just
south of Plaza Mayor. It serves
an unbeatable tapa of *bacalao
frito* (battered cod).

LA CHATA

C/Cava Baja 24 Ⓜ La Latina. Daily 2–4.30pm
& 8.30pm–12.30am. Closed Tues & Wed
lunchtime & Sun eve. MAP P.30–31, POCKET MAP B14

One of the city's most traditional
and popular tiled tapas bars,
with hams hanging from the
ceiling and taurine memorabilia
on the walls. Serves a good
selection of dishes, including
cebolla rellena and *pimientos del
piquillo rellenos* (stuffed onions
and peppers).

LA CHATA

MERCADO DE SAN MIGUEL

Plaza de San Miguel ⓜ Sol. Sun–Wed
10am–midnight, Thurs–Sat 10am–2am.
MAP P.30–31, POCKET MAP B12

Transformed from a
neighbourhood market into a
hip location for an *aperitivo*,
this beautiful wrought-iron
mercado is worth exploring at
almost any time of day. There's
something for everyone, from
vermouth and champagne to
salt cod, oysters and sushi.

LA TABERNA DE LOS CIEN VINOS

C/Nuncio 16 ⓜ La Latina. Tues–Sat
1–3.45pm & 8–11.45pm, Sun 1–3.45pm.
MAP P.30–31, POCKET MAP B14

A vast array of Spanish
wines (the selection changes
monthly) plus plenty of tapas
to choose from, including
leek pie, smoked salmon and
roast beef. Not suitable for the
indecisive.

TAPASENTAO

C/Almendro 27 ⓜ La Latina. Tues
8pm–midnight, Wed, Thurs & Fri 1–4.30pm
& 8pm–midnight, Sat & Sun 1pm–2am, Sun
1pm–midnight. Closed second half Aug.
MAP P.30–31, POCKET MAP A14

Fill in a card ticking your
choices from the very tasty
and reasonably priced dishes.
Recommended are the chorizo
with wafer-thin chips, three-
cheese salad and the fried
mushrooms. There is a less
crowded branch nearby at
C/Príncipe Anglona 1.

TXIRIMIRI

C/Humilladero 6 ⓜ La Latina.
Daily 12.30–4.30pm, 8.30pm–midnight.
MAP P.30–31, POCKET MAP C7

Fantastic range of tapas and
pintxos in this friendly bar
beside the Mercado de la
Cebada. Mouth-watering combi-
nations include langoustine
croquetas, mushroom risotto and
their speciality, Unai hamburger.

CORAZÓN LOCO

C/Almendro 22 ⓜ La Latina. 12.30pm–1.30am,
Mon & Tues opens at 7pm. Sat & Sun till
2.30am. MAP P.30–31, POCKET MAP A14

The front bar of this popular
La Latina watering hole is
invariably packed, but there
is a quieter, cosier brick-lined
dining area at the back which
serves a good range of tapas.

JUANA LA LOCA

Plaza Puerta de Moros 4 ⓜ La Latina.
Tues–Sat noon–4.30pm & 8.30pm–1am,
Sun noon–4.30pm. Closed Aug. MAP P.30–31,
POCKET MAP C7

Fashionable hangout serving
inventive tapas – tortilla
with caramelized onion, tuna
carpaccio, ostrich steaks – and
a great selection of very tasty,
but fairly pricey, canapés.

MATRITUM

C/Cava Alta 17 ⓜ La Latina. Mon–Wed,
8.30pm–midnight, Thurs–Sun 1–4.30pm &
8.30pm–midnight. Closed Aug. MAP P.30–31,
POCKET MAP B14

Delicious designer-style tapas,
from fig salad with mozarella,
anchovies and mint oil to
scallops and vegetables in a
cava sauce. There's a collection
of carefully selected wines too.

Bars

DELIC

Costanilla San Andrés 14 ⓂLa Latina.
Mon 8pm–2am, Tues–Sat 11am–2am, Sun
11am–midnight. Closed first half of Aug.
MAP P.30–31, POCKET MAP A14

Serving home-made cakes,
fruit juices and coffee, this
is a pleasant café by day,
transforming into a crowded but
friendly cocktail bar by night.

MARÍA PANDORA

Plaza Gabriel Miró 1 ⓂLa Latina.
Tues–Thurs 7pm–2am, Fri & Sat 6pm–3am,
Sun 4pm–2am. Closed second half of Aug.
MAP P.30–31, POCKET MAP B7

An incongruous mix of
champagnería (champagne bar)
and library, where quality *cava*
can be enjoyed with the perfect
accompaniment of chocolates
and mellow jazz.

EL TEMPRANILLO

C/Cava Baja 38 ⓂLa Latina. Daily 1–4pm
& 9pm–2am. Closed two weeks in Aug.
MAP P.30–31, POCKET MAP B14

Popular little wine bar serving
a vast range of domestic
wines by the glass. A great
place to discover your favourite
Spanish *vino* – and the tapas
are excellent too.

EL VENTORRILLO

C/Bailén 14 ⓂLa Latina or Ópera.
Daily 11am–1am, Fri & Sat till 2am.
MAP P.30–31, POCKET MAP C7

This popular *terraza* is great for
a relaxing drink while enjoying
the *vistillas* (little views) over
the cathedral and mountains,
but avoid the over-priced tapas.

EL VIAJERO

Plaza de la Cebada 11 ⓂLa Latina. Tues–Sat
1.30pm–2.30am, Sun noon–8pm. Closed
first half Jan, second half Aug. MAP P.30–31,
POCKET MAP B14

Bar, club, restaurant and
summer *terraza* all in one,
spread over different floors
of this fashionable La Latina
nightspot. The food (meat,
pizza and pasta) is good too,
but pricey.

Live music

LAS CARBONERAS

Plaza Conde de Miranda ⓂSol
☎ 915 428 677, ⓦwww.tablaolascarboneras
.com. Mon–Sat: shows 10.30pm, plus
Mon–Thurs at 10.30pm and Fri & Sat at
8.30pm & 11pm. MAP P.30–31, POCKET MAP B13

A relative newcomer to the
restaurant/*tablao* scene, geared
to the tourist market and
slightly cheaper than its rivals
(around €50 with dinner), but
a very good alternative if you
want to get a taste of flamenco.

CORRAL DE LA MORERÍA

C/Morería 17 ⓂLa Latina or Ópera
☎ 913 658 446, ⓦwww.corraldelamoreria
.com. Daily 8pm–2am: shows at 10pm &
midnight. MAP P.30–31, POCKET MAP C7

An atmospheric, if expensive,
venue for serious flamenco
acts. Around €40 to see the
show and over double that
if you want to dine in the
restaurant as well.

CORRAL DE LA MORERÍA

Palacio Real and Ópera

Although the barrio only became fashionable in the mid-nineteenth century, the attractions found in the compact area around Ópera metro station date back as far as the 1500s. The imposing and suitably lavish Palacio Real (Royal Palace) dominates this part of the city, bordered by the somewhat disappointing Catedral de la Almudena and the tranquil gardens of the Campo del Moro. The restored Teatro Real and Plaza de Oriente bring some nineteenth-century sophistication to the area, while the two monastery complexes of la Encarnación and las Descalzas Reales conceal an astounding selection of artistic delights. For after-dark attractions, the area is home to two of the city's leading clubs as well as a handful of pleasant cafés and restaurants.

PALACIO REAL

C/Bailén Ⓜ Ópera or Sol Ⓜ www.patrimonio nacional.es. April–Sept Mon–Sat 9am–6pm, Sun & hols 9am–3pm; Oct–March Mon–Sat 9.30am–5pm, Sun 9am–2pm; closed for state occasions and on Jan 1 & 6, May 1 & 15, Nov 9, Dec 24, 25 & 31; €10; free for EU citizens Oct–March Wed–Thurs 3–5pm & April–Sept 4–6pm. Wed free for EU citizens. MAP P.40, POCKET MAP C5

The present Palacio Real (Royal Palace) was built by Felipe V after the ninth-century Arab-built Alcázar was destroyed by fire in 1734. The Bourbon monarch, who had been brought up in the more luxurious surroundings of Versailles, took the opportunity to replace it with an altogether grander affair. He did not, however, live to see its completion and the palace only became habitable in 1764 during the reign of Carlos III. Nowadays it's used only for ceremonial purposes, with the present royal family preferring the more modest Zarzuela Palace, 15km northwest of the city.

The ostentation lacking in the palace's exterior is more than compensated for inside, with swirling marble floors, celestial frescoes and gold furnishings. It's a flamboyant display of wealth and power that was firmly at odds with Spain's declining status at the time.

THE PALACIO REAL

Look out for the grandiose **Salón del Trono** (Throne Room), the incredible oriental-style **Salón de Gasparini** (the Gasparini Room) and the marvellous **Sala de Porcelan**a (Porcelain Room), decorated with one thousand gold, green and white interlocking pieces.

The palace outbuildings and annexes include the recently refurbished **Armería Real** (Royal Armoury), containing a fascinating collection of guns, swords and armour. There's also an eighteenth-century **farmacia** (pharmacy) and a **Galería de Pinturas** which displays works by Caravaggio, Velázquez and Goya and also hosts temporary exhibitions.

JARDINES DE SABATINI

Ⓜ Ópera. Daily: April–Sept 9am–10pm; Oct–March 9am–9pm. MAP P.40, POCKET MAP B4–C4

The Jardines de Sabatini (Sabatini Gardens) make an ideal place from which to view the northern facade of the palace or to watch the sun go down. They contain a small ornamental lake, some fragrant magnolia trees and manicured hedges, while, in summer, they're often used as a concert venue.

CATEDRAL DE LA ALMUDENA

Ⓜ Ópera. Daily: 9am–8.30pm, Aug 10am–9pm. Not open for visits during Mass: Mon–Sat 10am, noon, 6pm & 7pm, Sun & hols 10.30am, noon, 1.30pm, 6pm & 7pm. MAP P.40, POCKET MAP B6

Planned centuries ago, Madrid's cathedral, Nuestra Señora de la Almudena, was plagued by lack of funds, bombed in the Civil War and finally opened in 1993. More recently it was the venue for the wedding of the heir to the throne, Prince Felipe, and his former newsreader bride, Letizia Ortiz.

The cathedral's cold Gothic interior housed within its stark Neoclassical shell is not particularly inspiring, though the garish ceiling designs and the sixteenth-century altarpiece in the Almudena chapel are exceptions. To one side of the main facade is a small **museum** (Mon–Sat 10am–2.30pm; €6, €4 for Madrid residents and students) containing some of the cathedral's treasures, though the main reason to visit is to gain access to the dome from where you can enjoy some fantastic views over the city. The entrance to the **crypt** (daily 10am–8pm) with its forest of columns and dimly lit chapels is on C/Mayor.

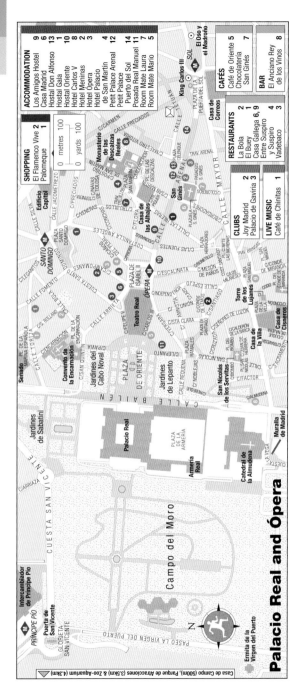

SHOPPING
El Flamenco Vive **2**
Palomeque **1**

ACCOMMODATION	
Los Amigos Hostel	9
Casa Madrid	6
Hostal Don Alfonso	13
Hostal Gala	1
Hostal Oriente	10
Hotel Carlos V	8
Hotel Meninas	2
Hotel Ópera	3
Hotel Palacio de San Martín	4
Petit Palace Arenal	12
Petit Palace Puerto del Sol	14
Posada Real Manuel	11
Room Mate Laura	7
Room Mate Mario	5

RESTAURANTS	
La Bola	2
El Buey	1
Casa Gallega	6, 9
Entre Suspiro y Suspiro	4
Vadebaco	3

CLUBS	
Joy Madrid	2
Palacio de Gaviria	3

LIVE MUSIC
Café de Chinitas **1**

CAFÉS	
Café de Oriente	5
Chocolatería San Ginés	7

BAR
El Anciano Rey de los Vinos **8**

Palacio Real and Ópera

CAMPO DEL MORO

Entrance on Paseo de la Virgen del Puerto
Ⓜ Príncipe Pío. April–Sept Mon–Sat
10am–8pm, Sun 9am–8pm; Oct–March
Mon–Sat 10am–6pm, Sun 9am–6pm;
closed occasionally for state occasions.
MAP P.40, POCKET MAP B5

One of the most underused – largely because of its inconvenient entrance down by the river – and beautiful of Madrid's parks, the Campo del Moro gets its name from being the site of the Moors' encampment, from where, in 1109, they mounted their unsuccessful attempt to reconquer Madrid. It later became a venue for medieval tournaments and celebrations. After the building of the Palacio Real several schemes to landscape the area were put forward, but it wasn't until 1842 that things got under way. Based around two monumental fountains, *Las Conchas* and *Los Tritones*, the grassy gardens are very English in style, featuring shady paths and ornamental pools, and provide an excellent refuge from the summer heat, as well as a splendid view of the palace.

PLAZA DE ORIENTE

Ⓜ Ópera. MAP P.40, POCKET MAP A11

The aristocratic, pedestrianized Plaza de Oriente is one of the most attractive open spaces in Madrid. The days when Franco used to address crowds here from the balcony of the royal palace now seem a distant memory, although a small number of neo-Fascists still gather here on the anniversary of his death, November 21.

The fountain in the centre was designed by Narciso Pascual y Colomer, who also transferred the bronze equestrian statue of Felipe IV here from the garden of the Buen Retiro Palace, near the Prado. Dating from 1640, this statue is reputedly the first-ever bronze featuring a rearing horse – Galileo is said to have helped with the calculations to make it balance. Other statues depict Spanish kings and queens, and were originally designed to adorn the palace facade, but were too heavy or, according to one version, too ugly, and were removed on the orders of Queen Isabel Farnese.

There's a very French feel to the buildings overlooking the square, with their glass-fronted balconies, underlined by the elegant neo-Baroque *Café de Oriente*, a favourite with the opera crowd.

PLAZA DE ORIENTE

TEATRO REAL

Plaza de Isabel II Ⓜ Ópera ☎915 160 660,
ticket line ☎902 244 848, Ⓦwww
.teatro-real.com. Open for visits Mon &
Wed–Fri 10.30am–1pm, Sat, Sun & hols
11am–1.30pm; closed mid-July to mid-Sept;
reservations ☎915 160 696. €5; tickets on
sale 10am–1pm at the box office. MAP P.40,
POCKET MAP A11–B11

When it opened in 1850,
the hulking grey hexagonal
opera house became the
hub of fashionable Madrid
and staged highly successful
works by Verdi and Wagner.
It fell into decay in the late
twentieth century and after a
ten-year refurbishment – that
should have lasted four – and
a staggering US$150 million
in costs, it finally reopened in
October 1997. With its lavish
red and gold decor, crystal
chandeliers, state-of-the-art
lighting and superb acoustics
it makes a truly magnificent
setting for opera, ballet and
classical concerts. Tickets range
from €9 to €300, but you'll
need to book well in advance
for the best seats.

CONVENTO DE LA ENCARNACIÓN

Plaza de la Encarnación 1 Ⓜ Ópera Ⓦwww
.patrimonionacional.es. Tours only (some in
English) Tues–Thurs & Sat 10.30am–12.45pm
& 4–5.45pm, Fri 10.30am–12.45pm, Sun &
hols 11am–1.45pm. €3.60; joint ticket with
Monasterio de las Descalzas Reales €6,
valid for a week; Wed free for EU citizens.
MAP P.40, POCKET MAP A10

Founded in 1611 by Felipe III
and his wife Margarita de
Austria, this convent was
intended as a retreat for titled
women and merits a visit for
its reliquary alone – one of
the most important in the
Catholic world. The solemn
granite facade is the hallmark of
architect Juan Gómez de Mora,
also responsible for the Plaza
Mayor. Much of the painting
contained within is uninspiring,
but there are some interesting
items, including an extensive
collection of royal portraits
and a highly prized collection
of sculptures of Christ. The
library-like **reliquary** contains
more than 1500 saintly relics
from around the world: skulls,
arms encased in beautifully
ornate hand-shaped containers
and bones from every conceivable part of the body. The most
famous of the lot is a small glass
bulb said to contain the blood of
St Pantaleón – a fourth-century
doctor martyr – which supposedly liquefies at midnight every
July 26 (the eve of his feast day).
Great tragedies are supposed
to occur if the blood fails to
liquefy. The tour ends with a
visit to the Baroque-style church
which features a beautifully
frescoed ceiling and a marble-
columned altarpiece.

MONASTERIO DE LAS DESCALZAS REALES

Plaza de las Descalzas 3 Ⓜ Callao, Sol
or Ópera Ⓦ www.patrimonionacional.es.
Tours only (some in English) Tues–Thurs
& Sat 10.30am–12.30pm & 4–5.30pm,
Fri 10.30am–12.30pm, Sun & hols
11.30am–1.30pm. €5; joint ticket with
Convento de la Encarnación €6, valid for a
week; Wed free for EU citizens. MAP P.40, POCKET
MAP C10–C11

One of the less well-known
treasures of Madrid, the
"Monastery of the Barefoot
Royal Ladies" was originally
the site of a medieval palace.
The building was transformed
by Juana de Austria into a
convent in 1564, and the
architect of El Escorial, Juan
Bautista de Toledo, was
entrusted with its design. Juana
was the youngest daughter of
the Emperor Charles V and,
at the age of 19, already the
widow of Prince Don Juan of
Portugal. Royal approval meant
that it soon became home to a
succession of titled ladies who

MONASTERIO DE LAS DESCALZAS REALES

brought with them an array of artistic treasures, helping the convent accumulate a fabulous collection of paintings, sculptures and tapestries. The place is still unbelievably opulent and remains in use as a religious institution, housing 23 shoeless nuns of the Franciscan order.

The magnificent main staircase connects a two-levelled cloister, lined with small but richly embellished chapels, while the Tapestry Room contains an outstanding collection of early seventeenth-century Flemish tapestries based on designs by Rubens.

The other highlight of the tour is the Joyería (Treasury), piled high with jewels and relics of uncertain provenance.

CASA DE LAS ALHAJAS

Plaza San Martín 1 ⓜ Ópera ⓦ www
.fundacioncajamadrid.es. Tues–Sun
10am–8pm. Free. MAP P.40, POCKET MAP C11
This three-floored exhibition space hosts a range of interesting and well-presented temporary shows run in conjunction with the Thyssen-Bornemisza museum (see p.72). Recent highlights have included exhibitions on Monet, Modigliani and Impressionist gardens.

Shops

EL FLAMENCO VIVE

C/Conde de Lemos 7 ⓜ Ópera or Sol. Mon–Sat
10.30am–2pm & 5–9pm. MAP P.40, POCKET MAP B12
A fascinating little slice of Andalucía in Madrid, specializing in all things flamenco, from guitars and CDs to dresses and books.

PALOMEQUE

C/Hileras 12 ⓜ Ópera or Sol.
Mon–Fri 9.30am–1.30pm & 4.30–8pm,

Sat 9.30am–1.30pm. MAP P.40, POCKET
MAP C11
Founded back in 1873, this somewhat incongrous religious superstore has kept its place amongst the fashion outlets, hotels and restaurants that line this busy shopping street. Inside you'll find all manner of spiritual paraphernalia from elaborate alabaster altarpieces and sculptures of angels to rosary beads and postcard collections of Spanish saints and virgins.

Cafés

CAFÉ DE ORIENTE

Plaza de Oriente 2 Ⓜ Ópera. Mon–Thurs &
Sun 8.30am–1.30am, Fri & Sat till 2.30am.
MAP P.40, POCKET MAP A11

Elegant, Parisian-style café
with a popular *terraza* looking
across the plaza to the palace.
The café was opened in the
1980s by a priest, Padre
Lezama, who ploughs his
profits into various charitable
schemes. There's an equally
smart bar, *La Botilleria* (open
noon–1am, an hour later on Fri
& Sat), next door.

CHOCOLATERÍA SAN GINÉS

Pasadizo de San Ginés 11 Ⓜ Sol or Ópera.
Daily 9.30am–7am. MAP P.40, POCKET MAP C12

A Madrid institution, this café,
established in 1894, serves
chocolate con churros (thick
hot chocolate with deep-fried
hoops of batter) to perfection
– just the thing to finish off a
night of excess. It's an almost
compulsory Madrileño custom
to end up here after the clubs
close, before heading home for
a shower and then off to work.

Restaurants

LA BOLA

C/Bola 5 Ⓜ Santo Domingo or Ópera
☎ 915 476 930. Mon–Sat 1–4pm &
8.30–11pm, Sun 1–4pm. MAP P.40, POCKET
MAP A10

Opened back in 1870, this
is the place to go for *cocido
madrileño* (soup followed by
chickpeas and a selection
of meats) cooked in the
traditional way over a wood
fire. Try the delicious *buñuelos
de manzana* (battered apples)
for pudding, and don't plan
on doing anything energetic
afterwards. Around €30 a head,
but they don't accept cards.

LA BOLA

EL BUEY

Plaza de la Marina Española 1
Ⓜ Santo Domingo or Ópera ☎ 915 413 041.
Mon–Sat 1–4pm & 9pm–midnight. MAP P.40,
POCKET MAP C4

A meat-eaters' paradise,
specializing in superb steak
that you fry yourself on a
hotplate. Great side dishes and
home-made desserts, with a
highly drinkable house red, all
for around €35 per head.

CASA GALLEGA

C/Bordadores 11 Ⓜ Ópera or Sol
☎ 915 419 055; also Plaza San Miguel 8
Ⓜ Ópera or Sol ☎ 915 473 055. Both daily
1–4pm & 8pm–midnight. MAP P.40, POCKET
MAP C11

Two airy and welcoming
marisquerías that have been
importing seafood on overnight
trains from Galicia since
opening in 1915. Costs vary
according to the market price
of the fish or shellfish that you
order. *Pulpo* (octopus) and
pimientos de Padrón (small
peppers, spiced up by the odd
fiery one) are brilliantly done
and inexpensive, but the more
exotic seasonal delights will
raise a bill to around €40 a head.

ENTRE SUSPIRO Y SUSPIRO

C/Caños de Peral 3 Ⓜ Ópera ☎ 915 420 644.
Mon–Fri 2–5pm & 9–1am, Sat 9–1am.
MAP P.40, POCKET MAP B10

Given Madrid's links with Latin America, this is one of surprisingly few decent Mexican restaurants in the city. Quesadillas, tacos and some imaginative takes on traditional dishes served up in pleasant surroundings, although it is rather cramped and prices are high at around €40 for a meal.

VADEBACO

C/Campomanes 6 Ⓜ Ópera ☎ 915 417 017.
Mon–Sat noon–4.30pm & 6pm–midnight, Sun
noon–4.30pm. MAP P.40, POCKET MAP B10

Creative tapas and over 350 different wines to choose from in this chic place. Cod samosas, mushroom ravioli and delicious desserts are just some of their dishes. Does a very good-value €12 lunchtime menu.

Bars

EL ANCIANO REY DE LOS VINOS

C/Bailén 19 Ⓜ Ópera. Mon, Tues & Thurs–Sun
10am–3pm & 6–11pm. MAP P.40, POCKET MAP C6

Traditional standing-room-only bar founded back in 1909, serving well-poured beer, *vermút*, a decent selection of wine and some good tapas.

Clubs

JOY MADRID

C/Arenal 11 Ⓜ Sol or Ópera Ⓦ www.joy
-estava.com. Daily midnight–6am. €10–15
including first drink. MAP P.40, POCKET MAP C11

This long-standing club is one of the staples of the Madrid night scene. It has a busy schedule of sessions every day of the week, catering for every-thing from House to 70's disco.

If you arrive early there are discounts on the entry fee.

PALACIO DE GAVIRIA

C/Arenal 9 Ⓜ Sol or Ópera Ⓦ www.palacio
gaviria.com. Daily 11pm–late. €10–15
including drink. MAP P.40, POCKET MAP C11

Nineteenth-century palace with a series of extravagant Baroque salons playing anything from house to tropical (a genre taking in everything from salsa to rumba). A great setting for a late drink, it hosts occasional "International Parties" (a common term here for parties aimed at students of different nationalities studying in Madrid) and dance classes too.

Live music

CAFÉ DE CHINITAS

C/Torija 7 Ⓜ Santo Domingo ☎ 915 595 135.
Ⓦ www.chinitas.com. Mon–Thurs 9pm–2am,
Fri & Sat 9pm–3am. Drinks and show €32.
MAP P.40, POCKET MAP C4

One of the oldest flamenco clubs in Madrid, hosting a dinner-dance spectacular. The music is authentic but keep an eye on how much you order as the bill can soon mount up. Reservations essential.

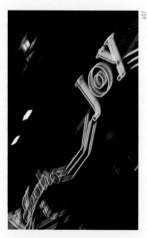

Rastro, Lavapiés and Embajadores

Lavapiés and Embajadores were originally tough, working-class districts built to accommodate the huge population growth of Madrid in the eighteenth and nineteenth centuries. Traditional sights are thin on the ground, but some original tenement blocks survive and the area is now famous for the Rastro street market. These barrios are also home to the *castizos* – authentic Madrileños – who can be seen decked out in traditional costume during local festivals. The character of these areas has changed, however, in recent years. Young Spaniards and large numbers of immigrants have arrived, meaning that Lavapiés and Embajadores are now Madrid's most racially mixed barrios, with teahouses, kebab joints and textile shops sitting alongside some of the most original bars and restaurants in the city. Petty crime can be a problem round here but the reality is not as dramatic as newspapers suggest.

IGLESIA COLEGIATA DE SAN ISIDRO

C/Toledo 37 Ⓜ Tirso de Molina or La Latina. Mon–Sat 7.45am–1pm & 6–8.45pm, Sun & hols 8.30am–2pm & 6–8.30pm. MAP P.48-49, POCKET MAP C14

Built from 1622 to 1633, this enormous twin-towered church was originally the centre of the Jesuit Order in Spain. After Carlos III fell out with the Order in 1767, he redesigned the interior and dedicated it to the city's patron, San Isidro. Isidro's remains – and those of his equally saintly wife – were brought here in 1769 from the nearby **Iglesia de San Andrés** (see p.33). The church was the city's cathedral from 1886 until 1993 when the **Catedral de la Almudena** (see p.39) was completed. It has a single nave with ornate lateral chapels and an impressive altarpiece.

MERCADO DEL RASTRO

Ⓜ La Latina. MAP P.48-49, POCKET MAP D8

Every Sunday morning the heaving, ramshackle mass of El Rastro fleamarket takes over Calle Ribera de Curtidores. On

SAN CAYETANO

offer is just about anything you might – or more likely might not – need, from second-hand clothes and military surplus items to caged birds and fine antiques. Real bargains are few and far between, but the atmosphere is always enjoyable and the bars around these streets are as good as any in the city. Be aware though, that petty theft is common here, so keep a close eye on your belongings. If you are looking for something more upmarket, head for the antiques shops in **Galerías Piquer** at C/Ribera de Curtidores 29, which are also open on a Sunday morning.

ESTADIO VICENTE CALDERÓN

Paseo Virgen del Puerto 67 Ⓜ Pirámides
☎ 913 664 707 Ⓦ www.clubatleticodemadrid
.com. Match tickets from €20; ☎ 902 530 500
and via the website. MAP P.48–49, POCKET MAP B1
Home to **Atlético Madrid**, one of the city's two big-name football teams, this 54,000-capacity stadium is quite a sight, with its smoked-glass sides rising high above the Manzanares river. Atlético may not have tasted the glory experienced by rivals Real Madrid, but they still rank as one of Spain's biggest teams. The stadium houses a club shop (Mon–Fri 10am–2pm &

2–8pm, Sat & Sun 10am–2pm, match days 11am–45 mins before kickoff) and a museum (Tues–Sun 11am–7pm; €10 with guided tour) detailing the history and achievements of the club.

LA CORRALA

C/Tribulete 12 Ⓜ Lavapiés. MAP P.48–49,
POCKET MAP E8
Built in 1839 and restored in the 1980s, this is one of many traditional *corrales* (tenement blocks) in Lavapiés, with balconied apartments opening onto a central patio. Plays, especially farces and *zarzuelas* (a mix of classical opera and music-hall), used to be performed regularly in Spanish *corrales*, and this one usually hosts performances in the summer.

SAN CAYETANO

C/Embajadores 15 Ⓜ Tirso de Molina or
La Latina. Variable hours, usually Mon–Sat
9.30am–12pm & 6–8pm, Sun 9am–2pm &
6–8pm. MAP P.48–49, POCKET MAP E8
José de Churriguera and Pedro de Ribera, both renowned for their extravagant designs, were involved in the design of the elaborate facade, which dates from 1761. Most of the rest of the church was destroyed in the Civil War and has since been rebuilt.

PLAZA LAVAPIÉS

Ⓜ Lavapiés. MAP P.48-49, POCKET MAP F8

In the Middle Ages, bustling Plaza Lavapiés was the core of Jewish Madrid, with the synagogue situated on the site now occupied by the Teatro Valle-Inclán. Today, with its Chinese, Arabic and African inhabitants, it remains a cosmopolitan place, and the plaza, along with Calle Argumosa running off from its southeastern corner, is an animated spot, with a variety of bars and cafés in various states of decay.

CALLE ATOCHA

Ⓜ Atocha or Antón Martín. MAP P.48-49, POCKET MAP E6-H8

Calle Atocha, one of the old ceremonial routes from Plaza Mayor to the basilica at Atocha, forms the northeastern border

of Lavapiés. At its southern end it's a mishmash of fast-food and touristy restaurants, developing, as you move north up the hill, into a strange mixture of cheap hostels, fading shops, bars, lottery kiosks and sex emporia. With its brash neon lighting and shiny black facade, the huge sex shop at no. 80, El Mundo Fantástico, stands unashamedly opposite a convent and the site of an old printing house that produced the first edition of the first part of *Don Quixote*.

CINE DORÉ

C/Santa Isabel 3 Ⓜ Antón Martín
☏ 914 672 600. Closed Mon. Films €2.50.
MAP P.48-49, POCKET MAP F14

At the end of the narrow Pasaje Doré alley is the Cine Doré, the **oldest cinema** in Madrid. Dating from 1922 with a later

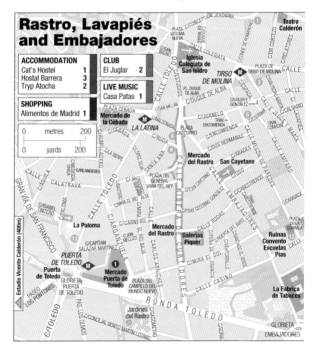

Modernista/Art Nouveau facade, it's now the **Filmoteca Nacional**, an art-house cinema with bargain prices and a pleasant, inexpensive café/restaurant (Tues–Sun 1.30pm–12.30am).

MUSEO DEL FERROCARRIL

Paseo de las Delicias 61 Ⓜ Delicias ☎ 902 228 822 Ⓦ www.museodelferrocarril .org. Tues–Sun 10am–3pm. Closed Aug. €5, Sat €1. MAP P.48–49, POCKET MAP H9

The Museo del Ferrocarril (Railway Museum) contains an impressive assortment of engines, carriages and wagons that once graced the train lines of Spain. The museum, which is housed in the handsome old station of Delicias, also has a fascinating collection of **model railways** and there's an atmospheric little café in one of the more elegant carriages.

CINE DORÉ

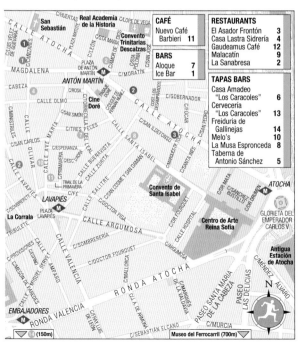

CAFÉ

Nuevo Café Barbieri	11

BARS

Aloque	7
Ice Bar	1

RESTAURANTS

El Asador Frontón	3
Casa Lastra Sidrería	4
Gaudeamus Café	12
Malacatín	9
La Sanabresa	2

TAPAS BARS

Casa Amadeo "Los Caracoles"	6
Cervecería "Los Caracoles"	13
Freiduría de Gallinejas	14
Melo's	10
La Musa Espronceda	8
Taberna de Antonio Sánchez	5

Shop

ALIMENTOS DE MADRID

Mercado Puerta de Toledo, 2° Ⓜ Puerta de Toledo. Mon–Sat 10.30am–9pm, Sun 10.30am–3pm. MAP P.48–49, POCKET MAP D9

This outlet in the Mercado de Toledo shopping centre showcases a wide variety of regional produce including wine, olive oil and honey.

Café

NUEVO CAFÉ BARBIERI

C/Avemaría 45 Ⓜ Lavapiés. Daily 3pm–2am, Fri & Sat till 3am. MAP P.48–49, POCKET MAP F8

A relaxed, slightly dilapidated café, with unobtrusive music, wooden tables, newspapers and a wide selection of coffees.

Restaurants

EL ASADOR FRONTÓN

Plaza Tirsode Moleia 7, 1° (entrance on C/Jesus y Maria) Ⓜ Tirso de Molina ☎ 913 692 325. Mon–Sat 1–4pm & 9pm–midnight, Sun 1–4pm. MAP P.48–49, POCKET MAP D14

Charming neighbourhood restaurant where locals come for a long lunch. There's a range of delicious Castilian dishes and some fine home-made desserts. Expect to pay around €40 for the works.

CASA LASTRA SIDRERÍA

C/Olivar 3 Ⓜ Antón Martín ☎ 913 690 837. Mon, Tues & Thurs–Sat 1–4pm & 8pm–midnight, Sun 1–5pm. Closed July. MAP P.48–49, POCKET MAP E14

Moderately priced Asturian fare: *chorizo a la sidra* (chorizo in cider), *fabada* (a stew of beans, chorizo and black pudding) and, of course, *sidra* (cider).

GAUDEAMUS CAFÉ

Edificio Escuelas Pias, C/Tribulete 14, 4° Ⓜ Lavapiés ☎ 915 282 594. Winter: Mon–Fri 3.30pm–midnight, Sat 6pm–midnight; summer: Mon–Sat 6pm–midnight. No cards. MAP P.48–49, POCKET MAP E8

Fabulous creative tapas-style dishes such as fried aubergines in rosemary honey and some really tasty chocolate desserts at this rooftop restaurant. It is not easy to find, though; make your way up past the library to the top floor. Menus from €26.

MALACATÍN

C/Ruda 5 Ⓜ La Latina ☎ 913 655 241. Mon–Fri 1–4pm & 8–11pm, Sat 1–5pm. Closed Aug. MAP P.48–49, POCKET MAP D8

Established in 1895 to serve wine to local workmen, this authentic *castizo* restaurant serves up generous helpings of what is arguably the best *cocido* in the city for a reasonable €18. You can sample it at the bar for €5 too.

LA SANABRESA

C/Amor de Diós 12 Ⓜ Antón Martín ☎ 914 290 338. Mon–Sat 1–4pm & 8.30–11.30pm, Fri & Sat till midnight. Closed Aug. MAP P.48–49, POCKET MAP G14

Unpretentious place with reasonably priced dishes. There are two *menús del día* for around €10 and a weekend set lunch for €12. Don't miss the grilled aubergines.

Tapas bars

CASA AMADEO "LOS CARACOLES"

Plaza Cascorro 18 Ⓜ La Latina. Mon–Thurs 11am–4pm, Fri & Sat 11am–4pm & 7–10.30pm, Sun 10am–4pm. MAP P.48–49, POCKET MAP D7

A favourite since the 1940s, this place has a range of tapas including the eponymous *caracoles* (snails), *callos* and *oreja*. On Sundays it's always heaving after the market.

CERVECERÍA "LOS CARACOLES"

C/Toledo 106 Ⓜ Puerta de Toledo. Tues–Sat 9am–10.30pm, Sun 9am–4pm. Closed July. MAP P.48–49, POCKET MAP C8

Rough-and-ready bar specializing in snails, washed down with local *vermút del grifo* (draught vermouth).

FREIDURIA DE GALLINEJAS

C/Embajadores 84 Ⓜ Embajadores. Mon–Sat 11am–11pm. Closed Aug. MAP P.48–49, POCKET MAP F9

This traditional tiled, family-run bar is famed for serving the best fried lambs' intestines in the city. A variety of different cuts are available as well as straightforward fried lamb.

MELO'S

C/Ave María 44 Ⓜ Lavapiés. Tues–Sat 9am–2am. Closed Aug. MAP P.48–49, POCKET MAP F8

Standing room only at this very popular Galician bar serving huge *zapatillas* (bread filled with *lacón* – shoulder of pork – and cheese) plus great *pimientos de Padrón* and some fine *croquetas*.

LA MUSA ESPRONCEDA

C/Santa Isabel 17 Ⓜ Atocha or Antón Martín. Daily 1.30–4pm & 8pm–midnight. MAP P.48–49, POCKET MAP G7

Great value tapas – classics such as tortilla and *croquetas* and creative bites such as brie wrapped in bacon – served in this friendly Lavapiés local.

TABERNA DE ANTONIO SÁNCHEZ

C/Mesón de Paredes 13 Ⓜ Tirso de Molina. Mon–Sat noon–4pm & 8pm–midnight, Sun noon–4pm. MAP P.48–49, POCKET MAP E7

Said to be the oldest *taberna* in Madrid, this seventeenth-century bar has a stuffed bull's head (in honour of Antonio Sánchez, the son of the founder, who was killed by a bull) and a wooden interior. Lots of *finos*, plus *jamón* tapas or *tortilla de San Isidro* (omelette with salted cod).

Bars

ALOQUE

C/Torrecilla del Leal 20 Ⓜ Antón Martín. Daily 7.30pm–1am. Closed Aug. MAP P.48–49, POCKET MAP F7

Relaxed wine bar where you can try top-quality *vinos* by the glass. The tapas, served up from the tiny kitchen at the back, are original and extremely good.

ICE BAR

C/Conde de Romanones 3 Ⓜ Tirso de Molina. Tues–Sat noon–4pm & 7.30pm–midnight, Sun 11am–3.30pm. Closed Aug. MAP P.48–49, POCKET MAP D13

The coldest if not the coolest bar in the city. For €15 (coat and cocktail included) you will be transported to a polar world complete with ice sculptures and frozen furniture.

Club

EL JUGLAR

C/Lavapiés 37 Ⓜ Lavapiés Ⓦ www.salajuglar .com. Sun–Wed 9.30pm–3am, Thurs–Sat 9.30am–3.30am. MAP P.48–49, POCKET MAP F8

Down-to-earth club playing funk and soul. As well as DJ nights, there's a Sunday flamenco session with a €10 entry fee.

Live music

CASA PATAS

C/Cañizares 10 Ⓜ Antón Martín or Tirso Molina Ⓣ 913 690 496 Ⓦ www.casapatas.com. Shows: Mon–Thurs 10.30pm, Fri & Sat 9pm & midnight. €25–30. MAP P.48–49, POCKET MAP E14

Authentic flamenco club with a bar and restaurant that gets its share of big names. The best nights are Thursday and Friday – check website for schedules.

Sol, Santa Ana and Huertas

The busy streets around Puerta del Sol, Plaza Santa Ana and Huertas are the bustling heart of Madrid and the reference point for most visitors to the capital. The city began to expand here during the sixteenth century and the area subsequently became known as the *barrio de las letras* (literary neighbourhood) because of the many authors and playwrights – including Cervantes – who made it their home. Today, the literary theme continues, with theatres, bookshops and cafés proliferating alongside the Círculo de Bellas Artes (Fine Arts Institute), the Teatro Español (historic theatre specializing in classic works) and the Congreso de Los Diputados (Parliament). For art lovers, there's the Real Academia de Bellas Artes de San Fernando museum, but for most visitors, though, the main attraction is the vast array of traditional bars, particularly concentrated around the picturesque Plaza Santa Ana.

PUERTA DEL SOL

Ⓜ Sol. MAP P.54, POCKET MAP D11

This half-moon-shaped plaza, thronged with people at almost any hour of the day, marks the epicentre of Madrid and, indeed, of Spain – **Kilometre Zero**, an inconspicuous stone slab on the south side of the square, is the spot from which all distances in the country are measured. Opposite is an equestrian bronze of King Carlos III, and to the east a statue of Madrid's emblem, *el oso y el madroño* (bear and strawberry tree).

The square has been a popular meeting place since the mid-sixteenth century, when it was the site of one of the main

gates into the city. Its most important building is the Casa de Correos, built in 1766 and originally the city's post office. Under Franco it became the headquarters of the much-feared security police and it now houses the main offices of the Madrid regional government. The neoclassical facade is crowned by the nation's most famous clock which officially ushers in the New Year: on December 31, Madrileños pack Puerta del Sol and attempt to scoff twelve grapes – one on each of the chimes of midnight – to bring themselves good luck for the next twelve months.

The square has also witnessed several incidents of national importance, including the slaughter of a rioting crowd by Napoleon's marshal, Murat, aided by the infamous Egyptian cavalry, on May 2, 1808. The massacre is depicted in Goya's canvas, *Dos de Mayo*, now hanging in the Prado (see p.66).

PLAZA SANTA ANA

Ⓜ Sol or Antón Martín. MAP P.54, POCKET MAP F13
The main reason for visiting vibrant Plaza Santa Ana is to explore the mass of bars, restaurants and cafés on the square itself and in the nearby streets that bring the area alive in the evenings.

The square was one of a series created by Joseph Bonaparte, whose passion for open spaces led to a remarkable remodelling of Madrid in the six short years of his reign. It's dominated by two distinguished buildings at either end: to the west, the *ME Madrid*, a giant white confection of a hotel; to the east, the nineteenth-century Neoclassical Teatro Español. There has been a playhouse on this site since 1583, and the current theatre is the oldest in Madrid, its facade

PLAZA SANTA ANA

decorated with busts of famous Spanish playwrights.

CASA DE LOPE DE VEGA

C/Cervantes 11 Ⓜ Antón Martín. Tues–Sat 9.30am–3pm. Closed mid-July to mid-Aug. Free guided tours; wait for a group to be formed; ring 914 299 216 to reserve a tour in English. MAP P.54, POCKET MAP G13
Situated in the heart of the Huertas district, the reconstructed home of the great Golden Age Spanish dramatist offers a fascinating glimpse of life in seventeenth-century Madrid. Lope de Vega, a prolific writer with a tangled private life, lived here for 25 years until his death in 1635 at the age of 72. The house itself has been furnished in authentic fashion using the inventory left at the writer's death and highlights include a chapel containing some of his relics, his study with a selection of contemporary books, an Arabic-style drawing room and a delightful courtyard garden.

Cervantes lived and died at no. 2 on the same street and though the original building has long gone, a plaque above a shop marks the site.

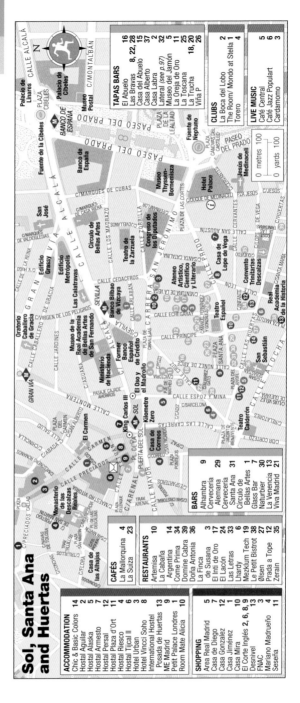

Sol, Santa Ana and Huertas

ACCOMMODATION
Chic & Basic Colors 14
Hostal Aguilar 2
Hostal Alaska 5
Hostal Armesto 7
Hostal Persal 12
Hostal Plaza d'Ort 11
Hostal Riesco 4
Hostal Tijcal II 6
Hotel Urban 3
Hotel Vinicci Soho 8
International Hostel
  Posada de Huertas 13
ME Madrid 9
Petit Palace Londres 1
Room Mate Alicia 10

CAFÉS
La Mallorquina 4
La Suiza 23

RESTAURANTS
Artemisa 10
La Cabaña 3
Argentina 14
Come Prima 34
Domine Cabra 39
Doña Antonia 36
La Finca
  de Susana 9
Casa de Diego 17
El Inti de Oro 24
Las Letras 33
Lhardy 6
Mezklum Tech 19
Le Petit Bistrot 38
Ölsen 27
Prada a Tope 12
Zerain 35

SHOPPING
Area Real Madrid 5
Casa de Diego 7
Casa González 12
Casa Jiménez 1
Casa Mira 10
El Corte Inglés 2, 6, 8, 9
Desnivel 3
FNAC 13
Mariano Madrueño 4
Seseña 11

BARS
Alhambra 9
Cervecería
  Alemana 29
Cervecería
  Santa Ana 31
Círculo de
  Bellas Artes 1
Glass Bar 7
Naturbier 30
La Venencia 13
Viva Madrid 21

TAPAS BARS
El Abuelo 16
Las Bravas 8, 22, 28
Casa del Abuelo 15
Casa Alberto 37
Casa Labra 2
Lateral (see p.97) 32
Museo del Jamón 5
La Oreja de Oro 11
La Toscana 25
La Trucha 18, 20
Viña P 26

CLUBS
La Boca del Lobo 2
The Room/ Mondo at Stella 1
Torero 4

LIVE MUSIC
Café Central 5
Café Jazz Populart 6
Cardamomo 3

BANCO ESPAÑOL DE CRÉDITO

ATENEO ARTÍSTICO, CIENTÍFICO Y LITERARIO

C/Prado 2 Ⓜ Antón Martín or Sevilla.
MAP P.54, POCKET MAP G12

The Ateneo (literary, scientific and political club) was founded after the 1820 Revolution and provided a focus for the new liberal political ideas circulating at that time. The exterior is neo-Plateresque in style, while the inside features a neoclassical lecture theatre, a wooden panelled corridor with portraits of past presidents of the club and a splendid reading room. It also has a café and hosts occasional exhibitions.

CONGRESO DE LOS DIPUTADOS

Plaza de las Cortes Ⓜ Sevilla Ⓦ www
.congreso.es. Sat 10.30am–12.30pm
(bring passport). Closed Aug & hols.
MAP P.54, POCKET MAP G12

The lower house of the **Spanish parliament** meets in a rather unprepossessing nineteenth-century building; its most distinguished feature is the two bronze lions that guard the entrance, made from a melted-down cannon captured during the African War of 1859–60. Sessions can be visited by appointment only, though you can turn up and queue for a free tour on Saturday mornings. This takes in several important rooms and the chamber with the bullet holes left by mad Colonel Tejero and his Guardia Civil associates in the abortive coup of 1981.

CALLE ALCALÁ

Ⓜ Sol or Sevilla. MAP P.54, POCKET MAP E11–J10

An imposing catalogue of Spanish architecture lines Calle Alcalá, an ancient thoroughfare that originally led to the university town of Alcalá de Henares. It starts at Puerta del Sol and in this first stretch look out particularly for the splendid early twentieth-century wedge-shaped Banco Español de Crédito adorned with **elephant heads** and plaques listing all the branches of the bank in Spain, soon to be turned into a luxury hotel, shopping centre and apartment block. The Banco de Bilbao Vizcaya, with its neoclassical facade complete with charioteers on top, and the baroque Ministerio de Hacienda (Inland Revenue) are similarly impressive.

IGLESIA DE SAN JOSÉ

C/Alcalá 41 Ⓜ Banco de España. Daily 7am–1.30pm & 6–8.30pm, Sun open from 9am. MAP P.54, POCKET MAP G10

The red-brick Iglesia de San José, near the junction with Gran Vía, dates back to the 1730s and was the last building designed by the prolific Pedro de Ribera. The interior holds the ornate Santa Teresa de Ávila chapel and an impressive collection of colourful images of Christ and the Virgin Mary.

IGLESIA DE LAS CALATRAVAS

C/Alcalá 25 Ⓜ Sevilla. Mon–Fri 8am–1pm & 6–8pm, Sat & Sun 11am–2pm & 6–8pm. MAP P.54, POCKET MAP F11

The pastel-pink Iglesia de las Calatravas was built in the seventeenth century for the nuns of the Calatrava, one of the four Spanish military orders. Inside, it contains a fantastically elaborate gold altarpiece by José Churriguera.

MUSEO DE LA REAL ACADEMIA DE BELLAS ARTES DE SAN FERNANDO

C/Alcalá 13 Ⓜ Sevilla ☎ 915 240 864 Ⓦ rabasf.insde.es. Tues–Fri 9am–5pm, Sat 9am–3pm, Sun & hols 9am–2.30pm. €5, free Wed. MAP P.54, POCKET MAP F11

Established by Felipe V in 1744 and housed in its present location since 1773, the Museo de la Real Academia de Bellas Artes de San Fernando is one of the most important art galleries in Spain. Its displays include sections on sculpture, architecture and music, some interesting French and Italian work and an extraordinary – but chaotically displayed – collection of Spanish paintings, including El Greco, Velázquez, Murillo and Picasso.

The Goya section has two revealing self-portraits, several depictions of the despised royal favourite *Don Manuel Godoy*, the desolate representation of *The Madhouse* and *The Burial of the Sardine* (a popular procession that continues to this day in Madrid).

The gallery is also home to the national copper engraving collection (Tues–Thurs 9am–5pm, Fri 9am–3pm; free), which includes some Goya etchings and several of the copper plates used for his *Capricho* series on show in the Prado.

CÍRCULO DE BELLAS ARTES

C/Marqués de Casa Riera 2 Ⓜ Banco de España. Exhibitions Tues–Fri 5–9pm, Sat 11am–2pm & 5–9pm, Sun 11am–2pm. €2. MAP P.54, POCKET MAP G11

REAL ACADEMIA DE BELLAS ARTES DE SAN FERNANDO

This striking 1920s Art Deco building, crowned by a statue of Pallas Athene, is home to one of Madrid's best arts centres. Inside there's a theatre, music hall, galleries, cinema and a café bar (see p.64). For many years a stronghold of Spain's intelligentsia, it attracts the city's arts and media crowd but is not exclusive, nor expensive. As the Círculo is theoretically a members-only club, it issues day membership on the door, for which you get access to all areas.

PLAZA DE CIBELES

Ⓜ Banco de España. MAP P.54, POCKET MAP J10

Encircled by four of the most monumental buildings in Madrid – the Palacio de Cibeles (the Madrid City Council offices), Banco de España (the Central Bank), the Palacio de Buenavista (the Army HQ) and the Palacio de Linares (the Casa de América) – Plaza de Cibeles is one of the city's most famous landmarks. At its centre, and marooned in a sea of never-ending traffic, is the late eighteenth-century fountain and statue of the goddess Cybele, riding in a chariot drawn by two lions. Built to celebrate the city's first public water supply, today the fountain sees celebrations of a different kind as the favoured location for Real Madrid fans to congregate after a victory (Atlético supporters bathe in the fountain of Neptune just down the road).

PALACIO DE CIBELES

Ⓜ Banco de España. MAP P.54, POCKET MAP J10

This grandiose wedding-cake of a building on the eastern side of Paseo del Prado, constructed between 1904 and 1917 by the prolific architect partnership of Antonio Palacios and Joaquín Otamendi, was once

PALACIO DE CIBELES

Madrid's main post office, but has recently been usurped by the Madrid City Council and is home for ever-burgeoning municipal offices. There's a huge glass-covered patio to the rear of the building that can be visited between 11am and 9pm on Sundays from May to September.

PALACIO DE LINARES

Plaza de Cibeles 2 Ⓜ Banco de España Ⓦ www.casamerica.es. Exhibitions usually Mon–Sat 11am–8pm, Sun 11am–3pm; guided tours Sat & Sun 11am, noon, 1pm. €7. Closed Aug. MAP P.54, POCKET MAP J10

This palatial eighteenth-century mansion, built by the Marqués de Linares, is now home to the Casa de América, a cultural organization that promotes Latin American art through concerts, films and exhibitions. At weekends there are guided tours through the sumptuous mansion decorated with some marvellous frescoes, crystal chandeliers and elaborate tapestries from the Real Fábrica (see p.76). The palacio also has a good bookshop, an expensive designer restaurant and an excellent summer garden terrace.

Shops

AREA REAL MADRID

C/Carmen 3 Ⓜ Sol. Mon–Sat 10am–9pm,
Sun 11am–8pm. MAP P.54, POCKET MAP D11

Club store where you can pick
up replica shirts and all manner
of – expensive – souvenirs
related to the club's history.
There is another branch (see
p.94) in the shopping centre on
the corner of Real's Bernabéu
stadium at C/Concha Espina 1.

CASA DE DIEGO

Puerta del Sol 12 Ⓜ Sol. Mon–Sat
9.30am–8pm. MAP P.54, POCKET MAP E11

Old-fashioned shop with
helpful staff selling a fabulous
array of Spanish fans (*abanicos*)
ranging from cheap offerings at
under €10 to beautifully hand-
crafted works of art costing
up to €200. Sells umbrellas,
walking sticks and shawls too.

CASA GONZALEZ

C/León 12 Ⓜ Antón Martín. Winter:
Tues–Thurs 9am–midnight, Fri & Sat
9am–1am; summer Tues–Sat 5pm–1am.
MAP P.54, POCKET MAP F13

Friendly little delicatessen
serving a great range of cheese
and meat and some very good
wines too. There is a small bar
too where you can sample the
excellent produce.

CASA JIMÉNEZ

C/Preciados 42 Ⓜ Callao. Mon–Sat
10am–1.30pm & 5–8pm, closed Sat pm in July
and all day Sat in Aug. MAP P.54, POCKET MAP C10

Traditional establishment that
has changed little since it first
opened its doors back in 1923.
Casa Jiménez is renowned for
its elaborately embroidered
mantones (shawls) made in
Seville (prices range from €100
to €600), as well as its gorgeous
fans starting at around €40.

CASA MIRA

Carrera de San Jerónimo 30 Ⓜ Sevilla. Daily
10am–2pm & 5–9pm. MAP P.54, POCKET MAP F12

The place to go for *turrón*
(flavoured nougat, eaten by
Spaniards at Christmas) and
marzipan. The family business
has been open for over a
150 years since the founder,
Luis Mira, arrived from
Asturias and set up a stall in
Puerta del Sol.

EL CORTE INGLÉS

C/Preciados 1–4 Ⓜ Sol. Mon–Sat 10am–9pm
& first Sun in the month. MAP P.54, POCKET
MAP D10–D11

The Spanish department store
par excellence. It's not cheap,
but the quality is very good,
the staff are highly professional
(the majority speak English)
and there's an upmarket food
department too.

CASA DE DIEGO

DESNIVEL

Plaza Matute 6 ⓜ Antón Martín. Mon–Sat 10am–2pm & 4.30–8.30pm. MAP P.54, POCKET MAP F14

A great selection of maps and guides if you fancy a hike in the nearby Sierra Guadarrama.

FNAC

C/Preciados 28 ⓜ Callao. Mon–Sat 10am–9.30pm, Sun noon–9.30pm. MAP P.54, POCKET MAP D10

French department store with excellent sections for books, videos, CDs and electrical equipment. Also sells concert tickets.

MARIANO MADRUEÑO

C/Postigo San Martín 3 ⓜ Callao. Mon–Fri 9.30am–2pm & 5–8pm, Sat 9.30am–2pm. MAP P.54, POCKET MAP C10

Traditional wine seller's, established in 1895, where there's an overpowering smell of grapes as you peruse its vintage-crammed shelves. Intriguing tipples include potent Licor de Hierbas from Galicia and home-made Pacharán (aniseed liqueur with sloe berries).

SESEÑA

C/Cruz 23 ⓜ Sol. Mon–Sat 10am–1.30pm & 4.30–8pm. MAP P.54, POCKET MAP E12

Open since 1901, this shop specializes in traditional Madrileño capes for royalty and celebrities. Clients have included Luis Buñuel, Gary Cooper and Hillary Clinton.

Cafés

LA MALLORQUINA

Puerta del Sol 2 ⓜ Sol. Daily 9am–9.15pm. MAP P.54, POCKET MAP D12

Classic Madrid café, great for breakfast or sweet snacks. Try one of their *napolitanas* (cream slices) in the upstairs salon that overlooks Puerta del Sol.

SESEÑA

LA SUIZA

Plaza Santa Ana 2 ⓜ Antón Martín or Sevilla. Daily 7am–midnight. MAP P.54, POCKET MAP F13

A traditional Madrid café serving delicious *leche merengada* (a sort of sweet whipped-milk ice cream) and a bewildering array of cakes. Its year-round terrace on the plaza is a perfect place to relax and watch the world go by.

Restaurants

ARTEMISA

C/Ventura de la Vega 4 ⓜ Sevilla ☎ 914 295 092. Daily 1.30–4pm & 9pm–midnight. MAP P.54, POCKET MAP F12

Long-standing vegetarian restaurant, serving a wide range of dishes including organic gazpacho, vegetable paella and some delicious aubergines. For non-vegetarians they also do a couple of chicken dishes. Mains will set you back €10–15.

LA CABAÑA ARGENTINA

C/Ventura de la Vega 10 ⓜ Sevilla ☎ 913 697 202. Daily 1.30–4pm & 9pm–midnight. MAP P.54, POCKET MAP F12

One of the best Argentine eateries in the city. Excellent-quality meat (*el bife lomo alto* is a house favourite) and classic desserts including *panqueques*. Friendly service and good value too at around €30 a head.

COME PRIMA

C/Echegaray 27 Ⓜ Antón Martín
☎ 914 203 042. Mon 9pm–midnight, Tues–Sat 1.30–4pm & 9pm–midnight. Closed Aug.
MAP P.54, POCKET MAP F13

Superior Italian restaurant, with fresh ingredients, excellent antipasti and authentic main courses including a great seafood risotto. Very popular, so make sure you book, and expect to pay around €35 a head.

DOMINE CABRA

C/Huertas 54 Ⓜ Antón Martín ☎ 914 294 365. Mon–Sat 2–4pm & 9–11.30pm, Sun 2–4pm. Closed Sat lunch & Sun in Aug & first half of Sept. MAP P.54, POCKET MAP G14

Interesting mix of traditional and modern, with Madrileño standards given the *nueva cocina* (new cuisine) treatment. Sauces are tasty – a rarity in Spain – and staff are friendly. There are good-value *menús* at around €13 and €18.

DOÑA ANTONIA

C/ Huertas 4 Ⓜ Antón Martín/Sol
☎ 911 568 208. Tues–Sun 1pm–midnight.
MAP P.54, POCKET MAP E13

Original tapas-style dishes such as chicken teriyaki and fried vegetables with rosemary oil as

MEJKLUM TECH

well as more traditional home cooking at this all-day restaurant in Huertas. Tea is served up in the afternoon together with some mouth-watering chocolate tart and cheesecake. Open till 2am at weekends.

LA FINCA DE SUSANA

C/Arlabán 4 Ⓜ Sevilla. Daily 1–3.45pm & 8.30–11.45pm. MAP P.54, POCKET MAP F11

One of three great-value restaurants set up by a group of Catalan friends (another, *La Gloria de Montera* is just off Gran Vía, see p.87). A varied *menú del día* for around €9 consists of simple dishes cooked with imagination. Efficient, but impersonal service. Arrive early to avoid queuing, as you can't book.

EL INTI DE ORO

C/Ventura de la Vega 12 Ⓜ Antón Martín
☎ 914 296 703. Daily 1.30–4pm & 8.30pm–midnight. Also at c/Amor de Dios 9 Ⓜ Antón Martín ☎ 914 291 958. MAP P.54, POCKET MAP F12

The friendly staff at this good-value Peruvian restaurant are more than ready to provide suggestions for those new to the cuisine. The pisco sour, a cocktail of Peruvian liquor, lemon juice, egg white and sugar is a recommended starter, while the *cebiche de merluza* (raw fish marinated in lemon juice) is a wonderful dish. A full meal costs around €30.

EL LACÓN

C/Manuel Fernández y González 8 Ⓜ Sol
☎ 914 296 042. Daily 1–4pm, 8pm–midnight. Closed Aug. MAP P.54, POCKET MAP F12

A large Galician bar-restaurant with plenty of seats upstairs. Great *pulpo, caldo gallego* (meat and vegetable broth) and empanadas. They also do boards of cold meats, vegetables, meat and fish. Main courses cost €12–15.

LAS LETRAS

C/Echegaray 26 ⓜ Antón Martín
☎ 914 294 843. Tues–Sat 1.30–4pm &
9–11.30pm, Sun 1.30–4pm. Closed Aug & Sun
in summer. MAP P.54, POCKET MAP F13

Small informal bar/restaurant
with designer touches to the
decor and food. The constantly
changing set menu usually
contains a good selection of
healthy options at a competitive €10.50.

LHARDY

Carrera de San Jerónimo 8 ⓜ Sol
☎ 915 213 385. Restaurant: Mon–Sat
1–3.30pm & 9–11.30pm, Sun 1–3.30pm.
Shop: Mon–Sat 10am–3pm & 5–9.30pm,
Sun 9am–2.30pm. Closed Aug. MAP P.54,
POCKET MAP E12

Once the haunt of royalty,
this is one of Madrid's most
beautiful and famous restaurants. It's greatly overpriced –
expect to pay over €60 per head
for a three-course meal – but
on the ground floor, there's a
wonderful bar/shop where you
can snack on canapés, *fino* and
consommé, without breaking
the bank.

MEZKLUM TECH

C/Príncipe 16 ⓜ Sevilla ☎ 915 218 911.
Mon–Sat 1–4pm & 9pm–midnight, Fri & Sat
open till 1am. MAP P.54, POCKET MAP F12

A self-consciously cool and
chic arrival on the Santa Ana
scene, *Mezklum* is decked out
in minimalist style with white,
pink and lilac tones and serves
a fine array of Mediterranean
dishes with good salads and
pasta. It has two lunchtime
menus priced at under €15;
evening meals are €25–30.

LE PETIT BISTROT

Plaza Matute 5 ⓜ Antón Martín
☎ 914 296 265. Tues–Sat 1.15–3.45pm &
9.15–11.45pm, Sun 11.30–2.30pm. MAP P.54,
POCKET MAP F14

A genuine French bistro in a
quiet plaza just off Huertas.

LE PETIT BISTROT

There's a very good set lunch
for around €15 and a slightly
more expensive, but hefty,
brunch on Sundays. Classics
such as French onion soup,
steak in béarnaise sauce and
profiteroles dripping in chocolate are all on offer.

ØLSEN

C/Prado 15 ⓜ Antón Martín
☎ 914 293 659. Daily 1–5pm &
8pm–midnight. MAP P.54, POCKET MAP G13

Slick Scandinavian restaurant
and vodka bar in the heart of
Huertas. Specialities include
gravalax, nordic sushi and
mouthwatering desserts, but
portions are quite small and
eating à la carte is expensive
(€40–50). A better option is the
lunchtime *menú* at €15.

PRADA A TOPE

C/Príncipe 11 ⓜ Sol ☎ 914 295 921.
Tues–Sun 12.30–5pm & 8pm–midnight.
MAP P.54, POCKET MAP F12

Quality produce from the
El Bierzo region of León. The
morcilla (black pudding),
empanada (pasty) and tortilla
are extremely tasty, while the
smooth house wines provide
the ideal accompaniment.

ZERAIN

C/Quevedo 3 Ⓜ Antón Martín ☎ 914 297 909.
Mon–Sat 1.30–4pm & 8.30pm–midnight.
Closed Aug. MAP P.54, POCKET MAP G13

Basque cider house and restaurant serving excellent meat and fish dishes. The *chuletón* (T-bone steak) is the speciality, but it also does a very good *tortilla de bacalao* (cod tortilla) and grilled *rape* (monkfish). A three-course meal will cost in the region of €40.

Tapas bars

EL ABUELO

C/Núñez de Arce 5 Ⓜ Sol. Wed–Sun
11.30am–3.30pm & 6.30–11.30pm. MAP P.54,
POCKET MAP E12

There's a *comedor* (dining room) at the back of this inexpensive bar, where you can order a selection of traditional *raciones* – the *croquetas* are great – and a jug of house wine.

LAS BRAVAS

C/Alvarez Gato 3 Ⓜ Sol. Other branches at
C/Espoz y Mina 13 Ⓜ Sol; & Pasaje Mathéu 5
Ⓜ Sol. Daily noon–4pm & 7pm–midnight.
MAP P.54, POCKET MAP E13

Standing room only at these three bars, where, as the name suggests, *patatas bravas* are the

thing to try. In fact, *Las Bravas* has patented its own version of the spicy sauce.

CASA DEL ABUELO

C/Victoria 12 Ⓜ Sol. Daily 11.30am–3.30pm
& 6.30–11.30pm. MAP P.54, POCKET MAP E12

A tiny, atmospheric bar serving just their own cloyingly sweet red wine (stick with a beer instead) and delicious cooked prawns – try them *al ajillo* (in garlic) or *a la plancha* (fried) – which are fried up in the tiny corner kitchen.

CASA ALBERTO

C/Huertas 18 Ⓜ Antón Martín
☎ 914 299 356. Tues–Sat noon–1am, Sun
noon–4pm (in summer). MAP P.54, POCKET
MAP F13

Traditional *tasca* that has resisted the passage of time since it was founded back in 1827. Good *caracoles* (snails), *gambas* (prawns) and great *croquetas*, ideally accompanied by a glass of house vermouth.

CASA LABRA

C/Tetuán 12 Ⓜ Sol ☎ 915 310 081. Mon–Sat
11am–3.30pm & 5.30–11pm. MAP P.54, POCKET
MAP D11

Dating from 1869 – and where the Spanish Socialist Party was founded ten years later – this

CASA ALBERTO

traditional and highly popular place (be prepared to queue) retains much of its original interior. Order a drink at the bar and a *ración* of *bacalao* (cod fried in batter) or some of the best *croquetas* in town. There's also a restaurant at the back serving classic Madrileño food.

MUSEO DEL JAMÓN

Carrera de San Jerónimo 6 Ⓜ Sol. Mon–Sat 9am–midnight, Sun 10am–midnight. MAP P.54, POCKET MAP E12

This is the largest branch of this unpretentious Madrid chain, from whose ceilings are suspended hundreds of *jamones* (hams). The best – and they're not cheap – are the *jabugos* from the Sierra Morena, though a filling ham sandwich is only around €2.

LA OREJA DE ORO

C/Victoria 9 Ⓜ Sol. May–July & Sept Mon–Sat 1–4pm & 8pm–1am; Oct–April Tues–Sun 1–4pm & 8pm–1am. Closed Aug. MAP P.54, POCKET MAP E12

Standing room only in this spit-and-sawdust bar. Try the excellent *pulpo a la Gallega* (sliced octopus served on a bed of potatoes seasoned with cayenne pepper) washed down with Ribeiro wine. Plenty of other seafood tapas on offer and of course the house

speciality *oreja* (pigs' ears) in a spicy sauce.

LA TOSCANA

C/Manuel Fernández y González 10 Ⓜ Antón Martín or Sevilla. Tues–Sat 1–4pm & 8pm–midnight. Closed Aug. MAP P.54, POCKET MAP F12

Home-made tapas in this popular and friendly Huertas classic. The *morcillo* (beef shank) is excellent, while the *croquetas*, *chistorra* and tuna salads are also very tasty.

LA TRUCHA

C/Manuel Fernández y González 3 Ⓜ Antón Martín or Sevilla ☎ 914 295 833. Branch at C/Nuñez de Arce 6 Ⓜ Sol ☎ 915 320 890. Mon–Sat 12.30–4pm & 7.30pm–midnight. Closed Sun. MAP P.54, POCKET MAP F12

Popular, tourist-oriented tapas bar cum moderately priced restaurant, where delicious smoked fish and *pimientos de Padrón* are the specialities.

VIÑA P

Plaza de Santa Ana 3 Ⓜ Sol or Antón Martín. Daily 1–4pm & 8pm–12.30am. MAP P.54, POCKET MAP F13

Touristy bar decked out with bullfighting paraphernalia and serving a great range of tapas. Try the asparagus, stuffed mussels and the mouthwatering *almejas a la marinera* (clams in a garlic and white wine sauce).

Bars

ALHAMBRA

C/Victoria 9 ⓜ Sol. Daily 11am–1.30am (2am at weekends). MAP P.54, POCKET MAP E12

A friendly tapas bar by day, *Alhambra* transforms itself into a fun disco bar by night with the crowds spilling over into the *El Buscón* bar next door.

CERVECERÍA ALEMANA

Plaza de Santa Ana 6 ⓜ Sol or Antón Martín. Mon & Wed–Sun 10.30am–12.30am, Fri & Sat till 2am. Closed Aug. MAP P.54, POCKET MAP F13

Refurbished but still stylish old beer house, once frequented by Hemingway. Order a *caña* (draught beer) and go easy on the tapas, as the bill can mount up fast.

CERVECERÍA SANTA ANA

Plaza de Santa Ana 10 ⓜ Sol or Antón Martín. Daily 11am–1.30am, Fri & Sat till 2.30am. MAP P.54, POCKET MAP F13

Has tables outside, and offers quality beer, friendly service and a good selection of tapas. Always packed at night.

CÍRCULO DE BELLAS ARTES

C/Alcalá 42 ⓜ Banco de España. Daily 8am–2am, Fri & Sat till 3am. MAP P.54, POCKET MAP G11

Great bar in this classy arts centre, complete with reclining nude sculpture, chandeliers

and sofas and a pleasant lack of pretensions. Service can be slow though. From May to October there's a comfortable *terraza* outside.

GLASS BAR

Carrera San Jeronimo 34 ⓜ Sevilla. Daily 11am–3am. MAP P.54, POCKET MAP F12

Housed in the ultra-chic *Hotel Urban*, this glamorous cocktail bar has become a compulsory stop for the well-heeled in-crowd. Designer tapas such as sushi, wild salmon and oysters accompany drinks. In summer a terrace bar opens on the sixth floor.

NATURBIER

Plaza de Santa Ana 9 ⓜ Sol or Antón Martín. Daily 8pm–2.30am. MAP P.54, POCKET MAP F13

Try this place's own tasty beer with a variety of German sausages to accompany it. There's usually room to sit in the cellar if the top bar is too crowded, although service is often slow.

LA VENENCIA

C/Echegaray 7 ⓜ Sevilla. Daily 7.30pm–1.30am. Closed Aug. MAP P.54, POCKET MAP F12

Rather dilapidated, wood-panelled bar that's great for sherry sampling. The whole range is here, served from wooden barrels, and accompanied by delicious olives and *mojama* (dry salted tuna).

CERVECERÍA ALEMANA

VIVA MADRID

C/Manuel Fernández y González 7 Ⓜ Antón Martín or Sevilla.Daily noon–2am, Fri & Sat till 3am. MAP P.54, POCKET MAP F12

A fabulous tiled bar offering cocktails, beer and speciality pricey coffees, plus basic tapas. Get here early if you want to see the tiles in their full glory, as it gets very crowded. Quite pricey but certainly worth the stop.

Clubs

LA BOCA DEL LOBO

C/Echegaray 11 Ⓜ Antón Martín or Sevilla Ⓦ www.labocadellobo.com. Wed–Sat 10.30pm–3.30am. MAP P.54, POCKET MAP F12

Dark, cavern-like club on this buzzing little street close to Santa Ana playing everything from electronic and funk to rock and salsa. Live gigs (in the dungeon-like cellar) and resident DJs.

THE ROOM/MONDO AT STELLA

C/Arlabán 7 Ⓜ Sevilla Ⓦ www.web-mondo .com; Ⓦ www.theroomclub.com. Thurs–Sat 1–6am. Entrance €12–15 including first drink. MAP P.54, POCKET MAP F11

Unrecognizable from its days as a Movida classic, *Stella* is now a sleek modern club with transparent dancefloor. It remains a big favourite with the city's serious party-goers, especially for *The Room* (Fri) and *Mondo* (Thurs & Sat) sessions.

TORERO

C/Cruz 26 Ⓜ Sol. Tues–Sat 11pm–5.30am (4.30am Wed). Entrance €10 including first drink. MAP P.54, POCKET MAP E13

Popular two-floored club right in the heart of the Santa Ana area. The bouncers are pretty strict, but once inside a fun place to be. Music ranges from salsa to disco.

THE ROOM

Live music

CAFÉ CENTRAL

Plaza del Ángel 10 Ⓜ Tirso de Molina ☎ 913 694 143 Ⓦ www.cafecentralmadrid .com. Mon–Sat 1pm–1.30am, Fri & Sat till 2.30am. €11–12 for gigs, otherwise free. MAP P.54, POCKET MAP E13

Small and relaxed jazz club that gets the odd big name, plus strong local talent. The Art Deco café, which does a €11 lunchtime menu, is worth a visit in its own right.

CAFÉ JAZZ POPULART

C/Huertas 22 Ⓜ Tirso de Molina ☎ 914 298 407 Ⓦ www.populart.es. Daily 6pm–2.30am. Usually free. MAP P.54, POCKET MAP F13

Friendly and laidback venue, with twice-nightly sets (11pm & 12.30am) usually from jazz and blues bands.

CARDAMOMO

C/Echegaray 15 Ⓜ Antón Martín or Sevilla ☎ 913 690 757 Ⓦ www.cardamomo.net. Daily 8pm–4am. Shows at 9pm. MAP P.54, POCKET MAP F12

This flamenco bar has evolved into a respected fully blown *tablao*. The show with a drink is €32, while dinner will set you back an extra €32. Check the website for the schedule.

Paseo del Arte and Retiro

Madrid's three world-class art galleries are all located within a kilometre of each other along what is known as the Paseo del Arte. The Prado, the most renowned of the three, houses an unequalled display of Spanish art, an outstanding Flemish collection and some impressive Italian work. The Thyssen-Bornemisza, based on one of the world's greatest private art collections, provides a dazzling excursion through Western art from the fourteenth to the late twentieth centuries. Finally, the Centro de Arte Reina Sofía displays contemporary art, including Picasso's iconic masterpiece *Guernica*. The area around the Paseo del Prado has two beautiful green spaces: the Jardines Botánicos and the Parque del Retiro, as well as lesser-known sights including the fascinating Real Fábrica de Tapices (Royal Tapestry Workshop) and the Museo Naval. It isn't an area renowned for its bars, restaurants and nightlife, but there are enough decent places for a drink or lunch.

MUSEO DEL PRADO

Ⓜ Atocha or Banco de España Ⓦ www
.museodelprado.es. Tues–Sun 9am–8pm,
hols 9am–2pm. €10, free Tues–Sat 6–8pm &
Sun 5–8pm. MAP P.68–69, POCKET MAP G13

The Prado is Madrid's premier tourist attraction and one of the oldest and greatest collections of art in the world, largely amassed by the Spanish royal family over the last two hundred years.

Tickets are purchased at the Puerta de Goya opposite the

GARDEN OF EARTHLY DELIGHTS

Hotel Ritz on C/Felipe IV and the entrance is round the back at the Puerta de los Jerónimos, which leads into the new extension. To avoid the large ticket queues, buy them from the museum website, though you will still have to collect them at the box office at the Puerta de Goya (separate fast-moving queue).

The museum, which has a new lease of life following the addition of a €152 million Rafael Moneo-designed extension, is set out according to national schools. However, these are undergoing gradual relocation and are not expected to find a settled home until at least 2012 (we've outlined the current set-up, but any variations will be shown on the floor plans available at the desk on your way into the museum).

The coverage of Spanish paintings begins on the ground floor with some striking twelfth-century Romanesque frescoes. Beyond is a stunning anthology that includes just about every significant Spanish painter from the adopted Cretan-born artist El Greco (Domenikos Theotokopoulos), who worked in Toledo in the 1570s, to Francisco de Goya, the outstanding painter of eighteenth-century Bourbon Spain. Don't miss the breathtaking collection of work by Diego Velázquez, including his masterpiece, *Las Meninas*.

No visit is complete without taking in Goya's deeply evocative works, *Dos de Mayo* and *Tres de Mayo*, and his disturbing series of murals known as the *Pinturas Negras* (*Black Paintings*) with their mix of witches, fights to the death and child-eating gods.

The Italian paintings include the most complete collection by painters from the Venice

MUSEO DEL PRADO

School in any single museum, among them Titian's magnificent equestrian portrait, *Emperor Carlos V at Mühlberg*. There are also major works by Raphael and epic masterpieces from Tintoretto, Veronese and Caravaggio.

The early Flemish works are even more impressive and contain one of Hieronymus Bosch's greatest triptychs, the hallucinogenic *Garden of Earthly Delights*. Look out, too, for the works of Pieter Bruegel the Elder, whose *Triumph of Death* must be one of the most frightening canvases ever painted, Rogier van der Weyden's magnificent *Descent from the Cross* and the extensive Rubens collection.

German and French painting is less well represented but still worth seeking out – especially the pieces by Dürer, Cranach and Poussin – while downstairs in the basement is a glittering display of the jewels that belonged to the Grand Dauphin Louis, son of Louis XIV and father of Felipe V, Spain's first Bourbon king.

The new wing houses temporary exhibition spaces, restoration workshops and a sculpture gallery as well as a restaurant, café and shops.

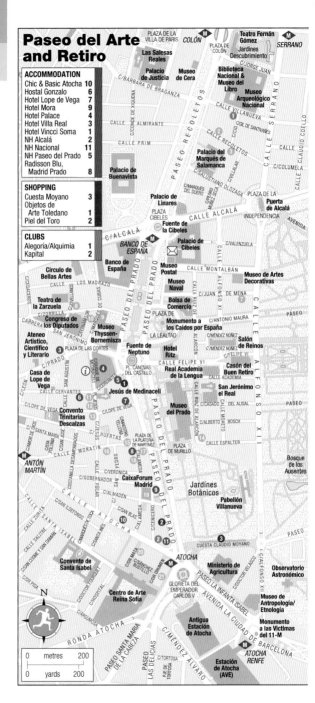

Paseo del Arte and Retiro

ACCOMMODATION
Chic & Basic Atocha	10
Hostal Gonzalo	6
Hotel Lope de Vega	7
Hotel Mora	9
Hotel Palace	4
Hotel Villa Real	3
Hotel Vincci Soma	1
NH Alcalá	2
NH Nacional	11
NH Paseo del Prado	5
Radisson Blu, Madrid Prado	8

SHOPPING
Cuesta Moyano	3
Objetos de Arte Toledano	1
Piel del Toro	2

CLUBS
Alegoría/Alquimia	1
Kapital	2

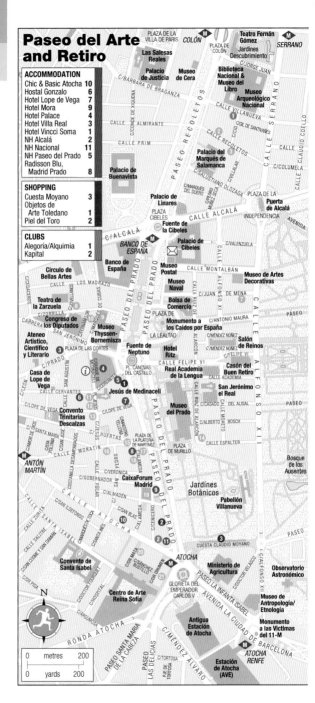

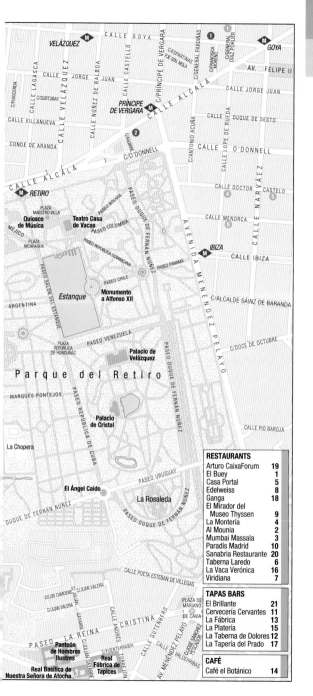

RESTAURANTS

Arturo CaixaForum	19
El Buey	1
Casa Portal	5
Edelweiss	8
Ganga	18
El Mirador del Museo Thyssen	9
La Montería	4
Al Mounia	2
Mumbai Massala	3
Paradís Madrid	10
Sanabria Restaurante	20
Taberna Laredo	6
La Vaca Verónica	16
Viridiana	7

TAPAS BARS

El Brillante	21
Cervecería Cervantes	11
La Fábrica	13
La Platería	15
La Taberna de Dolores	12
La Tapería del Prado	17

CAFÉ

Café el Botánico	14

CENTRO DE ARTE REINA SOFÍA

Ⓜ Atocha Ⓦ www.museoreinasofia.es. Mon & Wed–Sat 10am–9pm, Sun 10am–2.30pm. €6, free Mon, Wed–Fri 7–9pm, Sat after 2.30pm & all day Sun and for under-18s and over-65s. MAP P.68–69, POCKET MAP G8

An essential stop on the Madrid art circuit is the Centro de Arte Reina Sofía, an immense exhibition space providing a permanent home for the Spanish collection of modern and contemporary art, including the Miró and Picasso legacies.

If the queues at the main entrance are too long, try the alternative one in the extension on the Ronda de Atocha.

As well as its collection of twentieth-century art, the museum has a theatre, cinema, excellent bookshops, a print, music and photographic library, a restaurant, bar and café in the basement and a peaceful inner courtyard garden. An informative, but expensive, guidebook examining some of the key works is available from the shops, priced €22. At the entrance, there are audio-guides in English (€5), which provide informative commentaries for the first-time visitor.

The **permanent collection** begins on the second floor with a section examining the origins of modern Spanish art, largely through the two artistic nuclei

> I f you plan to visit all three art museums on the Paseo del Prado during your stay, it's well worth buying the **Paseo del Arte ticket** (€17.60), which is valid for a year and allows one visit to each museum at a substantial saving although it does not include the temporary exhibitions. It's available at any of the three museums.

that developed in Catalunya and the Basque Country at the end of the nineteenth century.

Midway round the collection is the Reina Sofía's main draw – Picasso's *Guernica* (see box opposite), an emblematic piece that has always evoked strong reactions. Strong sections on Cubism in the first of which Picasso is again well represented – and the Paris School follow. Dalí and Miró make heavyweight contributions too in the Surrealism section, while an impressive collection of Spanish sculpture is in the final suite of rooms.

The collection continues on the fourth floor, although here it's no match for the attractions of the previous exhibits. This section covers Spain's postwar years up to the present day and includes Spanish and international examples of abstract and avant-garde movements such as Pop Art, Constructivism and Minimalism, one of the highlights being Francis Bacon's *Figura Tumbada* (*Reclining Figure*). Worth hunting out is the section on photography during the years of Franco's dictatorship with some powerful and revealing images of the era from Catalans Francesc Català Roca and Francisco Ontañon.

There are also some striking pieces by the Basque abstract sculptor Chillida and Catalan Surrealist painter Antoni Tàpies. The fourth-floor galleries finish on a high with more offerings from Picasso and Miró, including the former's *El pintor y la modelo* (The Painter and the Model, 1963) series, painted when he was over 80 years old.

Jean Nouvel's 79 million-euro state-of-the-art extension, known as the **Area Nouvel**, is built around an open courtyard

CENTRO DE ARTE REINA SOFÍA

topped by a striking delta-shaped, metallic, crimson-coloured roof. It is home to the temporary exhibition spaces, an auditorium, a library and bookshop. Also housed here is *Arola Madrid*, a café/restaurant run under the auspices of leading Catalan chef Sergi Arola. Coffee and cakes are affordable, but lunch or supper will set you back at least €50.

Guernica

Superbly displayed and no longer protected by the bullet-proof glass and steel girders that once imprisoned it, Picasso's *Guernica* is a monumental icon of twentieth-century Spanish art and politics which, despite its familiarity, still has the ability to shock. Picasso painted it in response to the bombing of the Basque town of Gernika in April 1937 by the German Luftwaffe, acting in concert with Franco, during the Spanish Civil War. In the preliminary studies, displayed around the room, you can see how he developed its symbols – the dying horse, the woman mourning, the bull and so on – and then return to the painting to marvel at how he made it all work. Picasso determined that the work be "loaned" to the Museum of Modern Art in New York while Franco remained in power, meaning that the artist never lived to see it displayed in his home country – it only returned to Spain in 1981, eight years after Picasso's death and six after the demise of Franco.

MUSEO THYSSEN-BORNEMISZA

Ⓜ Banco de España Ⓦ www.museothyssen
.org. Tues–Sun 10am–7pm. €8 for permanent
collection, €5–8 for temporary exhibitions,
combined ticket €10–13. MAP P.68–69, POCKET
MAP H12

MUSEO THYSSEN-BORNEMISZA

This fabulous private collection, assembled by Baron Heinrich Thyssen-Bornemisza, his son Hans Heinrich and his former beauty-queen wife Carmen was first displayed here in 1993 and contains pieces by almost every major Western artist since the fourteenth century.

An extension, built on the site of an adjoining mansion and cleverly integrated into the original format of the museum, houses temporary exhibitions and Carmen's collection, which is particularly strong on nineteenth-century landscape, North American, Impressionist and Post-Impressionist work.

To follow the collection chronologically, begin on the second floor with pre-Renaissance work from the fourteenth century. This is followed by a wonderful array of Renaissance portraits by, amongst others, Ghirlandaio, Raphael and Holbein, including the latter's commanding *Henry VIII*. Beyond are some equally impressive pieces by Titian, Tintoretto, El Greco, Caravaggio and Canaletto, while a superb collection of landscapes and some soothing Impressionist works by Pissarro, Monet, Renoir, Degas and Sisley are housed in the new galleries.

The first floor continues with an outstanding selection of work by Gauguin and the Post-Impressionists. There's excellent coverage, too, of the vivid Expressionist work of Kandinsky, Nolde and Kirchner.

Beyond, the displays include a comprehensive round of seventeenth-century Dutch painting of various genres and some splendid nineteenth-century American landscapes. There are strong contributions from Van Gogh – most notably one of his last and most gorgeous works, *Les Vessenots* – and more from the Expressionists, including the apocalyptic *Metropolis* by George Grosz.

The ground floor covers the period from the beginning of the twentieth century with some outstanding Cubist work from Picasso, Braque and Mondrian to be found within the "experimental avant-garde" section. There are also some marvellous pieces by Miró, Pollock and Chagall. Surrealism is, not surprisingly, represented by Dalí, while the final galleries include some eye-catching work by Bacon, Lichtenstein and Freud.

PARQUE DEL RETIRO

Ⓜ Retiro, Ibiza, Atocha Renfe, Atocha or
Banco de España. MAP P.68–69, POCKET MAP K4–K7

The origins of the wonderful Parque del Retiro (Retiro Park) go back to the early seventeenth century when Felipe IV produced a plan for a new palace and French-style gardens, the Buen Retiro. Of the buildings, only the ballroom (Casón del Buen Retiro) and the Hall of Realms (the Salón de Reinos) remain.

The park's 330-acre expanse offers the chance to jog, roller-blade, cycle, picnic, row on the lake, have your fortune told, and – above all – **promenade**. The busiest day is Sunday, when half of Madrid turns out for the *paseo*.

Promenading aside, there's almost always something going on in the park, including concerts in the Quiosco de Música, performances by groups of South American pan-piping musicians by the lake and, on summer weekends, puppet shows by the Puerta de Alcalá entrance.

Travelling art exhibitions are frequently housed in the graceful **Palacio de Velázquez** (April–Sept Mon & Wed–Sun 11am–9pm; Oct–April Mon & Wed–Sun 10am–6pm; free) and the splendid **Palacio de Cristal** (same hours during exhibitions, but closed when raining; free), while the **Teatro Casa de Vacas** (Ⓦwww.casadevacas.es) hosts shows, concerts and plays. Look out, too, for the magnificently ostentatious statue to Alfonso XII by the lake and the Ángel Caído, supposedly the world's only public statue to Lucifer, in the south of the park. The Bosque de los Ausentes, 191 olive trees and cypresses planted by the Paseo de la Chopera in memory of the victims who died in the train bombings at the nearby Atocha station on March 11, 2004, is close by.

PUERTA DE ALCALÁ

Ⓜ Retiro or Banco de España. MAP P.68–69. POCKET MAP J4

The Puerta de Alcalá is one of Madrid's most emblematic landmarks. Built in neoclassical style in 1769 by Francesco Sabatini to commemorate Carlos III's first twenty years on the throne, it was the biggest city gate in Europe at the time. Once on the site of the city's easternmost boundary, it's now marooned on a small island on the traffic-choked Plaza de la Independencia.

JARDÍNES BOTÁNICOS

Plaza de Murillo 2 Ⓜ Atocha Ⓦ www.rjb.csic .es. Daily 10am–dusk. €2.50, under-10s free. MAP P.68–69. POCKET MAP H7

The delightful botanical gardens were opened in 1781 by Carlos III. The king's aim was to collect and grow species from all over his Spanish Empire, develop a research centre, and supply medicinal herbs and plants to Madrid's hospitals. Abandoned for much of the last century, they were restored in the 1980s and are now home to some 30,000 species from around the globe. Don't miss the hothouse with its amazing cacti or the bonsai collection of former prime minister Felipe González. Temporary exhibitions take place in the Pabellón Villanueva within the grounds.

PARQUE DEL RETIRO

CAIXAFORUM MADRID

Paseo del Prado 36 Ⓜ Atocha. Daily
10am–8pm. Free. MAP P.68-69, POCKET MAP H7

An innovative exhibition space,
opened in 2008 by the Catalan
savings bank, which comple-
ments the existing attractions
on the Paseo del Arte. The
centre, which hosts a variety
of high-quality art shows, is
flanked by an eye-catching
vertical garden designed
by French botanist Patrick
Blanc in which some 15,000
plants form an organic carpet
extending across the wall.
There is a decent art bookshop
inside and a top-floor café/
restaurant (see p.77).

MUSEO DE ARTES DECORATIVAS

C/Montalbán 12 Ⓜ Banco de España
Ⓦ mnartesdecorativas.mcu.es. Tues–Sat
9.30am–3pm, plus Thurs & Fri 5–8pm in
winter and spring, Sun 10am–3pm. €3, Free
on Sun, Oct & Nov. MAP P.68-69, POCKET MAP J5

The national collection of
decorative arts is housed in
an elegant nineteenth-century
mansion. The highlight is its
collection of *azulejos* (tiles)
and other ceramics with a
magnificent eighteenth-century
tiled Valencian kitchen on
the top floor. The rest of the
exhibits include an interesting
but unspectacular collection of

furniture, a series of reconstructed rooms and *objets d'art*
from all over Spain.

MUSEO NAVAL

Paseo del Prado 5 Ⓜ Banco de España.
Tues–Sun 10am–2pm; closed mid-July to
Sept and public hols. Free (bring ID).
MAP P.68-69, POCKET MAP J11

As you might expect, the Naval
Museum is strong on models,
charts and navigational aids
relating to Spanish voyages
of discovery. Exhibits include
the first map to show the New
World, drawn in 1500 by Juan
de la Cosa, cannons from the
Spanish Armada and part of
Cortés' standard used during
the conquest of Mexico. The
room dedicated to the *Nao
San Diego*, sunk during a
conflict with the Dutch off the
Philippines in 1600, contains
fascinating items recovered
during the salvage operation in
the early 1990s.

SAN JERÓNIMO EL REAL

C/Ruiz de Alarcón 19 Ⓜ Atocha or Banco de
España. Mon–Fri 8am–1.30pm & 6–8pm,
Sat & Sun 9am–1.30pm & 6.30–8pm,
Oct–July opens one hour earlier in the
afternoon. MAP P.68-69, POCKET MAP H6

Madrid's high-society church
was built on the site of a
monastery founded in the

MUSEO DE ARTES DECORATIVAS

early sixteenth century by the Catholic monarchs, Fernando and Isabel. It later became the venue for the swearing-in of the heirs to the throne and setting for many royal marriages and coronations (including the current king, Juan Carlos, in 1975). Despite remodelling and the addition of two Gothic towers, the old form of the church is still visible; but the seventeenth-century cloisters have fallen victim to the Prado extension.

PLAZA DE LA LEALTAD (MONUMENTO A LOS CAÍDOS POR ESPAÑA)

Ⓜ Banco de España. MAP P.68–69, POCKET MAP H6

This aristocratic plaza contains the **Monument to Spain's Fallen**. Originally a memorial to the Madrileños who died in the 1808 anti-French rebellion (the urn at the base contains their ashes), it was later changed to commemorate all those who have died fighting for Spain, and an eternal flame now burns here. On one side of the plaza stands the opulent *Ritz Hotel*, work of Charles Mewès, architect of the *Ritz* hotels in Paris and London, while opposite is the Madrid stock exchange.

ESTACIÓN DE ATOCHA

Ⓜ Atocha or Atocha Renfe. MAP P.68–69, POCKET MAP J9

The grand Estación de Atocha is now sadly infamous as the scene of the horrific train bombings that killed 191 people and injured close to 2000 in March 2004. A glass memorial to the victims stands just outside one of the entrances on Paseo de la Infanta Isabel. The tower channels light into an underground chamber (access via the station) lined with an inner membrane on which are written messages of condolence. The old station alongside was revamped in 1992 and is a glorious 1880s glasshouse, resembling a tropical garden. It's a wonderful sight from the walkways above, as a constant spray of water rains down on the jungle of vegetation. At the platforms beyond sit the gleaming AVE trains.

MUSEO NACIONAL DE ANTROPOLOGÍA/ETNOLOGÍA

C/Alfonso XII 68 Ⓜ Atocha or Atocha Renfe. Ⓦ mnantropologia.mcu.es. Tues–Sat 9.30am–8pm, Sun 10am–3pm. €3, free Sat after 2pm & Sun. MAP P.68–69, POCKET MAP J8

The National Anthropology and Ethnography Museum was founded by the eccentric Dr Pedro González Velasco to house his private collection. The displays give an overview of different cultures, particularly those linked to Spanish history. The most interesting exhibits include a macabre collection of deformed skulls, a Guanche mummy (the original inhabitants of the Canary Islands), some shrivelled embryos and the skeleton of a 2.35m tall circus giant, which Velasco had agreed to buy from the owner after his death – payment in advance of course.

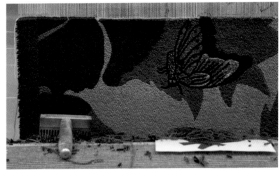

REAL FÁBRICA DE TAPICES

REAL FÁBRICA DE TAPICES

C/Fuentarrabía 2 Ⓜ Atocha Renfe or
Menéndez Pelayo Ⓦ www.realfabricade
tapices.com. Mon–Fri 10am–2pm; closed
Aug. €4. Tours every half-hour. MAP P.68–69,
POCKET MAP K9

The Royal Tapestry Workshop
makes for a fascinating visit.
Founded in 1721 and moved
to its present site in the
nineteenth century, the factory
uses processes and machines

unchanged for hundreds of
years. The handful of workers
that remain can be seen coolly
looping handfuls of bobbins
around myriad strings and
sewing up worn-out masterpieces with exact matching
silk. With progress painfully
slow – one worker produces a
square metre of tapestry every
three and a half months – the
astronomical prices soon seem
easily understandable.

Shops

CUESTA MOYANO

Cuesta de Claudio Moyano Ⓜ Atocha.
MAP P.68–69, POCKET MAP H8

A row of little wooden kiosks
on a hill close to the Retiro
selling just about every book
you could think of, from
second-hand copies of Captain
Marvel to Cervantes. Other
items include old prints of
Madrid and relics from the
Franco era.

OBJETOS DE ARTE TOLEDANO

Paseo del Prado 10 Ⓜ Atocha or Banco de
España. Mon–Sat 9.30am–8pm. MAP P.68–69,
POCKET MAP H13

Souvenir shop stocking "typical
Spanish"-style goods including
fans, Lladró porcelain, T-shirts
and tacky flamenco accessories.

PIEL DEL TORO

Paseo del Prado 42 Ⓜ Atocha or Banco de
España. Mon–Fri 10am–8.30pm, Sat & Sun
11am–8pm. MAP P.68–69, POCKET MAP H7

A colourful range of T-shirts,
sweatshirts and baseball
caps, all emblazoned with the
emblem of a bull. Despite the
clichéd image they make good,
lightweight presents.

Café

CAFÉ EL BOTÁNICO

C/Ruiz de Alarcón 27 Ⓜ Atocha or Banco
de España. Daily 9am–midnight. MAP P.68–69,
POCKET MAP H7

An ideal place for a coffee or an
afternoon drink after a Prado
visit; it sits in a quiet street next
to the botanical gardens and
serves good beer and a small
selection of delicious tapas.

Restaurants

ARTURO CAIXAFORUM

Paseo del Prado 36 Ⓜ Banco de España
☎ 913 896 795. Mon–Sun 1–4pm. MAP P.68–69,
POCKET MAP H7

Located in a stylish arts centre, this café/restaurant combines designer decor with well-presented Mediterranean-style food. Prices are reasonable if you opt for the €12 lunchtime menu which includes a choice of three dishes for each course.

EL BUEY

C/General Diez Portier 9 Ⓜ Goya
☎ 914 314 492. Mon–Sat 1–4pm & 9pm–midnight, Sun 1–4pm. MAP P.68–69,
POCKET MAP K3

Excellent Argentine-style meat dishes in this cramped little restaurant near the Retiro. Prices – €30 a head – are decent considering the quality.

CASA PORTAL

C/Dr Castelo 26 Ⓜ Ibiza ☎ 915 742 026.
Tues–Sat 1.30–4pm & 8.30–11.30pm. Closed hols & Aug. MAP P.68–69, POCKET MAP K4

Although it has undergone a change of ownership, *Casa Portal* retains its reputation for superlative Asturian cooking – go for the *fabada* (beans, *chorizo* and black pudding stew) or *besugo* (bream), washed down with some cider. The shellfish is excellent too. Around €35–40 per person.

EDELWEISS

C/Jovellanos 7 Ⓜ Banco de España
☎ 915 323 383. 1–4pm & 8pm–midnight, closed Sun eve. MAP P.68–69, POCKET MAP G11

Renowned German restaurant with an array of central European specialities and large portions. Expect to pay around €35 a head, although there's a €20 lunchtime menu including *Bratwurst*.

GANGA

C/Alameda 6 Ⓜ Atocha ☎ 913 964 273.
Daily 1–4pm & 8pm–midnight. MAP P.68–69,
POCKET MAP J14

Friendly Indian restaurant living up to its name – "ganga" is "bargain" in Spanish – and serving traditional dishes, including a very decent balti and chicken tikka. Expect to pay between €8 to €10 for a main course.

EL MIRADOR DEL MUSEO THYSSEN

Paseo del Prado 8 Ⓜ Banco de España
☎ 914 293 984. Tues–Sat 8pm–1am July & Aug only. MAP P.68–69, POCKET MAP H12

Summer-only terrace restaurant on the top floor of the art museum with some great views over the city. Specializes in Mediterranean cuisine; dishes include smoked salmon with pear paté. Reservations are essential, and it will cost €40–50 a head.

LA MONTERÍA

C/Lope de Rueda 35 Ⓜ Ibiza ☎ 915 741 812.
Mon–Sat 2–4pm & 8.30pm–11pm. MAP P.68–69,
POCKET MAP K4

This inconspicuous little restaurant on the eastern edge of the Retiro serves some of the tastiest food in the area. The house speciality *salmorejo* is excellent, as are the battered prawns, while mains include partridge and monkfish with rice options. Expect to pay at least €35 a head.

AL MOUNIA

C/Recoletos 5 Ⓜ Banco de España
☎ 914 350 828. Tues–Sat 1.30–3.30pm & 9pm–midnight. Closed Aug. MAP P.68–69,
POCKET MAP H4

Moroccan cooking at its best in the most established Arabic restaurant in town. The couscous, lamb and desserts are a must. Mains cost over €20; lunchtime menus start at €37.

VIRIDIANA

MUMBAI MASSALA

C/Recoletos 14 Ⓜ Banco de España or Retiro ☎ 914 357 194. Daily 1.30–4pm & 9–11.30pm. MAP P.68–69, POCKET MAP J4

The decor is palatial in this upmarket Indian restaurant, serving a wide range of very good, but expensive, curries – all the usual favourites are available. Evening prices are in the region of €40 a head, but a better alternative is the lunchtime menu for just €14.75.

PARADÍS MADRID

C/Marqués de Cubas 14 Ⓜ Banco de España ☎ 914 297 303. Mon–Fri 1–4pm & 8.30pm–midnight, Sat eve only. MAP P.68–69, POCKET MAP H12

Upmarket Catalan restaurant often frequented by politicians from the nearby parliament. High-quality Mediterranean food with superb starters, fish and rice dishes. Expect to pay €45–50.

SANABRIA RESTAURANTE

C/Doctor Mata 3 Ⓜ Atocha ☎ 914 673 390. Daily 8am–midnight. MAP P.68–69, POCKET MAP H8

Great-value restaurant just around the corner from the Reina Sofía. Six choices for

each course of the *menú del día*, generous helpings and a very filling *fabada* (bean stew).

TABERNA LAREDO

C/Menorca 14 Ⓜ Ibiza ☎ 915 733 061. Mon–Sat 11am–5pm & 8pm–midnight. Closed Aug. MAP P.68–69, POCKET MAP K4

Delicious salads, risottos and fish dishes served up with style at this acclaimed bar/restaurant close to the Retiro. The €42 sampler menu is a very good option. Reservations essential.

LA VACA VERÓNICA

C/Moratín 38 Ⓜ Antón Martín ☎ 914 297 827. Mon–Fri 2–4pm & 9pm–midnight, Sat 9pm–midnight. MAP P.68–69, POCKET MAP H14

A wide range of dishes at this slightly bohemian little restaurant. Try the *filet Verónica* and the *carabinero con pasta* (pasta with red prawns). The *menú del día* is €15.

VIRIDIANA

C/Juan de Mena 14 Ⓜ Banco de España ☎ 915 234 478 or 915 311 039. Mon–Sat 1.45–4pm & 8.30pm–midnight. Closed Easter & Aug. MAP P.68–69, POCKET MAP J6

A bizarre temple of Madrid *nueva cocina* (new cuisine), decorated with photos from Luis Buñuel's film of the same name and offering mouthwatering creations from a constantly changing menu, plus a superb selection of wines. The bill for a three-course meal is likely to come close to €100 a head but it's an unforgettable experience.

Tapas bars

EL BRILLANTE

Glorieta del Emperador Carlos V 8 Ⓜ Atocha. Daily 6.30am–12.30am. MAP P.68–69, POCKET MAP H8

Down-to-earth bar with long opening hours and a range

of tapas and *bocadillos* (filled baguette). *Calamares* is the house special. A great place for a quick snack in between museum visits.

CERVECERÍA CERVANTES

Plaza de Jesús 7 Ⓜ Antón Martín or Banco de España. Mon–Sat 12.30–5pm & 7.30–11.45pm, Sun noon–4pm. MAP P.68–69, POCKET MAP H13

Great beer and excellent fresh seafood tapas in this busy little bar just behind the *Palace Hotel*. The *gambas* (prawns) go down a treat with a cool glass of the beer, while the *tosta de gambas* (a sort of prawn toast) is a must.

LA FÁBRICA

Plaza de Jesús 2 Ⓜ Antón Martín or Banco de España. Mon–Thurs & Sun 11am–1am, Fri & Sat 11am–2am. MAP P.68–69, POCKET MAP H13

Bustling, friendly bar serving a delicious range of canapés, chilled beer and good vermouth. There's seating at the back for tapas if you want to linger for longer.

LA PLATERÍA

C/Moratín 49 Ⓜ Antón Martín or Atocha. Mon–Fri 7.30am–1am, Sat & Sun 9.30am–1am. MAP P.68–69, POCKET MAP H14

This bar has a popular summer *terraza* geared to a tourist clientele and a good selection of reasonably priced tapas available all day. Service can be a little brusque though.

LA TABERNA DE DOLORES

Plaza de Jesús 4 Ⓜ Antón Martín or Banco de España. Daily 11am–midnight. MAP P.68–69, POCKET MAP H13

The canapés are splendid at this standing-room-only tiled bar, decorated with beer bottles from around the world. The beer is great and the food specialities include roquefort and anchovy and smoked-salmon canapés.

LA TAPERÍA DEL PRADO

Plaza Platerías de Martínez 1 Ⓜ Antón Martín or Banco de España ☎ 914 294 094. Daily 7.30am–12.30am. MAP P.68–69, POCKET MAP J14

Modern bar serving up a range of tapas and *raciones*, plus a decent set lunch at around €10. Portions are on the small side.

Clubs

ALEGORÍA/ALQUIMIA

C/Villanueva 2 (entrance on C/Cid) Ⓜ Colón ☎ 915 772 785 ⓦ www.alegoria-madrid.es. Daily 9pm–5am. Entrance €9. MAP P.68–69, POCKET MAP J3

Modelled on an English gentleman's club, this restaurant, bar and disco comes complete with leather sofas, a wood-panelled library and models of old sailing ships hanging from the ceiling.

KAPITAL

C/Atocha 125 Ⓜ Atocha ⓦ www.grupo-kapital.com. Thurs–Sun midnight–6am. From €12. MAP P.68–69, POCKET MAP H8

Seven-floor club catering for practically every taste, with three dancefloors, lasers, go-go dancers, a cinema and a *terraza*. Musical menu of disco, merengue, salsa, *sevillanas* and even some karaoke, plus its own "after hours" session from 8pm on Sundays.

ALEGORÍA

Gran Vía, Chueca and Malasaña

The Gran Vía, one of Madrid's main thoroughfares, effectively divides the old city to the south from the newer parts in the north. Heaving with traffic, shoppers and sightseers, it's the commercial heart of the city, and a monument in its own right, with its turn-of-the-twentieth-century, palace-like banks and offices. North of here, and bursting with bars, restaurants and nightlife, are two of the city's most vibrant barrios: Chueca, focal point of Madrid's gay scene, and Malasaña, former centre of the Movida Madrileña, the happening scene of the late 1970s and early 1980s, and still a somewhat alternative area, focusing on lively Plaza Dos de Mayo. As well as the bustling atmosphere, a couple of museums and a number of beautiful churches in the area provide even more reasons for a visit.

GRAN VÍA

Gran Vía. MAP P.82-83, POCKET MAP D10-G10

The Gran Vía (Great Way), built in three stages at the start of the twentieth century, became a symbol of Spain's arrival in the modern world. Financed on the back of an economic boom, experienced as a result of the country's neutrality in World War I, the Gran Vía is a showcase for a whole gamut of architectural styles, from Modernist to Neo-Rococo.

The finest section is the earliest, constructed between 1910 and 1924 and stretching from C/Alcalá to the Telefónica skyscraper. Particularly noteworthy are the Edificio Metrópolis (1905–11), complete with cylindrical facade, white

stone sculptures, zinc-tiled roof and gold garlands, and the nearby Grassy building (1916–17). The vast 81-metre-high slab of the Telefónica building was Spain's first skyscraper. During the Civil War it was used as a reference point by Franco's forces to bomb the area. The stretch down to Plaza de Callao is dominated by shops, cafés and cinemas, while the plaza itself is now the gateway to the shoppers' haven of C/Preciados. On the corner is the classic Art Deco Capitol building (1930–33), its curved facade embellished with lurid neon signs. Cast your eyes skywards on the final stretch downhill towards Plaza de España to catch sight of an assortment of statues and decorations that top many of the buildings.

PLAZA DE CHUECA

PLAZA DE CHUECA

Ⓜ Chueca. MAP P.82–83, POCKET MAP G3

The smaller streets north of Gran Vía are home to all manner of vice-related activities and are notorious for petty crime. However, in Plaza de Chueca there's a strong neighbourhood feel and a lively gay scene at night. The area has been rejuvenated in recent years and now holds some enticing streets lined with offbeat restaurants, small private art galleries and unusual corner shops. Calle Almirante has some of the city's most fashionable clothes shops and Calle Augusto Figueroa is the place to go for shoes.

LAS SALESAS REALES

Plaza de las Salesas Ⓜ Colon. 9am–1.30pm & 6–9pm. MAP P.82–83, POCKET MAP H3

The Santa Bárbara church was originally part of the convent complex of las Salesas Reales, founded in 1747. The church is set behind a fine forecourt,

while inside, there's a grotto-like chapel, delightful frescoes and stained-glass windows, and some striking green marble altar decoration. The tombs of Fernando VI, his wife Bárbara de Bragança and military hero General O'Donnell lie within.

SOCIEDAD DE AUTORES

C/Fernando VI 4 Ⓜ Alonso Martinez. MAP P.82–83, POCKET MAP G3

Home to the Society of Authors, this is the most significant Modernista building in Madrid. Designed in 1902 by the Catalan architect José Grasés Riera, its facade features a dripping decoration of flowers, faces and balconies.

PLAZA DEL DOS DE MAYO

Ⓜ Tribunal or Bilbao. MAP P.82–83, POCKET MAP E2

Plaza del Dos de Mayo is the centre of a lively bar scene, with people spilling onto the streets that converge on the square. The plaza commemorates the rebellion against occupying French troops in 1808, while the neighbourhood gets its name from a young seamstress, Manuela Malasaña, who became one of the rebellion's heroines.

Gran Vía, Chueca and Malasaña

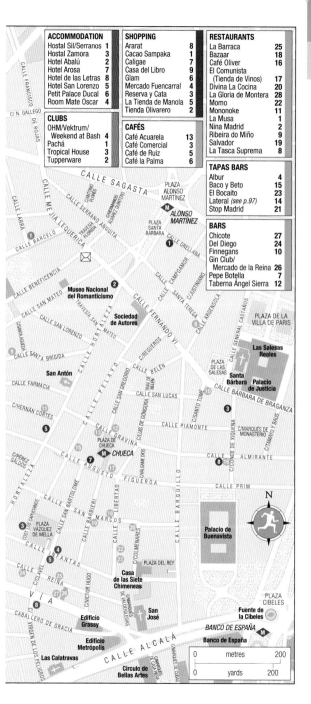

GRAN VÍA, CHUECA AND MALASAÑA

MUSEO NACIONAL DEL ROMANTICISMO

C/San Mateo 13 ⓂTribunal
Ⓦmuseoromanticismo.mcu.es. May–Oct
Tues–Sat 9.30am–8.30pm (closes 6.30pm
Nov–April), Sun 10am–3pm. €3, free on Sat
after 2pm, Sun. MAP P.82–83, POCKET MAP F2

The freshly renovated Museo del Romanticismo, aims to show the lifestyle and outlook of the late-Romantic era through the re-creation of a typical bourgeois residence in the turbulent reign of Isabel II (1833–1868), and this it does brilliantly. Overflowing with a marvellously eclectic and often kitsch hoard of memorabilia, the mansion is decorated with some stunning period furniture and ceiling frescoes, together with more bizarre exhibits such as the pistol which the satirist Mariano José de Larra used to shoot himself in 1837 after being spurned by his lover.

MUSEO DE HISTORIA DE MADRID

C/Fuencarral 78 ⓂTribunal Ⓦwww.munimadrid
.es/museomunicipal. Tues–Fri 9.30am–8pm, Sat
& Sun 10am–2pm; Aug Tues–Fri 9.30am–2pm,
Sat & Sun 10am–2pm. Free (closed for
refurbishment). MAP P.82–83, POCKET MAP F2

Just around the corner from the Museo del Romanticismo, the Museo de Historia de Madrid is in the final throes of yet another lengthy restoration programme. The former city almshouse was remodelled in the early eighteenth century by Pedro de Ribera and features one of his trademark elaborately decorated Baroque doorways superimposed on a striking red brick facade. Inside, the museum contains a chronological collection of paintings, photos, models, sculptures and porcelain, all relating to the history and urban development of Madrid since 1561 (the date it was designated imperial capital by Felipe II). The centre-piece is a fascinating 3-D model of the city made in 1830 by military engineer León Gil de Palacio.

SAN ANTONIO DE LOS ALEMANES

Corredera de San Pablo 16 ⓂChueca or
Callao. Daily 9am–1pm & 6–8pm. Closed Aug.
€2. MAP P.82–83, POCKET MAP E3

One of the city's hidden treasures, this little church was designed in 1624 by the Jesuit architect Pedro Sánchez and Juan Gómez de Mora. The elliptical interior is lined with dizzying floor-to-ceiling pastel-coloured frescoes by Neapolitan artist Luca Giordano which depict scenes from the life of St Anthony.

SAN ANTONIO DE LOS ALEMANES

Shops

ARARAT

C/Almirante 10 Ⓜ Chueca. Mon–Sat
11am–2pm & 5–8.30pm. MAP P.82–83,
POCKET MAP G3

Spanish and foreign designers
for women at reasonable prices.
You can find formal and party
wear as well as younger, more
modern styles too.

CACAO SAMPAKA

C/Orellana 4 Ⓜ Alonso Martinez. Mon–Sat
10am–9.30pm; closed Aug 8–21. MAP P.82–83,
POCKET MAP G2

Every conceivable colour, shape
and flavour of chocolate is
available in this chocoholics'
paradise. There are even books
about the stuff. The only
surprise is that the restaurant
has some non-chocolate snacks
on the menu.

CALIGAE

C/Augusto Figueroa 27 Ⓜ Chueca.
Mon–Fri 10am–2pm & 5–8pm, Sat
10.30am–2pm & 5–8pm. MAP P.82–83,
POCKET MAP G3

One of a string of shoe shops
on this busy Chueca street
selling discounted designer
footwear. If you're on the
lookout for some sandals,
fashion trainers, party shoes
or boots, then this is the place
to come.

CASA DEL LIBRO

Gran Vía 29 Ⓜ Gran Vía and C/Maestro
Victoria 3 Ⓜ Sol. Mon–Sat 9.30am–9.30pm.
MAP P.82–83, POCKET MAP E4

The Casa del Libro's Gran
Vía branch is the city's
biggest bookshop, with four
floors covering just about
everything, including trans-
lations of classic Spanish
works. The Maestro Victoria
branch has a good section
of maps, guides and books
about Madrid.

GLAM

GLAM

C/Fuencarral 35 Ⓜ Gran Vía. Mon–Fri
11am–9pm, Sat 11am–9.30pm, Sun
4.30–9pm. MAP P.82–83, POCKET MAP F3

Club/street-style clothes that
wouldn't look out of place in an
Almodóvar film. There's a shoe
shop with wacky trainers and
trendy footwear next door.

MERCADO FUENCARRAL

C/Fuencarral 45 Ⓜ Gran Vía. Mon–Sat
10am–10pm. MAP P.82–83, POCKET MAP F3

Shopping mall catering for
the young fashion-conscious
crowd, filled with clubwear
shops, record stores, jewellers, a
café and even a tattoo parlour.

RESERVA Y CATA

C/Conde de Xiquena 13 Ⓜ Chueca. Mon
5–9pm, Tues–Fri 11am–3pm & 5–9pm, Sat
11am–3pm. MAP P.82–83, POCKET MAP G3

Staff at this friendly specialist
shop will help you select from
some of the best new wines in
the Iberian peninsula.

LA TIENDA DE MANOLA

C/Hortaleza 49 Ⓜ Chueca. Mon–Fri
10am– 2.30pm & 6–8.30pm, Sat
9.30am–2.30pm. MAP P.82–83, POCKET MAP F3

Great little cheese shop tucked
between the fashion outlets
that line this road. You can pick
up cheese from all over Spain.

TIENDA OLIVARERO

C/Mejia Lequerica 1 ⓜ Alonso Martinez.
Mon–Fri 10am–2pm & 5–8pm, Sat
10am–2pm. MAP P.82–83, POCKET MAP G2

This outlet for an olive-growers'
co-operative has useful
information sheets to help you
buy the best olive oils from
around Spain.

Cafés

CAFÉ ACUARELA

C/Gravina 10 ⓜ Chueca. Daily 3pm–3am, Fri
& Sat till 4am. MAP P.82–83, POCKET MAP G3

Comfy café, with over-the-
top Baroque decor and great
cocktails. Popular with a mostly
gay/lesbian crowd.

CAFÉ COMERCIAL

Glorieta de Bilbao 7 ⓜ Bilbao. Daily
8am–1am, Fri & Sat till 2am. MAP P.82–83,
POCKET MAP F1

A Madrileño institution and
one of the city's most popular
meeting points, this is a lovely
traditional café full of mirrors,
large tables and a cross-section
of Madrid society.

CAFÉ DE RUIZ

C/Ruiz 11 ⓜ Bilbao. Daily 11am–2am.
MAP P.82–83, POCKET MAP E2

Classic Malasaña café and a
great place to while away an
afternoon. Discreet background
music and good cakes are
followed by cocktails in the
evening.

CAFÉ LA PALMA

C/Palma 62 ⓜ Noviciado ⓦ www.cafe
lapalma.com. Daily 4pm–3am. MAP P.82–83,
POCKET MAP D2

Part traditional café, part arts
and music venue, *Café La
Palma* acts as a venue for a
myriad of local artists ranging
from singer-songwriters to
storytellers. It also has popular
DJ sessions on many evenings.

Restaurants

LA BARRACA

C/Reina 29 ⓜ Bilbao ☎ 915 327 154.
Daily 1.30–4.30pm & 8.30pm–midnight.
MAP P.82–83, POCKET MAP F4

Step off the dingy street into
this little piece of Valencia for
some of the best *paella* in town.
The starters are excellent and
there's a great lemon sorbet
for dessert too. A three-course
meal with wine costs around
€35 a head.

BAZAAR

C/Libertad 21 ⓜ Chueca. Daily 1–4pm &
8.30–11.45pm. MAP P.82–83, POCKET MAP G4

Fusion-style Mediterranean
and Asian cuisine. Lunchtime
menu is just €10; evening meals
for around €20. The down side
is the production-line-style
service. No reservations, so
arrive early.

CAFÉ OLIVER

C/Almirante 12 ⓜ Chueca ☎ 915 217 379.
Mon–Sat 1.30–4.30pm & 9pm–midnight,
Sun 11.30am–4pm. MAP P.82–83, POCKET
MAP G3

Stylish surroundings and food
in this trendy bistro. There's
a €14 lunchtime menu with
dishes such as peppers stuffed
with hake and seafood pasta,
while the €25 Sunday brunch
is very popular if rather
overpriced.

EL COMUNISTA (TIENDA DE VINOS)

C/Augusto Figueroa 35 ⓜ Chueca
☎ 915 217 012. Mon–Sat 1–4.30pm &
9.30–11.45pm, Sun 9.30–11.45pm.
Closed mid-Aug to mid-Sept. MAP P.82–83,
POCKET MAP G4

Long-established *comedor* that
has changed little since it was
given its unofficial name as a
student haunt under Franco.
The *sopa de ajo* (garlic soup)
is delicious.

DIVINA LA COCINA

C/Colmenares 13 Ⓜ Chueca ☎ 915 313 765.
Mon–Sun 1–4pm & 9pm–midnight (open till
1am on Sat & Sun). MAP P.82–83, POCKET MAP G4

Fashionable restaurant on a little
street close to Gran Vía. Lunch
menus from €12.90; evening
menus are more expensive
(around €18). Meals include
stuffed courgettes, ostrich
burgers and superb cheesecakes.

LA GLORIA DE MONTERA

C/Caballero de Gracia 10 Ⓜ Gran Vía. Daily
1–4.30pm & 8.30–11.45pm. MAP P.82–83,
POCKET MAP F10

Cool and airy sister restaurant
to *La Finca de Susana* (see
p.60). *Menú* at €9.90 with
well-presented dishes. No
reservations.

MOMO

C/Libertad 8 Ⓜ Chueca ☎ 915 327 348.
Daily 1–4pm & 9.30pm–midnight. MAP P.82–83,
POCKET MAP G4

The place to go for a *menú del
día* with a little bit extra. For
€10 you get three courses, with
drinks and coffee. Unusually,
they also do a set dinner in the
evening for €15.

MONONOKE

C/Hernán Cortés 19 Ⓜ Chueca
☎ 915 229 806. Mon–Sat 1.30–4pm &
8.30pm–midnight. MAP P.82–83, POCKET MAP F3

Very friendly staff in this
small Japanese restaurant in
the heart of Chueca. Great
value with a selection of sushi,
sashimi, tempura and tori
teriyaki menus all available for
under €20.

LA MUSA

C/Manuela Malasaña 18 Ⓜ Bilbao
☎ 914 487 558. Daily 1.30–4.30pm &
8.30pm–midnight. MAP P.82–83, POCKET MAP E1

A firm favourite on the
Malasaña scene. Good tapas,
generous helpings, strong wine
list and chic decor are all part
of the recipe for success. The
only problem is the crowds.

NINA MADRID

C/Manuela Malasaña 10 Ⓜ Bilbao
☎ 915 910 046. Mon–Fri 1.30–4.30pm &
8.30–11.30pm, Sat & Sun 12.30–5.30pm &
8.30–11.30pm. MAP P.82–83, POCKET MAP E1

A stylish restaurant serving
a €12 *menú del día*, weekend
brunches (€23) and an evening
sampler menu for €28. A la
carte dishes are nowhere near
as good value.

RIBEIRA DO MIÑO

C/Santa Brígida 1 Ⓜ Tribunal ☎ 915 219 854.
Tues–Sun 1–5pm & 8pm–midnight.
MAP P.82–83, POCKET MAP F3

Great-value *marisquería*,
serving a seafood platter for
two at €31; try the slightly
more expensive Galician white
wine, Albariño, to accompany
it. Reservations essential.

LA BARRACA

SALVADOR

C/Barbieri 12 Ⓜ Chueca ☎ 915 214 524.
Mon–Sat 1.30–4pm & 9pm–midnight. Closed
Aug. MAP P.82–83, POCKET MAP G4

Chueca mainstay with bullfighting decor and dishes such as *rabo de toro* (bull's tail), *gallina en pepitoria* (chicken in almond sauce) and *arroz con leche* (rice pudding). Lunch around €20.

LA TASCA SUPREMA

C/Argensola 7 Ⓜ Alonso Martinez
☎ 913 080 347. Mon–Sat 1.30–4pm.
Closed Aug. MAP P.82–83, POCKET MAP G3

Popular neighbourhood local, only open at lunchtime and worth booking ahead for. Castilian home cooking includes, on Monday and Thursday, *cocido* and excellent *pimientos de piquillo* (piquant red peppers).

Tapas bars

ALBUR

C/Manuela Malasaña 15 Ⓜ Bilbao.
Daily noon–1am (2am Fri & Sat). MAP P.82–83,
POCKET MAP E1

The decor is rustic and the food excellent here, but the service can be a little slow. The grilled vegetables and the cheese platters are worth sampling. Lunchtime menu is €11.

BACO Y BETO

C/Pelayo 24 Ⓜ Chueca. Mon–Fri 8pm–1am,
Sat 2–4pm & 8pm–1am. MAP P.82–83, POCKET
MAP F3

Creative tapas in this small bar in the heart of Chueca. Try the sirloin canapé soaked in bitter orange and the home-made *croquetas*.

EL BOCAITO

C/Libertad 6 Ⓜ Chueca. Mon–Fri 1–4.30pm
& 8.30pm–midnight, Sat 8.30pm–midnight.
Closed Aug. MAP P.82–83, POCKET MAP G4

Watch the busy staff prepare the food in the kitchen that straddles the two bars as you munch away on a variety of delicious tapas. Look out for the *Luisito* (chilli, squid, mayonnaise and a secret sauce all topped with a prawn), the hottest canapé you're ever likely to encounter. If you prefer to sit down, there is a restaurant at the back.

STOP MADRID

C/Hortaleza 11 Ⓜ Gran Vía. Daily noon–2am.
MAP P.82–83, POCKET MAP F4

Corner bar with hams hanging from the windows and wine bottles lining the walls. Tapas consist largely of *jamón* and *chorizo*, with the "Canapé Stop" of ham and tomato doused in olive oil an excellent option.

Bars

CHICOTE

Gran Vía 12 Ⓜ Gran Vía. Mon–Sat
5pm–1.30am. MAP P.82–83, POCKET MAP F10

Opened back in 1931 by Perico Chicote, ex-barman at the *Ritz*. Sophia Loren, Frank Sinatra, Ava Gardner, Luis Buñuel, Orson Welles and Hemingway have all passed through the doors of this cocktail bar. It's lost much of its old-style charm as it has tried to keep up to date, though it's still worth a visit for nostalgia's sake.

DEL DIEGO

C/Reina 12 Ⓜ Gran Vía. Mon–Sat 9pm–3am.
Closed Aug. MAP P.82–83, POCKET, MAP F10

New York-style cocktail bar set up by former *Chicote* waiter Fernando del Diego and now better than the original place. The expertly mixed cocktails are served up in a friendly, unhurried atmosphere.

Margaritas, mojitos and manhattans; the house special, a vodka-based Del Diego is a must.

FINNEGANS

Plaza de Las Salesas 9 🚇 Alonso Martinez. Daily 1pm–2am. MAP P.82–83, POCKET MAP G3

Irish bar with several rooms, complete with bar fittings and wooden floors brought over from the Emerald Isle. English-speaking staff and TV sports.

GIN CLUB/MERCADO DE LA REINA

Gran Vía 12 🚇 Gran Vía. Gin Club 1.30pm–late, bar & tapas: 9am–midnight (Fri & Sat 1am), restaurant: 1.30–4pm & 8.30pm–midnight. MAP P.82–83, POCKET MAP G10 & F10

Multipurpose tapas bar, restaurant and *bar de copas*. The bar serves a wide range of *pinchos* and *raciones* as well as a house special (upmarket) hamburger meal at €10.50. The restaurant is rather more pricey with main courses around €15. At the back, with its mirror ceilings, black leather chairs, is a cocktail bar, the *Gin Club*, offering over twenty different brands, as well as a good mojito.

PEPE BOTELLA

C/San Andrés 12 🚇 Bilbao. 11am–2am. MAP P.82–83, POCKET MAP E2

Elegant little bar perched on the edge of the Plaza Dos de Mayo. Friendly staff, marble-topped tables, low-volume music and no fruit machine.

TABERNA ÁNGEL SIERRA

C/Gravina 11 🚇 Chueca. Daily noon–1am. MAP P.82–83, POCKET MAP G3

One of the great bars in Madrid, where everyone drinks *vermút* accompanied by free, exquisite pickled anchovy tapas. *Raciones* are also available, though they're pretty pricey.

Clubs

OHM/VEKTRUM/WEEKEND AT BASH

Plaza Callao 4 🚇 Callao 🌐 www.tripfamily .com. Wed 11pm–6am, Thurs–Sat midnight–6am, Sun midnight–5am. €12–15, including first drink. MAP P.82–83, POCKET MAP D4

Bash is a major venue on the Madrid club scene. *OHM* is the main techno-house session on Friday and Saturday nights and very popular with the gay crowd. There's funk and hip-hop on Wednesday, electro and techno on Thursday, and *Weekend* is the Sunday session.

PACHÁ

C/Barceló 11 🚇 Tribunal. Wed–Sat midnight–5am. €12–15 with drink. MAP P.82–83, POCKET MAP F2

Eternal survivor on the Madrid clubbing scene, *Pachá* runs an early session for under-age clubbers 6.30–10.30pm on Fridays and Saturdays and then gets going with the real thing from midnight. House and techno on Saturdays; the music is more varied on other nights. Unpredictable door policy.

TROPICAL HOUSE

Gran Vía 54 🚇 Gran Vía. Tues, Thurs & Sun 8pm–late. €7 with drink; women are given free entry if you pick one of the invitations given out at the door. MAP P.82–83, POCKET MAP D4

Dance the night away to tropical vibes or simply watch the salsa experts. Thursday night is salsa night, and on Sundays and Thursdays it's ballroom-style dance followed by disco.

TUPPERWARE

C/Corredera Alta de San Pablo 26 🚇 Tribunal. Daily 9pm–3.30am. MAP P.82–83, POCKET MAP F2

The place to go for the latest on the indie scene, with grunge and classics from the punk era.

Salamanca and Paseo de la Castellana

Exclusive Barrio de Salamanca was developed in the second half of the nineteenth century as an upmarket residential zone under the patronage of the Marquis of Salamanca. Today it's still home to Madrid's smartest apartments and designer emporiums, while the streets are populated by the chic clothes and sunglasses brigade, decked out in fur coats, Gucci and gold. Shopping aside, there's a scattering of sights here, including the pick of the city's smaller museums and Real Madrid's imposing Santiago Bernabéu stadium. Bordering Salamanca to the west is the multi-lane Paseo de la Castellana, peppered with corporate office blocks, where, in summer, the section north of Plaza de Colón is littered with trendy *terrazas*.

PLAZA DE COLÓN

Ⓜ Colón. MAP P.92, POCKET MAP H3

Overlooking a busy crossroads and dominating the square in which they stand are a Neo-Gothic monument to Christopher Columbus (Cristóbal Colón), given as a wedding gift to Alfonso XII, and an enormous Spanish flag. Directly behind are the Jardínes del Descubrimiento (Discovery Gardens), a small park containing three huge stone blocks representing Columbus's ships, the *Niña*, *Pinta* and *Santa María*. Below the plaza, underneath a cascading wall of water, is the **Teatro Fernán Gómez**, a venue

MUSEO ARQUEOLÓGICO NACIONAL

for theatre, film, dance, music and occasional exhibitions.

BIBLIOTECA NACIONAL AND MUSEO DEL LIBRO

Paseo de Recoletos 20 Ⓜ Colón Ⓦ www .bne.es. Tues-Sat 10am-9pm, Sun & hols 10am-2pm. Free. MAP P.92, POCKET MAP J3

The National Library contains over six million volumes, including every work published in Spain since 1716. The Museo del Libro (Book Museum) within displays a selection of the library's treasures, including Arab, Hebrew and Greek manuscripts, and has an interesting interactive exhibition on the development of written communication (in Spanish only).

MUSEO ARQUEOLÓGICO NACIONAL

C/Serrano 13 Ⓜ Serrano or Colón Ⓦ man .mcu.es. Tues-Sat 9.30am-8pm, Sun 9.30am-3pm. Check website for entrance fees. MAP P.92, POCKET MAP J3

Given a new lease of life after a long overdue restoration programme, the archeological museum's vast collections trace the cultural evolution of humankind. Most exhibits are from Spain and include striking **Celto-Iberian busts** known as *La Dama de Elche* and *La Dama de Baza*. There are some suitably enigmatic sphinx-like sculptures found in Alicante and a wonderfully rich hoard of Visigothic treasures found at Toledo. Good coverage is also given to Roman, Egyptian, Greek and Islamic finds.

MUSEO DE CERA

Paseo de Recoletos 41 Ⓜ Colón Ⓦ www.museoceramadrid.com. Mon–Fri 10am-2.30pm & 4.30-8.30pm, Sat, Sun & hols 10am-8.30pm. €16 (€12 for 4-10 year olds). MAP P.92, POCKET MAP H3

Over 450 different personalities – including a host of VIPs,

heads of state and, of course, Real Madrid football stars – are displayed in this expensive and tacky museum, which is nevertheless popular with children. There's also a chamber of horrors and a film history of Spain (supplement charged).

MUSEO DE ARTE PÚBLICO

Paseo de la Castellana 41 Ⓜ Rubén Darío. MAP P.92, POCKET MAP J1

An innovative use of the space underneath the Juan Bravo flyover, this open-air art museum is made up of a haphazard collection of sculptures, cubes, walls and fountains, including work by Eduardo Chillida, Joan Miró and Julio González.

MUSEO SOROLLA

Paseo del General Martínez Campos 37 Ⓜ Rubén Darío, Gregorio Marañón or Iglesia Ⓦ museosorolla.mcu.es. Tues-Sat 9.30am-8pm, Sun 10am-3pm. €3, free Sun. MAP P.92, POCKET MAP J1

Part museum and part art gallery, this tribute to an artist's life and work is one of Madrid's most underrated treasures. Situated in Joaquín Sorolla's former home, it's a delightful oasis of peace and tranquillity, its cool and shady Andalusian-style courtyard and gardens decked out with statues, fountains, assorted plants and fruit trees. The ground floor has been kept largely intact, re-creating the authentic atmosphere of the artist's living and working areas. The upstairs rooms, originally the sleeping quarters, have been turned into a gallery, where sunlight, sea, intense colours, women and children dominate Sorolla's impressionistic paintings. On your way out in the Patio Andaluz, there's a collection of his sketches and gouaches.

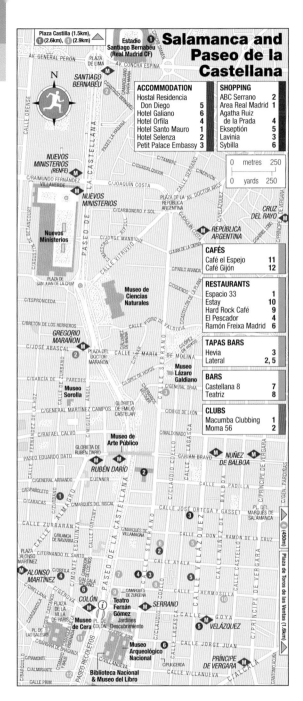

Salamanca and Paseo de la Castellana

ACCOMMODATION

Hostal Residencia Don Diego	5
Hotel Galiano	6
Hotel Orfila	1
Hotel Santo Mauro	1
Hotel Selenza	2
Petit Palace Embassy	3

SHOPPING

ABC Serrano	2
Area Real Madrid	1
Agatha Ruiz de la Prada	4
Ekseptión	5
Lavinia	3
Sybilla	6

CAFÉS

Café el Espejo	11
Café Gijón	12

RESTAURANTS

Espacio 33	1
Estay	10
Hard Rock Café	9
El Pescador	4
Ramón Freixa Madrid	6

TAPAS BARS

Hevia	3
Lateral	2, 5

BARS

Castellana 8	7
Teatriz	8

CLUBS

Macumba Clubbing	1
Moma 56	2

MUSEO LÁZARO GALDIANO

C/Serrano 122 ⓜ Gregorio Marañón ⓦ www
.flg.es. Mon & Wed–Sun 10am–4.30pm. €4,
free Sun. MAP P.92, POCKET MAP J1

When businessman and
publisher José Lázaro Galdiano
died in 1947, he left his private
collection – a vast treasure trove
of paintings and *objets d'art* – to
the state. Spread over the four
floors of his former home, the
collection contains jewellery,
outstanding Spanish archeological pieces and some beautifully
decorated thirteenth-century
Limoges enamels. There's
also an excellent selection of
European paintings with works
by Bosch, Rembrandt, Reynolds
and Constable, plus Spanish
artists including Zurbarán,
Velázquez, El Greco and Goya.
Other exhibits include several
clocks and watches, many of
them once owned by Emperor
Charles V.

MUSEO DE CIENCIAS NATURALES

C/José Gutiérrez Abascal 2 ⓜ Gregorio
Marañón ⓦ www.mncn.csic.es. Tues–Fri
10am–6pm, Sat 10am–8pm (July & Aug
10am–3pm), Sun 10am–2.30pm. €5, free Sun.
MAP P.92, POCKET MAP J1

The Natural History Museum's
displays are split between two
buildings. One contains a fairly
predictable collection of stuffed
animals, skeletons and audio-
visual displays on the evolution
of life on earth, the other is
home to some rather dull fossil
and geological exhibits.

ESTADIO SANTIAGO BERNABÉU

C/Concha Espina 1 ⓜ Santiago Bernabéu
☏ 913 984 300, tickets ☏ 902 324 324,
ⓦ www.realmadrid.com. Ticket office
Mon–Fri 3–9pm (match days from 11am).
Tickets from €30 go on sale a week before
each match. Tour and trophy exhibition:
Mon–Sat 10am–7pm, Sun 10.30am–6.30pm
(closes five hours before games on
match days); €16, under-14s €11. MAP P.92,
POCKET MAP J1

The magnificent 80,000-seater
Bernabéu stadium provides a
suitably imposing home for
one of the most glamorous
teams in football, Real Madrid.
Venue of the 1982 World Cup
final, the stadium has witnessed
countless triumphs of "Los
blancos", who have notched up
31 Spanish league titles and
nine European Cup triumphs
in their 109-year history. Real
have broken the world transfer
record three times in the last
decade, and their latest star
is Portugal forward Cristiano
Ronaldo. Tickets for big games
can be tricky to get hold of,
but the club runs a telephone
and internet booking service
(see opposite).

You can catch a glimpse of
the hallowed turf on the over-
priced stadium tour during
which you visit the changing
rooms, walk around the edge of
the pitch and sit in the VIP box
before heading to the trophy
room with its endless cabinets
of gleaming silverware. The
stadium also has a reasonably
priced café (*Realcafé*) and a
more expensive restaurant
(*Puerta 57*) both open to the
public and affording views over
the pitch (though they are not
open during games).

TROPHIES AT ESTADIO SANTIAGO BERNABÉU

PLAZA CASTILLA

PLAZA CASTILLA

Ⓜ Plaza de la Castilla. MAP P.92, POCKET MAP J1
The Paseo de la Castellana ends
with a flourish at Plaza Castilla
with the dramatic leaning
towers of the Puerta de Europa
and the four giant skyscrapers
constructed on Real Madrid's
former training ground, the
result of a controversial deal
that allowed the club to solve
many of its financial problems.
The two tallest towers, one of
which is designed by Norman
Foster, soar some 250 metres
into the sky.

PLAZA DE TOROS DE LAS VENTAS

C/Alcalá 237 Ⓜ Ventas ☎ 913 562 200,
Ⓦ www.las-ventas.com. Box office
March–Oct Thurs–Sun 10am–2pm & 5–8pm;
BBVA ticket line ☎ 902 150 025, Ⓦ www
.taquilatoros.com and from authorized
agents in booths along C/Victoria near Sol.
€5–120. MAP P.92

Situated on the easternmost
tip of the Barrio de
Salamanca, Madrid's 23,000-
capacity, Neo-Mudéjar
bullring, Las Ventas, is the
most illustrious in the world.
The season lasts from March
to October and *corridas*
(bullfights) are held every
Sunday at 7pm and every day
during the three main *ferias*
(fairs): La Comunidad (early
May), San Isidro (mid-May
to June) and Otoño (late Sept
to Oct). Tickets go on sale at
the ring a couple of days in
advance, though many are
already allocated to season-
ticket holders. The cheapest
seats are *gradas*, the highest
rows at the back, from where
you can see everything that
happens without too much of
the detail; the front rows are
known as the *barreras*. Seats
are also divided into *sol* (sun),
sombra (shade) and *sol y
sombra* (shaded after a while),
with *sombra* seats the most
expensive.

There's a taurine **museum**
attached to the bullring
(March–Oct Tues–Fri
9.30am–2.30pm, Sun & fight
days 10am–1pm; Nov–Feb
Mon–Fri 9.30am–2pm;
free) with an intriguing if
rather anarchic collection
of bullfighting memorabilia
including stunning *trajes de
luces*, the beautifully decorated
suits worn by the *toreros*.

Shops

ABC SERRANO

Paseo de la Castellana 34 and C/Serrano 61
both Ⓜ Rubén Darío. Mon–Sat 10am–9pm,
Sun noon–8pm. MAP P.92, POCKET MAP F2
Upmarket shopping mall
housed in the beautiful former
headquarters of the **ABC**

newspaper. There are fashion
and household outlets, as
well as a couple of bars and
restaurants, and a popular
rooftop terrace.

AREA REAL MADRID

Bernabéu Stadium; C/Padre Damián,
Puerta 55 Ⓜ Santiago Bernabéu. Daily
10.30am–8.30pm. MAP P.92, POCKET MAP J1

Club store where you can pick up replica shirts of the star players and all manner of – expensive – souvenirs related to the club's history.

AGATHA RUIZ DE LA PRADA

C/Serrano 27 ⓜ Serrano. Mon–Sat 10am–8.30pm. MAP P.92, POCKET MAP J2

Movida-era designer who shows and sells her gaudily coloured clothes and accessories at this outlet. There's a children's line, stationery and household goods too.

EKSEPTIÓN

C/Velázquez 28 ⓜ Velázquez. Mon–Sat 10.30am–2.30pm & 5–8.30pm. MAP P.92, POCKET MAP K3

A dramatic catwalk bathed in spotlights leads into this shop selling some of the most expensive women's clothes in Madrid. Next door are younger, more casual clothes in the Eks shop for both men and women. There's also a branch selling discount last-season fashions at half-price at Avda Concha Espina 14 (Mon–Sat 11.30am–8pm).

LAVINIA

C/José Ortega y Gasset 16 ⓜ Nuñez de Balboa. Mon–Sat 10.30am–9pm. MAP P.92, POCKET MAP K1

A massive wine shop with a great selection from Spain and the rest of the world. The perfect place to get that Ribera del Duero, Albariño or Rueda that you wanted to take home.

SYBILLA

C/Jorge Juan 12 ⓜ Serrano. Mon–Sat 10.30am–2.30pm. Mon–Sat 10am–2pm & 4.30–8.30pm. MAP P.92, POCKET MAP K3

Top designer Sybilla broke through in the 1980s and remains at the forefront of the women's fashion scene in Spain – with prices to match.

Also does a jewellery line and accessories for the home. If shopping gets too tiring, there are armchairs and sofas to collapse into.

Cafés

CAFÉ EL ESPEJO

Paseo de Recoletos 31 ⓜ Colón. Daily 8am–1am. MAP P.92, POCKET MAP H3

Opened in 1978, but you wouldn't guess it from the antiquated decor – mirrors, gilt and a wonderful, extravagant glass pavilion, plus a leafy outside *terraza*. An ideal spot to buy a coffee and watch the world go by.

CAFÉ GIJÓN

Paseo de Recoletos 21 ⓜ Colón. Daily 8am–1.30am. MAP P.92, POCKET MAP H4

Famous literary café dating from 1888, decked out in Cuban mahogany and mirrors. A centre of the *Movida* in the 1980s, it still hosts regular artistic *tertulias* (discussion groups). There's a cellar restaurant, a very pleasant summer *terraza* and a set menu at lunchtime.

AGATHA RUIZ DE LA PRADA

CAFÉ EL ESPEJO

Restaurants

ESPACIO 33

Paseo de la Castellana 259, Edificio Torre Espacio ⓜ Begoña ☎ 914 276 891. Mon–Fri 1.30–4.30pm, Fri & Sat 8.30pm–12.30am. MAP P.92, POCKET MAP J1

For stunning views of Madrid and the Sierra, try dining out 160 metres up in the air on the 33rd floor of one of the four massive skyscrapers that tower above the Castellana. This sleek, modern restaurant serves up some high-quality Mediterranean food for around €45 for a three-course meal.

ESTAY

C/Hermosilla 46 ⓜ Velázquez ☎ 915 780 470, Mon–Sat 1–4pm & 8pm–midnight. MAP P.92, POCKET MAP K2

Basque-style cuisine in miniature (canapés and mini casseroles) in this pleasant and roomy restaurant. A great range of *pintxos*, including *jamón* with roquefort cheese, langoustine vol-au-vents and a fine wine list too. A meal will cost €25–30.

HARD ROCK CAFÉ

Paseo de la Castellana 2 ⓜ Colón ☎ 914 364 340. Daily 12.30pm–2am. MAP P.92, POCKET MAP J1

A children's favourite, with its tried-and-tested formula of rock memorabilia, Tex-Mex and burgers at under €20 a head. The best thing about it is the summer *terraza* overlooking Plaza Colón.

EL PESCADOR

C/José Ortega y Gasset 75 ⓜ Lista ☎ 914 021 290. Mon–Sat 12.30–4pm & 7.30pm–midnight. Closed Aug. MAP P.92, POCKET MAP K1, POCKET MAP K2

One of the city's top seafood restaurants, with specials flown in from the Atlantic each morning. Prices are high (around €55 per head), but you'll rarely experience better-quality seafood than this. If funds don't stretch to a full meal, you can try a *ración* in the bar instead.

RAMÓN FREIXA MADRID

C/Claudio Coello 67 ⓜ Serrano ☎ 917 818 262. Tues–Sat 1–4pm & 8.30–midnight. MAP P.92, POCKET MAP J2

Catalan chef Ramón Freixa's flagship restaurant in Madrid situated in the luxury surroundings of the *Selenza* hotel (see p.128) in the heart of Salamanca. Creative and impeccably presented dishes from an ever-changing menu featuring superb game, fish and new twists on Spanish classics. A la carte dishes range €25–55, while there is a selection of taster menus available from

€70. Only space for 35 diners, so book well in advance, especially if you want a table in the summer terrace.

Tapas bars

HEVIA

C/Serrano 118 Ⓜ Rubén Darío or Gregorio Marañón. Mon–Sat 9am–1.30am. MAP P.92, POCKET MAP J1

Plush venue for plush clientele feasting on pricey but excellent tapas and canapés – the hot Camembert is delicious, as is the *surtido de ahumados* (selection of smoked fish).

LATERAL

Paseo de la Castellana 132 Ⓜ Santiago Bernabéu. Daily 10am–midnight. MAP P.92, POCKET MAP J1

A swish tapas bar serving classic dishes such as *croquetas* and *pimientos rellenos* (stuffed peppers) with a modern twist. It's close to the Bernabéu and gets crowded on match days but there are other branches at C/Velázquez 57, C/Fuencarral 43 and Plaza Santa Ana 12.

Bars

CASTELLANA 8

Paseo de la Castellana 8 Ⓜ Colón. Daily 11.30am–2.30am. MAP P.92, POCKET MAP J2

Restaurant and café by day, cocktail bar and club by night, *Castellana 8* has a laidback atmosphere, cool decor and a terrace perfect for chilling out on a hot summer evening.

TEATRIZ

C/Hermosilla 15 Ⓜ Serrano. Bar 9pm–3am, restaurant 1.30–4.30pm & 9pm–1am; closed Sat lunch, Sun & Aug. MAP P.92, POCKET MAP J2

This former theatre refurbished by Catalan designer Javier Mariscal and Frenchman Philippe Starck, and is

extremely stylish. There's a tapas bar at the entrance, a bar on the stage and a restaurant in the stalls. Drinks are pretty pricey but there's no entrance charge. Sip and enjoy the elegant makeover.

Clubs

MACUMBA CLUBBING

Estación de Chamartín Ⓜ Chamartín Ⓦ www.spaceofsound.com. Elite Noche: Sat midnight–6am. Space of Sound: Sun 9am–6pm. €15 including first drink. MAP P.92, POCKET MAP J1

Guest DJs from London's *Ministry of Sound* come for the Saturday Elite Noche all-nighter and if you just can't stop till you get enough, the Space of Sound "after hours" club allows you to strut your stuff through Sunday too.

MOMA 56

C/José Abascal 56 Ⓜ Gregorio Marañón Ⓦ www.moma56.com. Wed–Sun midnight–6am. Around €15. MAP P.92, POCKET MAP J1

An exclusive club, popular with *pijos* (rich kids) and the upmarket glamour crowd. Also inside are a restaurant and a bar serving cocktails and light Mediterranean fusion food.

RAMON FREIXA MADRID

Plaza de España and beyond

Largely constructed in the Franco era and dominated by two early Spanish skyscrapers, the Plaza de España provides an imposing full stop to Gran Vía and a breathing space from the densely packed streets to the east. Beyond the square lies a mixture of aristocratic suburbia, university campus and parkland, distinguished by the green swathes of Parque del Oeste and Casa de Campo. Sights include the eclectic collections of the Museo Cerralbo, the fascinating Museo de América, the Ermita de San Antonio de la Florida, with its stunning Goya frescoes and, further out, the pleasant royal residence of El Pardo. Meanwhile, the spacious *terrazas* along Paseo del Pintor Rosales provide ample opportunity for refreshment.

PLAZA DE ESPAÑA

 Plaza de España. MAP P.100, POCKET MAP C3

The Plaza de España was the Spanish dictator Franco's attempt to portray Spain as a dynamic, modern country. The gargantuan apartment complex of the **Edificio de España**, which heads the square, looks like it was transplanted from 1920s New York, but was in fact completed in 1953. Four years later, the 32-storey **Torre de Madrid** took over for some time as the tallest building in Spain. Together they tower over an elaborate monument to Cervantes in the middle of the square, set by an uninspiring pool. The plaza itself can be a little seedy at night, although it does play

DON QUIXOTE IN PLAZA ESPAÑA

host to occasional festivities and an interesting craft fair during the fiesta of San Isidro (on or around May 15).

MUSEO DE CERRALBO

C/Ventura Rodríguez 17 Ⓜ Plaza de España Ⓦ museocerralbo.mcu.es. Tues, Wed, Fri & Sat 9.30am–3pm, plus Thurs 5–8pm, Sun & hols 10am–3pm; July & Aug Tues–Sat 9.30am–2pm, Sun & hols 11am–2pm. €3, free Sun. MAP P.100, POCKET MAP B3

Reactionary politician, poet, traveller and archeologist, the seventeenth Marqués de Cerralbo endowed his elegant nineteenth-century mansion with a substantial collection of paintings, furniture and armour. Bequeathed to the state on his death, the house opened as a museum in 1962 and the cluttered nature of the exhibits is partly explained by the fact that the marqués's will stipulated that objects should be displayed exactly as he had arranged them. The highlight is a fabulous over-the-top mirrored ballroom with a Tiepolo-inspired fresco, golden stuccowork and marbled decoration.

CENTRO CULTURAL CONDE DUQUE

C/Conde Duque 9–11 Ⓜ Ventura Rodríguez Ⓦ www.esmadrid.com/condeduque. MAP P.100, POCKET MAP C2

Constructed in the early eighteenth century, this former barracks of the royal guard has been converted into a dynamic cultural centre, housing the city's collection of **contemporary art** and hosting a variety of temporary exhibitions.

PLAZA DE COMENDADORAS

Ⓜ Noviciado. MAP P.100, POCKET MAP D2

Bordered by a variety of interesting craft shops, bars and cafés, this tranquil square is named after the convent that occupies one side of it. The convent is run by nuns from the military order of Santiago and the attached church is decked out with banners celebrating the victories of the Order's knights. A large painting of their patron, St James the Moor-slayer, hangs over the high altar. The plaza itself comes alive in the summer months when the *terrazas* open and locals gather for a chat and a drink.

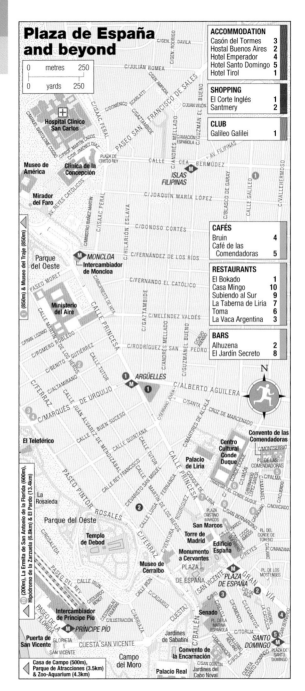

MIRADOR DEL FARO

MINISTERIO DEL AIRE

Ⓜ **Moncloa.** MAP P.100, POCKET MAP B1

The Air Ministry is a product of the post-Civil War Francoist building boom. Work on the mammoth edifice began in 1942, and even the Third Reich's architect, Albert Speer, was consulted. However, with the defeat of the Nazis, plans were soon changed and a Habsburg-style structure was built instead – nicknamed the "Monasterio" del Aire because of its similarity to El Escorial. The neighbouring Arco de la Victoria was constructed in 1956 to commemorate the Nationalist military triumph in the Civil War.

MIRADOR DEL FARO

Ⓜ **Moncloa.** MAP P.100, POCKET MAP B1

Reopened after a long, 5.6 million-euro refurbishment, this futuristic 92-metre high viewing tower provides stunning views over the northern section of the city, including the university campus and the mountains beyond. There are plans to open a café/restaurant on the top floor.

MUSEO DE AMÉRICA

Avda de los Reyes Católicos 6 Ⓜ Moncloa Ⓦ museodeamerica.mcu.es. May–Oct Tues–Sat 9.30am–8.30pm, Sun 10am–3pm; Nov–April Tues–Sat 9.30am–6.30pm, Sun 10am–3pm. €3. MAP P.100, POCKET MAP B1

This fabulous collection of pre-Columbian American art and artefacts includes objects brought back at the time of the Spanish Conquest, as well as more recent acquisitions and donations. The layout is thematic, with sections on geography, history, social organization, religion and communication. The Aztec, Maya and Inca civilizations are well represented and exhibits include: the Madrid Codex, one of only three surviving hieroglyphic manuscripts depicting everyday Maya life; the Tudela Codex, with indigenous paintings describing the events of the Spanish Conquest; and the Quimbayas Treasure, a breathtaking collection of gold objects from a funeral treasure of the Colombian Quimbaya culture, dated 900–600 BC.

MUSEO DE AMÉRICA

MUSEO DEL TRAJE

Avda de Juan de Herrera 2 ⓜ Moncloa
ⓦ museodeltraje.mcu.es. Tues–Sat
9.30am–7pm, Sun & hols 10am–3pm (July
& Aug open late from 9.30am–10.30pm on
Thurs). €3, free Sat after 2.30pm and all day
Sun. MAP P.100, POCKET MAP B1

A fascinating excursion
through the history of clothes
and costume. Exhibits include
garments from a royal tomb
dating back to the thirteenth
century, some stunning
eighteenth-century ballgowns
and a selection of Spanish
regional costumes as well as
shoes, jewellery and underwear.
Modern Spanish and inter-
national designers are also
featured, with a Paco Rabane
mini-skirt and elegant shoes
from Pedro del Hierro. There
is an upmarket restaurant in
the grounds, which has a cool
garden terrace in the summer
(see p.106).

PARQUE DEL OESTE

ⓜ Moncloa. MAP P.100, POCKET MAP A3

Featuring a pleasant stream,
assorted statues and shady
walks, this delightful park
offers a welcome respite from
the busy streets of the capital.
In summer there are numerous
terrazas overlooking it on
Paseo del Pintor Rosales. The
beautiful rose garden – is at its most
fragrant in May and June,
while further down the hill
is a small cemetery where
the 43 Spaniards executed by
occupying French troops on
May 3, 1808 – and immortalized by Goya in his famous
painting in the Prado (see p.66)
– lie buried.

TEMPLO DE DEBOD

C/Ferraz 1 ⓜ Plaza de España. April–Sept
Tues–Fri 10am–2pm & 6–8pm, Sat &
Sun 10am–2pm; Oct–March Tues–Fri
9.45am–1.45pm & 4.15–6.15pm, Sat & Sun
10am–2pm. Free. MAP P.100, POCKET MAP B3

A fourth-century BC Egyptian
temple in the middle of Madrid
may seem an incongruous
sight. It's here, however, as a
thank-you from the Egyptian
government for Spanish help
in salvaging archeological sites
threatened by the construction
of the Aswan High Dam.
Reconstructed here stone
by stone in 1968, it has a
multimedia exhibition on the
culture of Ancient Egypt inside.
Archeologists have called for
it to be enclosed and insulated
from the open air as pollution is
taking a heavy toll on the stone.

EL TELEFÉRICO

DUCK IN CASA DE CAMPO

EL TELEFÉRICO

Paseo del Pintor Rosales Ⓜ Argüelles
Ⓦ www.teleferico.com. April–Sept Mon–Fri
noon–early eve (exact times vary), Sat & Sun
noon–around 8pm; Oct–March Sat, Sun &
hols noon–dusk. €3.70 single, €5.35 return.
MAP P.100, POCKET MAP A2

The Teleférico **cable car**
shuttles passengers from the
edge of the Parque del Oeste
high over the Manzanares
river to a restaurant/bar in the
middle of Casa de Campo (see
below). The round trip offers
some fine views of the park,
the Palacio Real, the Almudena
Cathedral and the city skyline.

LA ERMITA DE SAN ANTONIO DE LA FLORIDA

Paseo de la Florida 5 Ⓜ Príncipe Pío Ⓦ www
.munimadrid.es/ermita. Tues–Fri 9.30am–8pm,
Sat & Sun 10am–2pm. MAP P.100, POCKET MAP A4

Built on a Greek-cross plan
between 1792 and 1798, this
little church is the burial site
of Goya and also features some
outstanding frescoes by him.
Those in the dome depict
St Anthony of Padua
resurrecting a dead man to
give evidence in favour of a
prisoner (the saint's father)
unjustly accused of murder.
The *ermita* also houses the
artist's mausoleum, although
his head was stolen by
phrenologists for examination
in the nineteenth century. The
mirror-image chapel on the
other side of the road was built
in 1925 for parish services so
that the original could become
a museum. On St Anthony's
Day (June 13) girls queue at
the church to ask the saint for
a boyfriend; if pins dropped
into the holy water then stick
to their hands, their wish will
be granted.

CASA DE CAMPO

Ⓜ Lago. MAP P.100, POCKET MAP A4

The Casa de Campo, an
enormous expanse of heath and
scrub, is in parts surprisingly
wild for a place so easily accessible from the city. Founded by
Felipe II in the mid-sixteenth
century as a royal hunting
estate, it was only opened
to the public in 1931 and
soon after acted as a base for
Franco's forces to shell the city.
Large sections have been tamed
for conventional pastimes and
there are picnic tables and café/
bars throughout the park, the
ones by the lake providing fine
views of the city. There are also
mountain-bike trails, a jogging
track, an open-air swimming
pool (June–Sept daily
10.30am–8pm; €4.35), tennis
courts and rowing boats for
rent on the lake, all near Metro
Lago. The park is best avoided
after dark as many of its roads
are frequented by prostitutes.

ZOO-AQUARIUM

Casa de Campo Ⓜ Batan Ⓦ www.zoomadrid
.com. Daily 11am–dusk (opens 10.30am on
holidays and at weekends). €18.80, 3–7 year
olds €15.25, under-3s free. MAP P.100, POCKET
MAP A4

Laid out in sections
corresponding to the five
continents, Madrid's zoo, on
the southwestern edge of Casa
de Campo, provides decent
enclosures and plenty of space
for over 2000 different species.
When you've had your fill of
big cats, koalas and venomous
snakes, you can check out
the aquarium, dolphinarium,
children's zoo or bird show.
Boats can be rented and there
are mini train tours too.

PARQUE DE ATRACCIONES

Casa de Campo Ⓜ Batan Ⓦ www.parquede
atracciones.es. April–Sept most days
noon–midnight; Oct–March weekends and
hols noon–7pm. Access only €10.60; entry
with unlimited access to rides adult €29, 3–6
year-olds €23. MAP P.100, POCKET MAP A4

This is Madrid's most popular
theme park, where highlights
for adults and teenagers
include the 100km/hr Abismo
rollercoaster, the swirling
Tarantula ride, the 63-metre
vertical drop La Lanzadera, the
stomach-churning La Máquina
and the whitewater raft ride

Los Rápidos. El Viejo Caserón
is a pretty terrifying haunted
house, but there are some more
sedate attractions too, as well
as an area for younger children.
Spanish acts perform in the
open-air auditorium in the
summer and there are frequent
parades too, plus plenty of
burger/pizza places to replace
lost stomach contents.

HIPÓDROMO DE LA ZARZUELA

Carretera La Coruña km 8 Ⓦ www.hipodromo
delazarzuela.es. €9 for a general entry,
under-14s free. There is a free bus that goes
from Paseo de Moret next to the Intercambiador
in Moncloa. MAP P.100, POCKET MAP A4

The **horseracing** track just out
of the city on the A Coruña
road is flourishing once again
after a decade of neglect, and
holds races every Sunday in
the spring and autumn. The
unstuffy atmosphere and a
beautiful setting make this a
fun day out for all the family.

EL PARDO

C/Manuel Alonso Ⓦ www.patrimonionacional
.es. April–Sept Mon–Sat 10.30am–5.45pm,
Sun 9.30am–1.30pm; Oct–March Mon–Sat
10.30am–4.45pm, Sun 10am–1.30pm; closed for
official visits. Guided tours €4, 5–16 year-olds
€2.30, free Wed for EU citizens. Buses (#601)
from Moncloa (daily 6.30am–midnight; every
10–15min; 25min). MAP P.100, POCKET MAP A4

PARQUE DE ATRACCIONES

Nine kilometres northwest of central Madrid lies Franco's former principal residence at El Pardo. A garrison still remains at the town, where most of the Generalíssimo's staff were based, but the place is now a popular excursion for Madrileños, who come here for long lunches at the excellent *terraza* restaurants. The tourist focus is the **Palacio del Pardo**, rebuilt by the Bourbons on the site of the hunting lodge of Carlos I and still used by visiting heads of state. Behind the imposing but blandly symmetrical facade, the interior houses the chapel where Franco prayed, and the theatre where he used to censor films. On display are a number of mementos of the dictator, including his desk, a portrait of Isabel la Católica and an excellent collection of tapestries. The country house retreat known as the Casita del Príncipe, designed by Prado architect Juan de Villanueva for Carlos IV and his wife María Luisa de Parma, is only open from Friday to Sunday between Easter and the end of September (ring ☎ 913 761 500 to make the obligatory prior reservation for a guided tour).

Shops

EL CORTE INGLÉS

C/Princesa 41 & 56 ⓜ Argüelles. Mon–Sat 10am–10pm. MAP P.100, POCKET MAP B1

One of many branches of Spain's biggest and most popular department store. It stocks everything from souvenirs and gift items to clothes and electrical goods. Prices are on the high side, but quality is usually very good.

SANTMERY

C/Juan Álvarez Mendizábal 27 ⓜ Ventura Rodríguez. Mon–Fri 9.30am–3pm & 5.30–10pm, Sat 9.30am–3pm. MAP P.100, POCKET MAP B2

Wine shop that doubles as a bar and delicatessen. You can sample some wines by the glass, but more exclusive ones have to be bought by the bottle. Try their house speciality *mousse de cabrales a la sidra* (blue cheese and cider paté) as well as the ham and cheese.

Cafés

BRUIN

Paseo Pintor Rosales 48 Ⓜ Argüelles. Daily noon–1am. MAP P.100, POCKET MAP A1

Old-fashioned ice-cream parlour – serving 35 different varieties – that makes a good stop-off point before heading into nearby Parque del Oeste. Iced drinks are also on sale and there's a very pleasant summer terrace too.

CAFÉ DE LAS COMENDADORAS

Plaza de las Comendadoras 1 Ⓜ Noviciado. Daily: winter 6pm–1.30am; summer noon–1.30am. MAP P.100, POCKET MAP D2

Relaxing café with a busy summer *terraza*, situated on one of the city's nicest squares. There are two other decent café-bars alongside if this one is too crowded.

Restaurants

EL BOKADO

Avda. Juan de Herrera 2 Ⓜ Ciudad Universitaria ☎ 915 490 041. Tues–Fri 1.30–4pm & 9pm–midnight, Sat 1.30–4.30pm & 9.30pm–12.30am. MAP P.100, POCKET MAP B1

Situated in the grounds of the Museo del Traje on the edge of the university area, this Basque-style restaurant serves up a range of imaginative fish, rice and meat dishes amid the minimalist surroundings of the museum. With a cool summer terrace looking out onto the gardens, it makes the perfect location for an alfresco meal when the temperatures start to soar. Expect to pay between €40 and €60.

CASA MINGO

Paseo de la Florida 34 Ⓜ Príncipe Pío ☎ 915 477 918. Daily 11am–midnight. Closed Aug. MAP P.100, POCKET MAP A4

Noisy, crowded and reasonably priced Asturian chicken-and-cider house. Tables are like gold dust, so loiter with your bottle of *sidra* in hand. The spit-roast chicken is practically compulsory, though the *chorizo* cooked in cider and *cabrales* (blue cheese) is also very good. Well worth the €15 or so a head.

SUBIENDO AL SUR

C/Ponciano 5 Ⓜ Noviciado. Mon 2–5pm, Tues–Sat 2–5pm & 9pm–midnight. MAP P.100, POCKET MAP D3

Homely café-restaurant serving up excellent cosmopolitan

CASA MINGO

food and snacks and offering a varied €9.50 lunchtime menu.

LA TABERNA DE LIRIA

C/Duque de Liria 9 Ⓜ Ventura Rodríguez or Plaza de España ☎ 915 414 519. Mon–Fri 1.30–3.30pm & 9.30–11.30pm, Sat 9.15–11.30pm. Closed Aug. MAP P.100, POCKET MAP C2

Excellent, but quiet restaurant close to Plaza de España serving Mediterranean-style dishes with a French touch. Great fish, inventive salads and delicious desserts. They provide some menu options from between €25 and €42 per head.

TOMA

C/Conde Duque 14 Ⓜ Ventura Rodríguez or Plaza de España ☎ 915 474 996. Tues–Sat 9pm–12.30am. MAP P.100, POCKET MAP C2

Intimate restaurant with just a handful of tables in a bright red room, where husband-and-wife team Paul and Angela serve up a constantly changing menu with a creative twist. Booking is essential and budget on around €30 a head. They provide an excellent Sunday brunch option too.

LA VACA ARGENTINA

Paseo del Pintor Rosales 52 Ⓜ Argüelles ☎ 915 596 605. Daily 1–5pm & 9pm–midnight. MAP P.100, POCKET MAP A1

One of a chain of restaurants serving Argentine-style grilled steaks (*churrasco*). This branch has good views of the Parque del Oeste from its summer terrace, but service can be slow. Average cost is around €30.

Bars

ALHUZENA

C/Martín de los Heros 72 Ⓜ Argüelles. Mon–Sat 8pm–2am. Closed Aug. MAP P.100, POCKET MAP A1

Rustic basement bar tucked away on this street very near

EL JARDÍN SECRETO

Argüelles metro serving some superb home-made tapas, including two varieties of *croquetas* and fried aubergines. For dessert they have some great chocolate crêpes and muffins with ice cream.

EL JARDÍN SECRETO

C/Conde Duque 2 Ⓜ Ventura Rodríguez or Plaza de España. Mon–Thurs 5.30pm–midnight, Fri & Sat 6pm–2am. MAP P.100, POCKET MAP C2

Cosy, dimly lit bar on the corner of a tiny plaza close to Plaza de España serving reasonably priced drinks and cocktails. Service is friendly and the atmosphere unhurried.

Club

GALILEO GALILEI

C/Galileo 100 Ⓜ Islas Filipinas Ⓦ www .salagalileogalilei.com. Daily 6pm–4.30am. €5–10. MAP P.100, POCKET MAP C1

Bar, concert venue and disco rolled into one. Latin music is regularly on offer, along with cabaret and flamenco.

Day-trips

If you want to take a break from the frenetic activity of the city centre, there are some fascinating day-trips all within easy reach of the Spanish capital.

If you only have time for one day-trip, make it **Toledo**. The city preceded Madrid as the Spanish capital and is today a monument to the many cultures – Visigothic, Moorish, Jewish and Christian – which have shaped the destiny of Spain. Immortalized by El Greco, who lived and worked here for most of his later career, the city is packed with memorable sights. A close second is stunning **Segovia**, with its stunning Roman aqueduct, fantasy castle and mountain backdrop. Third on the list is **El Escorial**, home to Felipe II's vast monastery-palace complex, a monument to out-monument all others, although the adjacent Valle de los Caídos, built under the orders of Franco, is even more megalomaniacal and far more chilling. And not forgetting **Aranjuez**, an oasis in the parched Castilian plain famed for its strawberries, lavish Baroque palace and gardens, and the plaza at nearby **Chinchón**, which provides a fabulous setting for a long, lazy lunch.

SEGOVIA

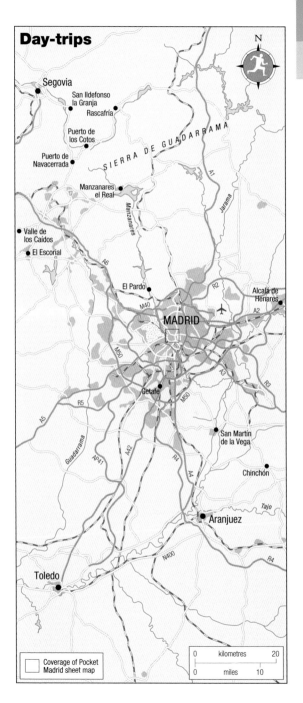

Toledo

EL ALCÁZAR AND MUSEO DEL EJÉRCITO

C/Unión s/n ⓦ www.museo.ejercito.es.
June–Sept Mon–Sat 10am–9pm, Sun
10am–3pm; Oct–May Mon–Sat 10am–7pm,
Sun 10am–3pm. €5, under-18 free, free Sun.

If one building dominates
Toledo, it's the imposing
fortress of the **Alcázar.**
Originally the site of a Roman
palace, Emperor Charles V
ordered the construction of
the current fortress in the
sixteenth century, though
it has been burned and
bombarded so often that
little remains of the original
building. The monument
enjoyed iconic status during
the Franco era after the
Nationalist forces inside,
under siege by the Repub-
lican town, were eventually
relieved by an army heading
for Madrid which took severe
retribution on the local
inhabitants. After a tortuous
relocation and refurbishment
programme, the Alcázar is
now home to an impressive
new army museum. Encom-
passing a new building
constructed over the archeological remains of the original
fortress, the museum provides
two fascinating routes – one
historic and one thematic –
through which the role of the
Spanish military is examined
in exhaustive detail. Exhibits
include everything from
medieval swords and suits of
armour to toy soldiers and
Civil War uniforms.

HOSPITAL Y MUSEO DE SANTA CRUZ

C/Cervantes 3. Mon–Sat 10am–6.30pm,
Sun 10am–2pm. Free.

A superlative Renaissance
building with a magnificent
Plateresque main doorway, this
museum houses some of the
greatest El Grecos in Toledo,
including *The Coronation of
the Virgin* and *The Assumption
of the Virgin*. As well as
outstanding works by Goya
and Ribera, there's also a huge
collection of ancient carpets
and faded tapestries, a military
display, sculpture, ceramics and
a small archeological collection.

Visiting Toledo

There are **buses** to Toledo from the bus station in Plaza Elíptica (Ⓜ Plaza Elíptica) in Madrid every thirty minutes, taking about 1hr. The city's bus station is in the modern part of the city; bus #5 runs from it to central Plaza de Zocódover. A high-speed train service from Atocha takes just 30min; it's €18 for a day return ticket, but purchase this in advance (from most travel agents around the city). Toledo's train station is a 20min walk or a bus ride (#5 or #6) from the heart of town. The main **tourist office** (Mon–Sat 9am–7pm, winter Mon–Fri closes 6pm, Sun & hols 9am–3pm; ☎ 925 220 843, Ⓦ www.turismocastillalamancha.com) is outside the city walls opposite the Puerta Nueva de Bisagra. There's another office (Mon–Sat 10am–5pm, Sun 10am–3pm) at the top of the escalators leading into the city from the Glorieta de La Reconquista, and a small information kiosk in the plaza next to the cathedral (daily 10am–6pm, Ⓦ www.toledo-turismo.com). You can save on the entry fees to some of the sights if you invest in the €8 Bono Turístico ticket.

LA CATEDRAL

C/Cardenal Cisneros. Mon–Sat 10.30am–6.30pm, Sun 2–6.30pm. Coro closed Sun am; museums closed Mon. €7, free Sun pm for Spanish citizens; audio-guides €3.

Toledo's stunning cathedral reflects the importance of the city that for so long outshone its neighbour, Madrid. A robust Gothic construction, which took over 250 years (1227–1493) to complete, it's richly decorated in Gothic, Renaissance and Baroque styles. The cavernous interior is home to some magnificent stained glass, an outstanding **Coro** (Choir), a wonderful **Gothic Capilla Mayor** (Main Chapel) and an extravagant high altar. The cathedral **museums** are worth a look for their impressive collections including paintings by El Greco, Goya and Velázquez, as well as one of El Greco's few surviving pieces of sculpture.

SANTO TOMÉ AND THE BURIAL OF THE COUNT OF ORGAZ

Plaza del Conde Ⓦ www.santotome.org. Daily: summer 10am–7pm; winter 10am–6pm. €2.30, free Wed after 4pm for EU citizens.

Housed alone, in a small annexe of the church of Santo Tomé, one of the most celebrated attractions of Toledo is El Greco's masterpiece, *The Burial of the Count of Orgaz*. The painting depicts the count's funeral, at which St Stephen and St Augustine appeared in order to lower him into the tomb. Combining El Greco's genius for the mystic with his great powers as a portrait painter and master of colour, the work includes a depiction of the artist himself – he can be spotted seventh from the left, looking out at the viewer with his son in the foreground.

MUSEO DEL GRECO

C/Samuel Levi. April–Sept Tues–Sat 9.30am–8.30pm, Sun 10am–3pm; May–Oct Tues–Sat 9.30am–6.30pm, Sun 10am–3pm. €3, €5 entry with Museo Sefardi, free Sat 4–6.30pm & Sun.

This museum in the former Jewish quarter close to Santo Tomé is devoted to the life and work of the ground-breaking sixteenth-century artist so closely associated with Toledo. An exhibition space houses his famous **View and Map of Toledo**, a full series of the Twelve Apostles, completed later than the set in the cathedral and subtly different in style and other outstanding works.

There are plenty of bars and restaurants scattered around the old town, although inevitably most of the options are pretty touristy. For a budget option try *Casa Ludeña* at Plaza Magdalena 13, close to the Alcázar, while *Alex* at Plaza de Amador de los Ríos 10, near the cathedral, offers regional specialities at reasonable prices. For a more sophisticated option try *Los Cuatro Tiempos* at C/Sixto Ramón Parro 5.

MUSEO DE VICTORIO MACHO

Plaza de Victorio Macho ⓦ www
.realfundaciontoledo.es. Mon-Sat 10am-7pm,
Sun 10am-3pm. €3.

Splendidly situated on a spur overlooking the Tajo, this museum contains the sculptures, paintings and sketches of Spanish artist Victorio Macho (1887–1966). The museum is set in a delightfully tranquil garden with the auditorium on the ground floor showing a documentary film (available in English) about the city and its history.

MUSEO SEFARDÍ/SINAGOGA DEL TRÁNSITO

C/Samuel Levi ⓦ museosefardi.net. Tues-Sat
9.30am-6pm (summer till 7pm),
Sun 10am-2pm. €3, free Sat pm & Sun.

Built along Moorish lines by Samuel Levi in 1366, the Sinagoga del Tránsito became a church after the fifteenth-century expulsion of the Jews and was restored to its original form only in the last century. The interior is a simple galleried hall, brilliantly decorated with polychromed stuccowork and superb filigree windows, while Hebrew inscriptions praising God, King Pedro and Samuel Levi adorn the walls. It also houses a small but engaging Sephardic

Museum (same hours) tracing the distinct traditions and development of Jewish culture in Spain.

SINAGOGA SANTA MARÍA LA BLANCA

C/Reyes Católicos 4. Daily: summer
10am-6.45pm; winter 10am-5.45pm. €2.30,
free Wed after 4pm for EU citizens.

The second of Toledo's two surviving synagogues, the tranquil Santa María la Blanca pre-dates the Sinagoga del Tránsito by over a century. Despite having been both a church and synagogue, the horseshoe arches and the fact that it was built by Mudéjar craftsmen give it the look of a mosque. The arches are decorated with elaborate plaster designs of pine cones and palm trees, while its Baroque *retablo* (altarpiece) dates from the time it was a church. The whole effect is stunning, all set off against a deep-red floor that contains some of the original decorative tiles.

MONASTERIO DE SAN JUAN DE LOS REYES

C/San Juan de los Reyes 2. Daily: summer
10am-6.30pm; winter 10am-5.30pm. €2.30,
free Wed after 4pm for EU citizens.

The exterior of this beautiful church is bizarrely festooned with the chains worn by Christian prisoners from Granada, who were released on the reconquest of the city in 1492. It was originally a **Franciscan convent** founded by the Reyes Católicos (Catholic Monarchs) Fernando and Isabel – who completed the Christian reconquest of Spain – and in which, until the fall of Granada, they had planned to be buried. Its double-storeyed cloister is outstanding, with an elaborate Mudéjar ceiling in the upper floor.

CONVENTO DE SANTO DOMINGO ANTIGUO

Plaza Santo Domingo Antiguo. Summer: Mon–Sat 11am–1.30pm & 4–7pm, Sun 4–7pm. €2.

The Convento de Santo Domingo Antiguo's chief claim to fame is as the resting place of El Greco, whose remains lie in the crypt that can be glimpsed through a peephole in the floor. The convent's religious treasures are displayed in the old choir, but more interesting is the high altarpiece of the church – El Greco's first major commission in Toledo. Unfortunately, most of the canvases have gone to museums and are here replaced by copies.

MEZQUITA DEL CRISTO DE LA LUZ

Cuesta de los Carmelitas Descalzos 10. Summer: Mon–Fri 10am–2pm & 3.30–6.40pm, Sat & Sun: 10am–6.40pm; winter: Mon–Fri 10am–2pm & 3.30–5.45pm, Sat & Sun 10am–5.45pm. €2.30, free Wed after 4pm for EU citizens.

Although this is one of the oldest Moorish monuments in Spain (the mosque was built by Musa Ibn Ali in the tenth century on the foundations of a Visigothic church), only the nave, with its nine different cupolas, is the original Arab construction. The apse was added when the building was converted into a church, and is claimed to be the first product of the Mudéjar style. The mosque itself, set in a tiny patio-like park and open on all sides to the elements, is so small that it seems more like a miniature summer pavilion, but it has an elegant simplicity of design that few of the town's great monuments can match.

TOWN HALL, TOLEDO

Segovia

THE AQUEDUCT

Plaza del Azoguejo.

Over 700m long and almost 30m high, Segovia's aqueduct is an impressive sight. Built without a drop of mortar or cement, it has been here since around the end of the first century AD – no one knows exactly when – though it no longer carries water to the city. For an excellent view of both the aqueduct and the city, climb the stairs beside it up to a surviving fragment of the city walls.

THE CATHEDRAL

Plaza Mayor. Daily: April–Sept 9.30am–6.30pm; Oct–March 9.30am–5.30pm. €3. Museum: Sun 9.30am–1.15pm.

Segovia's cathedral was the last major Gothic building constructed in Spain. Pinnacles and flying buttresses are tacked on at every conceivable point, although the interior is surprisingly bare and its space is cramped by a great green marble choir in the very centre. The cathedral's treasures are almost all confined to the museum.

THE ALCÁZAR

Plaza Reina Victoria Eugenia Ⓦ www .alcazardesegovia.com. Daily: April–Sept 10am–7pm; Oct–March 10am–6pm. €4, free for EU citizens third Tues in the month.

At the edge of town and overlooking the valley of the Eresma river is the Alcázar, an extraordinary fantasy of a castle with its narrow towers and flurry of turrets. Although it dates from the fourteenth and fifteenth centuries, it was almost completely destroyed by a fire in 1862 and rebuilt as a deliberately exaggerated version of the original. Inside, the rooms are decked out with armour, weapons and tapestries, but the major attractions are the splendid wooden sculptured ceilings and the magnificent panoramas.

VERA CRUZ

Carretera Zamarramala. Summer Tues 4–7pm, Wed–Sun 10.30am–1.30pm & 4–7pm; winter Tues–Sun 10.30am–1.30pm & 4–7pm. Closed Nov. €2, free Tues.

This remarkable twelve-sided church stands in the valley facing the Alcázar. Built by the Knights Templar in the early thirteenth century on the pattern of the Church of the Holy Sepulchre in Jerusalem,

Visiting Segovia

Segovia is an easy day-trip from Madrid, with up to ten fast trains daily (28min) from Atocha and Chamartín stations, as well as **buses** every thirty minutes operated by La Sepulvedana and leaving from Paseo de la Florida 11 (Metro Príncipe Pío; 1hr 45min). The city's own train station is some distance out of town – take bus #8 to the central Plaza Mayor; the bus station is on the same route. There are two **tourist offices** in the Plaza Mayor, a local one at no. 6 (daily 9am–8pm; Ⓦ www.turismodesegovia .com) and a regional one at no. 10 (Easter & July–Sept daily 9am–9pm; rest of year daily 9am–2pm & 5–8pm; Ⓦ www.turismocastillayleon.com). There is a visitor reception centre in the busy Plaza de Azoguejo (daily 10am–8pm) by the aqueduct. A regular bus service from Segovia to La Granja is operated by La Sepulvedana. It leaves from the bus station at Paseo Ezequiel González 12.

THE AQUEDUCT, SEGOVIA

it once housed part of the supposed True Cross (hence its name). Today, you can climb the tower for a highly photogenic view of the city, while nearby is a very pleasant riverside walk along the banks of the tranquil Eresma river.

CONVENTO DE SAN ANTONIO REAL

C/San Antonio Real. Tues–Sat 10am–2pm & 4.30–7pm, Sun 10.30am–2pm. €2.

If you follow the line of the aqueduct away from the old city for about ten minutes, you will come to a little gem of a palace originally founded by Enrique IV in 1455 and containing an intriguing collection of Mudéjar and Hispano-Flemish art. The convent has some of the most beautiful **artesonado** (wooden sculptured) ceilings in the city and there's a wonderfully detailed fifteenth-century wooden Calvary in the main church.

LA GRANJA

Ⓦ www.patrimonionacional.es. Palace: April–Sept Tues–Sun 10am–6pm; Oct–March Tues–Sat 10am–1.30pm & 3–5pm, Sun 10am–2pm. Guided tour €5, unguided €4.50, free Wed for EU citizens. Gardens daily: summer 10am–9pm; winter 10am–6pm.

The summer palace of La Granja was built by the first Bourbon king of Spain, Felipe V, no doubt in another attempt to alleviate his homesickness for Versailles. Its chief appeal lies in its mountain setting and extravagant wooded grounds and gardens, but it's also worth casting an eye over the plush furnishings and fabulous tapestries of the palace which, though damaged by a fire in 1918, has been successfully restored.

Outside, the highlight of the eighteenth-century gardens is a series of majestic fountains. They're a fantastic spectacle, with some of the jets rising forty metres, but they usually only operate at 5.30pm at weekends and on Wednesdays between Easter and July, with special displays on May 30, July 25 and August 25 (€3.40).

Segovia is renowned for its delicious Castilian roasts; some of the best places to sample the local specialities are the *Mesón José María* at c/Cronista Lecea 11, just off the Plaza Mayor, *Mesón de Cándido* below the aqueduct at Plaza Azoguejo 5 and *Casa Duque* at nearby C/Cervantes 12.

El Escorial and Valle de los Caídos

EL ESCORIAL

Ⓦ www.patrimonionacional.es. Tues–Sun: April–Sept 10am–6pm; Oct–March 10am–5pm. €8 unguided, €10 guided; combined ticket with El Valle de los Caídos €8.50 unguided, €11 guided; free Wed for EU citizens.

El Escorial was the largest Spanish building of the Renaissance, built to celebrate a victory over the French in 1557 and divided into different sections for secular and religious use. Linking the two zones is the Biblioteca (Library), a splendid hall with vivid, multicoloured frescoes by Tibaldi, and containing some gorgeously executed Arabic manuscripts.

The enormous, cold, dark interior of the Basílica contains over forty altars, designed to allow simultaneous Masses to be held. Behind the main altar lies some of Felipe II's mammoth collection of saintly relics, including six whole bodies, over sixty heads and hundreds of bone fragments set in fabulously expensive caskets.

Many of the monastery's religious treasures are contained in the Sacristía and Salas Capitulares and include paintings by Titian, Velázquez and José Ribera. Below these rooms is the Panteón Real, where past Spanish monarchs lie in their gilded marble tombs. The royal children are laid in the Panteón de los Infantes and there's also a babies' tomb with room for sixty infants.

What remains of El Escorial's art collection – works by Bosch, Dürer, Titian, Zurbarán, among others that escaped transfer to the Prado – is kept in the elegant Museos Nuevos. Don't miss the Sala de Batallas, a long gallery lined with an epic series of paintings depicting important imperial

EL ESCORIAL

battles. Finally, there are the treasure-crammed Salones Reales (Royal Apartments), containing the austere quarters of Felipe II, with the chair that supported his gouty leg and the deathbed from which he was able to contemplate the high altar of the Basílica.

LA SILLA DE FELIPE

Around 3km out of town is the Silla de Felipe – "Felipe's Seat" – a chair carved into a rocky outcrop with a great view of the palace, and from where the king is supposed to have watched the building's construction. You can reach it on foot by following the path which starts by the arches beyond the main entrance to the Biblioteca; keep to the left as you go down the hill and then cross the main road and follow the signs. If you have a car, take the M-505 Ávila road and turn off at the sign after about 3km.

VALLE DE LOS CAÍDOS

Tues–Sun: April–Sept 10am–6pm; Oct–March 10am–5pm. €5; combined ticket with El Escorial €8.50 unguided, €11 guided; free Wed for EU citizens.

Almost at first glance, this basilica complex, constructed by Franco after his Civil War victory, belies its claim to be a memorial to the dead of both sides. The grim, pompous architectural forms employed, the constant inscriptions "Fallen for God and for Spain" and the proximity to El Escorial clue you in to its true function – the glorification of General Franco and his regime. The dictator himself lies buried behind the high altar, while the only other named tomb is that of his guru, the Falangist leader, José Antonio Primo de Rivera. The "other side" is present only in the fact that the whole thing was built by the Republican army's survivors.

From the entrance to the basilica, a shaky funicular (Tues–Sun: April–Sept 11am–1.30pm & 4–6pm; Oct–March 11am–1.30pm & 3–5.30pm; €2.50) ascends to the base of a vast cross, reputedly the largest in the world, offering superlative views over the Sierra de Guadarrama and of the giant, grotesque religious figures propping up the cross.

Good restaurants in El Escorial include *La Fonda Genara* at Plaza de San Lorenzo 2 (daily 1–4pm & 9–11.30pm; ☎918 901 636), a relaxed place filled with theatrical mementos and offering a wide range of delicious Castilian cuisine. *Menús* available for around €10–15, otherwise around €30 per person.

Visiting El Escorial

There are around 25 **trains** a day to El Escorial from Madrid (5.45am–11.30pm from Atocha, calling at Chamartín), or **buses** (#661 and #664 from the intercambiador at Moncloa) run every fifteen minutes on weekdays and hourly at weekends. To visit the Valle de los Caídos from El Escorial, take a local bus run by Herranz (#660), which starts from their office in Plaza de la Virgen de Gracía, just north of the visitors' entrance to the monastery. It runs from El Escorial at 3.15pm, returning at 5.30pm (Tues–Sun; €8 return including entrance to the monument).

Aranjuez and Chinchón

THE PALACIO REAL

ⓦ www.patrimonionacional.es. Tues–Sun: April–Sept 10am–6.15pm; Oct–March 10am–5.15pm. €4.50 unguided, €5 guided; free Wed for EU citizens.

The centrepiece of Aranjuez is the Palacio Real and its gardens. The present building dates from the 1700s and was an attempt by Spain's Bourbon monarchs to create a Spanish Versailles. The palace is noted for its exotic decor highlighted in the fabulously elaborate Porcelain and Smoking Rooms.

JARDÍN DE LA ISLA AND JARDÍN DEL PRÍNCIPE

Daily: 8am–dusk. Free.

Two palace gardens worthy of a visit are the Jardín de la Isla with its fountains and neatly tended gardens, and the more attractive Jardín del Príncipe, which inspired Rodrigo's famous *Concierto de Aranjuez*, offering shaded walks

🍽 *El Rana Verde* close to the palace and on the banks of the river at Plaza Santiago Rusiñol is probably Aranjuez's best-known restaurant and serves a selection of *menús* from €17.

along the river and plenty of spots for a siesta.

CASA DEL LABRADOR

Jardín del Príncipe. Tues–Sun: June–Sept 10am–6pm; Oct–March 10am–5pm; visits by appointment only ☎ 918 910 305. €5; free Wed for EU citizens.

At the far end of the Jardín del Príncipe is the Casa del Labrador (Peasant's House), which is anything but what its name implies. The house contains more silk, marble, crystal and gold than would seem possible to cram into so small a place, as well as a huge collection of fancy clocks. Although the hotchpotch of styles will offend purists, this miniature palace still provides a fascinating insight into the tastes of the Bourbon dynasty.

THE SMOKING ROOMS AT PALACIO REAL, ARANJUEZ

Visiting Aranjuez and Chinchón

From the end of April to July and September to mid-October, a weekend service on an old wooden steam train, the **Tren de la Fresa**, runs between Madrid and Aranjuez. It leaves Atocha station at 10.05am and departs from Aranjuez at 6pm (information ☎ 902 228 822). The €25 fare (children aged 4–12 years €17) includes a guided bus tour in Aranjuez, entry to the monuments and *fresas con nata* on the train. Standard trains leave every 15–30min from Atocha, with the last train returning from Aranjuez at about 11.30pm. **Buses** run every half-hour during the week and every hour at weekends from Estación Sur. You'll find a helpful **tourist office** in the Casa de Infantes (daily 10am–6pm; ☎ 918 910 427, ✆www.aranjuez .es).There are hourly buses (#337) from Madrid **to Chinchón** from the bus station at Avda Mediterraneo 49 near the Plaza Conde Casal, or you can reach the town from Aranjuez on the sporadic service from c/Almíbar 138 (Mon–Fri 4 daily, Sat 2 daily). There's a small **tourist office** in the Plaza Mayor (Mon–Fri 10am–8pm, Sat & Sun 10am–3pm; ☎ 918 935 323, ✆www.ciudad-chinchon.com).

CASA DE LOS MARINOS (FALÚAS REALES)

Tues–Sun: April–Sept 10am–6.15pm; Oct–March 10am–5.15pm. €3 unguided, €5 guided; free Wed for EU citizens.

The small Casa de los Marinos is a museum containing the brightly coloured launches in which royalty would take to the river. You can do the modern equivalent and take a 45-minute boat trip through the royal parks from the jetty by the bridge next to the palace (summer: Tues–Sun 11am–sunset; €7).

PLAZA DE TOROS

Mon, Wed & Sun 11am, noon & 1pm; Fri & Sat 11am, noon, 1pm, 5pm & 6pm (in winter last two visits are replaced by one at 4.30pm). Free.

Aranjuez's beautiful eighteenth-century Plaza de Toros houses an exhibition space, part of which is made up of a **bullfighting museum**, while the rest traces the town's history and royal heritage. Nearby, on C/Naranja and C/Rosa, there are a number of *corrales*, traditional-style wooden-balconied tenement blocks.

CHINCHÓN

A stroll around the elegant little town of Chinchón, followed by lunch at one of its restaurants, is a popular pastime for Madrileños. Noteworthy monuments include a fifteenth-century castle (not open to visitors), a picture-postcard medieval Plaza Mayor and the Iglesia de la Asunción, with a panel by Goya of *The Assumption of the Virgin*, but it is as the home of *anís* that the town is best known. To sample the local aniseed spirit try one of the local bars or the Alcoholera de Chinchón, a shop on the Plaza Mayor – most visitors come for a tasting before eating at one of the town's traditional *mesones* (see box below).

For a classic Castillian lunch in Chinchón try the *Mesón el Comendador* or *La Balconada* overlooking the main plaza or the nearby *Mesón Cuevas del Vino*.

Accommodation

Madrid has a plentiful supply of accommodation and most of it is very central. With increasing competition in the sector, many hotels have been busy upgrading facilities in recent years and there is now a much wider range of stylish, medium-priced hotels, including the design-conscious High Tech and Room Mate chains. The city has a sprinkling of exclusive top-range hotels too, while if you're after a budget place to stay go for one of the *hostales* – small, frequently family-run establishments housed in large, centrally located apartment blocks.

The main factor to consider in choosing a place is location. To be at the heart of the old town, choose the areas around Puerta del Sol, Plaza de Santa Ana or Plaza Mayor; for nightlife, Malasaña or Chueca will appeal; if you are looking for a quieter location and a bit more luxury, consider the Paseo del Prado, Recoletos or Salamanca areas; and if you are with children the areas by the main parks are good options. Another thing to bear in mind is noise. Madrid is a high-decibel city so avoid rooms on lower floors or choose a place away from the action. As for facilities, air conditioning is usual and a welcome extra in summer.

Prices given in our reviews are for the cheapest double room available.

Booking accommodation

Madrid's increasing popularity as a weekend-break destination means that it's best to book accommodation in advance. Phoning or emailing is recommended; most places will understand English. It's also advisable to reconfirm the booking a few days in advance.

Hotels in the more expensive categories run special weekend offers, so it's always worth checking their websites for details. Many travel agents have voucher schemes which are a great way of making huge savings on standard rates – they're available at travel agents and online at sites such as Ⓦ www.bancotel.com or www.halconviajes.com /weekendplan/.

If you do arrive without a reservation, accommodation services at the airport, the Estación Sur de Autobuses, and Atocha and Chamartín train stations can be a useful fallback.

Madrid de los Austrias

BED & BREAKFAST ABRACADABRA

> C/Bailén 39, 1º Ⓜ Ópera or La Latina ☎ 656 859 784, Ⓦ www.abracadabra bandb.com. MAP P.30–31, POCKET MAP C7. A homely seven-bedroom B&B run by a very friendly couple who have refurbished the place in rustic, colonial style. Some rooms have en-suite bathrooms. Continental breakfast included in the rate. Doubles with shared bathroom from €52. **En-suite doubles from €68.**

CHIC & BASIC MAYERLING >

C/Conde de Romanones 6 Ⓜ Tirso de Molina ☎ 914 201 580, Ⓦ www .chicandbasic.com. MAP P.30–31, POCKET MAP D13. A stylish hotel with 22 rooms, housed in a former textile warehouse close to C/Atocha. Clean lines and black and white decor predominate in the simple, neat rooms. Continental breakfast is included and there's free internet and wi-fi as well as a sun terrace. **Doubles from €80.**

HOSTAL LA MACARENA > C/Cava de

San Miguel 8, 2º Ⓜ Sol ☎ 913 659 221, Ⓦ www.silserranos.com. MAP P.30–31, POCKET MAP B13. Family-run *hostal* in a back street just beside Plaza Mayor. The neat, well-kept rooms are on the small side, but all have bathroom, satellite TV and a/c. It can be a little noisy, but the location is perfect. **Doubles from €59.**

HOSTAL LA PERLA ASTURIANA

> Plaza de Santa Cruz 3 Ⓜ Sol ☎ 913 664 600, Ⓦ www.perlaasturiana .com. MAP P.30–31, POCKET MAP C13. Small, basic rooms in nicely located *hostal*, though despite refurbishment it has been left behind a bit by modern standards. Doubles and triples have a/c. **Doubles from €58.**

HOSTAL TIJCAL > C/Zaragoza 6, 3º

Ⓜ Sol ☎ 913 655 910, Ⓦ www .hostaltijcal.com. MAP P.54, POCKET MAP D6. Quirky *hostal* offering salmon-pink rooms (some have good views) with bathroom, TV, very comfortable beds and a/c. Triples and quadruples also available. A sister *hostal*,

Tijcal II, is at C/Cruz 26 (☎ 604 628, ☏ 915 211 477). Doubles from €54.

HOTEL PLAZA MAYOR > C/Atocha 2

Ⓜ Sol ☎ 913 600 606, Ⓦ www .h-plazamayor.com. MAP P.30–31, POCKET MAP D13. A stone's throw from the Plaza Mayor and housed in a refurbished historic building, this good-value and friendly hotel has 33 bright, a/c rooms. **Doubles from €75.**

PETIT PALACE POSADA DEL PEINE

> C/Postas 17 Ⓜ Sol ☎ 915 238 151, Ⓦ www.hthotels.com. MAP P.30–31, POCKET MAP C12. This upmarket branch of the *High Tech* hotel chain is situated in a refurbished building right next to the Plaza Mayor and was once the site of a seventeenth-century inn. Sleek rooms with minimalist decor and stylish fittings. Buffet breakfast. **Doubles from €100.**

Ópera

LOS AMIGOS HOSTEL > C/Arenal 26,

4º Ⓜ Ópera ☎ 915 592 472, Ⓦ www. losamigoshostel.com. MAP P.40, POCKET MAP B11. Great backpacking option just a few minutes from Sol. Dormitories (€17–19 per bed) cater for 4–6 people, and there are a couple of communal rooms, plus free wi-fi. The staff speak English, and bed linen and use of kitchen are included. **Doubles with bathroom from €50.**

CASA MADRID > C/Arrieta 2, 2º

Ⓜ Ópera ☎ 915 595 791, Ⓦ www .casademadrid.com. MAP P.40, POCKET MAP B10. Exclusive boutique hotel, with seven stunning rooms decorated with hand-painted frescoes, classical statues and fresh flowers. Ideal for an expensive romantic escape, but not really the place for children. **Doubles from €248.**

HOSTAL DON ALFONSO > Plaza

Celenque 1, 2º Ⓜ Sol ☎ 915 319 840 Ⓦ www.hostaldonalfonso.es. MAP P.40, POCKET MAP C11. Just off the pedestrianized shopping street C/Arenal and a stone's throw from Sol, this clean, simply furnished *hostal* has 14 doubles, two triples and some singles, all with bathrooms, a/c and TV. **Doubles from €50.**

HOSTAL GALA > C/Costanilla de los Ángeles 15 Ⓜ Callao ☎ 915 419 692, Ⓦ www.hostalgala.com. MAP P.40, POCKET MAP B10. A tasteful *hostal* close to the shopping areas of C/Preciados and Gran Vía. The 22 rooms have a/c, power showers and small balconies. **Doubles from €70.**

HOSTAL ORIENTE > C/Arenal 23 Ⓜ Ópera ☎ 915 480 314, Ⓦ www .hostaloriente.es. MAP P.40, POCKET MAP B11. Well-appointed *hostal* close to the Opera house. The nineteen classically decorated rooms are comfortable and have newly equipped bathrooms. **Doubles from €65.**

HOTEL CARLOS V > C/Maestro Vitoria 5 Ⓜ Callao ☎ 915 314 100, Ⓦ www.hotelcarlosv-madrid.com. MAP P.40, POCKET MAP D11. Traditional hotel behind the Descalzas Reales monastery. Some of the a/c rooms on the fifth floor have balconies (at extra cost), though there isn't much of a view. There's an elegant lounge and café, and the hotel has a deal with a nearby car park allowing guests to use it at reduced rates. **Doubles from €78.**

HOTEL MENINAS > C/Campomanes 7 Ⓜ Ópera ☎ 915 412 805, Ⓦ www .hotelmeninas.com. MAP P.40, POCKET MAP B10. A stylish 37-room hotel in a quiet street near the Teatro Real. Professional staff, fantastic attic rooms and flat-screen TVs. Guests can use the gym and sauna at the nearby *Hotel Ópera* (see below). Breakfast included for web reservations. Prices vary according to availability but usually doubles from **€100.**

HOTEL ÓPERA > C/Cuesta de Santo Domingo 2 Ⓜ Ópera ☎ 915 412 800, Ⓦ www.hotelopera.com. MAP P.40, POCKET MAP B10. In a pleasant location near the Plaza de Oriente, this slick hotel has 79 smart rooms (some with terraces) at reasonable rates. In keeping with the name, the waiters in the restaurant entertain diners with arias from operas and zarzuelas. **Doubles from €149.**

HOTEL PALACIO DE SAN MARTÍN > Plaza de San Martín 5 Ⓜ Ópera

☎ 917 015 000, Ⓦ www.hotel -inturpalaciosanmartin.com. MAP P.40, POCKET MAP C10. Situated in an attractive square by the Descalzas Reales monastery, this elegant hotel offers 94 spacious rooms, a small gym and sauna, plus a fine rooftop restaurant. **Doubles from €100.**

PETIT PALACE ARENAL > C/Arenal 16 Ⓜ Sol ☎ 915 644 355, Ⓦ www .hthoteles.com. MAP P.40, POCKET MAP C11. A member of the *High Tech* hotel chain with 64 sleek, modern rooms. All have a/c and there are special family rooms too. Another member of the chain, the *Puerta del Sol*, is close by at C/Arenal 4. **Doubles from €90.**

POSADA REAL MANUEL > Plaza de Oriente 2, 3º Ⓜ Ópera ☎ 915 598 450, Ⓦ www.posadarealmanuel.com. MAP P.40, POCKET MAP A11. This seven-room *posada* has a fabulous location with great views over the plaza towards the Palacio Real. **Doubles from €72.**

ROOM MATE MARIO > C/Campomanes 4 Ⓜ Ópera ☎ 915 488 548, Ⓦ www.room -matehotels.com. MAP P.40, POCKET MAP B10. Hip designer hotel close to the Teatro Real. Staff are friendly and the ultra-cool rooms, though compact, are well equipped with neat bathrooms, flat-screen TVs and DVD. Buffet breakfast included in price. There is a similarly trendy member of the chain, the *Laura*, at Travesía de Trujillos 3 (☎ 917 011 670) in the plaza by the Descalzas monastery. **Doubles from €90.**

Rastro, Lavapíes and Embajadores

CAT'S HOSTEL > C/Canizares 6 Ⓜ Antón Martín ☎ 913 692 807, Ⓦ www.catshostel.com. MAP P.48–49, POCKET MAP E14. Certainly not your run-of-the-mill hostel, *Cat's* has an Andalusian patio and subterranean bar. Doubles are available on request, otherwise accommodation is in clean, a/c four–twelve-bed dorms. Price includes breakfast. **Dorm bed from €18.**

HOSTAL BARRERA > C/Atocha 96, 2º
Ⓜ Antón Martín ☎ 915 275 381,
Ⓦ www.hostalbarrera.com. MAP
P.48–49, POCKET MAP G7. Upmarket
fourteen-room *hostal* a short distance
from Atocha station and with an
English-speaking owner. The smart a/c
rooms are a cut above most found in this
category and the bathrooms are modern.
One of the best in this part of town.
Doubles from €60.

TRYP ATOCHA > C/Atocha 83
Ⓜ Antón Martín ☎ 913 300 500,
Ⓦ www.trypatocha.solmelia.com.
MAP P.48–49, POCKET MAP G14. This
large, business-style hotel, which is not
far from Huertas, has 150 modern rooms
with all the facilities you'd expect. Family
rooms with bunks for children start at
€155. **Doubles from €89.**

Sol, Santa Ana and Huertas

CHIC & BASIC COLORS >
C/Huertas 14, 2º izda Ⓜ Antón Martín
☎ 914 296 935, Ⓦ www.chicandbasic
.com. MAP P.54, POCKET MAP F13. Swish
hostal in the heart of Huertas with ten
design-conscious en-suite rooms, all
complete with a/c and plasma TVs. There
is a self-service breakfast and a common
room where you can read the paper.
Doubles from €75.

HOSTAL AGUILAR > Carrera de San
Jerónimo 32, 2º Ⓜ Sol ☎ 914 295 926
or 914 293 661, Ⓦ www.hostalaguilar
.com. MAP P.54, POCKET MAP F12.
Large *hostal* offering airy rooms all
with bath, TV and a/c. It specializes in
multi-bed rooms including quadruples
(€84), making it an ideal budget place for
families. **Doubles from €50.**

HOSTAL ALASKA > C/Espoz y Mina 7,
4º dcha Ⓜ Sol ☎ 915 211 845, Ⓦ www
.hostalalaska.com. MAP P.54, POCKET
MAP E12. Doubles, triples and a single
in this friendly *hostal*. All seven of the
basic, brightly decorated rooms have
bathrooms, a/c and TV. There's an
apartment available on the fifth floor with

Our picks

Friendly – *Hostal Gonzalo* p.126
Good value – *Hostal Gala* p.123
Boutique – *Abalú* p.128
Designer chic – *Urban* p.126
Romantic – *Casa Madrid* p.123
Celeb-spotting – *Santo Mauro*
p.128
Family – *Tirol* p.129

a bedroom, sofa-bed and kitchen (€100
for four). **Doubles from €52.**

HOSTAL ARMESTO > C/San Agustín 6,
1º dcha Ⓜ Antón Martín ☎ 914 299
031, Ⓦ www.hostalarmesto.com. MAP
P.54, POCKET MAP G13. Eight-room
hostal with some nicely decorated rooms,
all with small bathrooms, a/c and TV. The
best ones overlook the delightful little
garden in the Casa de Lope de Vega next
door. Very well positioned for the Huertas/
Santa Ana area. **Doubles from €50.**

HOSTAL PERSAL > Plaza del Angel 12
Ⓜ Sol ☎ 913 694 643, Ⓦ www
.hostalpersal.com. MAP P.54, POCKET
MAP E13. Eighty-room *hostal* that's
closer to a hotel in terms of services and
facilities. The simple, clean rooms all
have a/c, bathrooms, TV and free wi-fi.
Triples and quadruples available from
€95 and €110 respectively. **Doubles
from €65.**

HOSTAL PLAZA D'ORT > Plaza del
Angel 13, 1º Ⓜ Sol ☎ 914 299 041,
Ⓦ www.plazadort.com. MAP P.54,
POCKET MAP E13. All the smallish rooms
in this very clean *hostal* have a shower
or bath, TV, telephone and internet
connection, and some have a/c too.
Doubles from €55.

HOSTAL RIESCO > C/Correo 2, 3º
Ⓜ Sol ☎ 915 222 692, Ⓦ www
.hostalriesco.es. MAP P.54, POCKET
MAP D12. Neat and simple rooms in this
friendly family-run *hostal* located in a
street just off Sol. All rooms (some of
which are triples) are en suite and have
a/c. **Doubles from €55.**

HOTEL URBAN > Carrera San Jeronimo 34 Ⓜ Sevilla ☎ 917 877 770, Ⓦ www.derbyhotels.es. MAP P.54, POCKET MAP G12. Über cool, fashion-conscious, five-star hotel in the heart of town. There are 96 designer rooms with all mod cons, a rooftop pool, a summer terrace and two "pijo" cocktail bars. It even has its own small museum consisting of items from owner Jordi Clos's collection of Egyptian and Chinese art. Look out for special deals on the website. **Doubles from €230.**

HOTEL VINCCI SOHO > C/Prado 18 Ⓜ Antón Martín ☎ 911 414 100, Ⓦ www.vinccihoteles.com. MAP P.54, POCKET MAP G13. A great location in the heart of Huertas for this new, four-star 170-room hotel. Smart wooden decor and furnishings and modern facilities, though bathrooms are rather small. Worth it only if you can get one of the cheaper offers on the website. **Doubles from €120.**

INTERNATIONAL HOSTEL POSADA DE HUERTAS > C/Huertas 21 Ⓜ Ciudad de los Ángeles ☎ 914 295 526, Ⓦ www.posadadehuertas.com. MAP P.54, POCKET MAP F13. A modern hostel right at the heart of things, close to Plaza Santa Ana. A/c dormitories range in size from four to ten berths (breakfast included). There's a common room with TV and internet access, laundry facilities and individual lockers. **From €17.**

ME MADRID > Plaza de Santa Ana 14 Ⓜ Sol ☎ 917 016 000, Ⓦ www.memadrid.com. MAP P.54, POCKET MAP E13. Once a favourite haunt of bullfighters, this giant white wedding cake of a hotel that dominates the plaza is now part of the exclusive *ME* chain. It comes complete with the de rigueur minimalist decor, designer furnishings, high-tech fittings, a super cool penthouse bar and a chic restaurant serving fusion-style food. Special offers can bring the price down to around €150, but usually **doubles from €200.**

PETIT PALACE LONDRES > C/Galdo 2 Ⓜ Sol ☎ 915 314 105, Ⓦ www.hthotels.com. MAP P.54, POCKET MAP D11. One of a chain of the smart *High Tech* hotels that offer very good rates and services. This one is in a refurbished mansion close to Sol and has the trademark smart, well-appointed rooms with a range of facilities. **Doubles from €120.**

ROOM MATE ALICIA > C/Prado 2 Ⓜ Sol ☎ 913 896 095, Ⓦ www.room-matehotels.com. MAP P.54, POCKET MAP F13. Perched on the corner of Plaza Santa Ana, the 34-room *Alicia* is in a great location, if a little noisy. Seriously cool decor by interior designer Pascua Ortega, stylish rooms and unbeatable value. There are suites from €160 with great views over the plaza and if you really want to push the boat out there is a two-floored duplex at around €300. **Doubles from €90.**

Paseo del Arte and Retiro

CHIC & BASIC ATOCHA > C/Atocha 113, 3º Ⓜ Atocha ☎ 913 692 895, Ⓦ www.chicandbasic.com. MAP P.68–69, POCKET MAP G7. Just across the roundabout from Atocha station, this branch of the *Chic & Basic* chain contains 36 sleek but simple rooms at a very competitive price. A sun terrace on the sixth floor and complimentary coffee in the "help yourself" zone. **Doubles from €95.**

HOSTAL GONZALO > C/Cervantes 34, 3º Ⓜ Antón Martín ☎ 914 292 714, Ⓦ www.hostalgonzalo.com. MAP P.68–69, POCKET MAP H13. One of the most welcoming *hostales* in the city, tucked away close to Paseo del Prado. Fifteen bright, en-suite rooms, all of which have a/c, TV and new bathrooms as well as free wi-fi. It's a very good-value, smart place run by a charming owner Antonio, and his brother Javier. **Doubles from €55.**

HOTEL LOPE DE VEGA > C/Lope de Vega 49 Ⓜ Atocha ☎ 913 600 011, Ⓦ www.hotellopedevega.com. MAP P.68–69, POCKET MAP H13. With a great location close to the main art galleries, this hotel is a good mid-priced option. Each of the seven floors is dedicated to a theme relating to playwright Lope de Vega, while the business-style rooms are neat and comfortable. **Doubles from €96.**

HOTEL MORA > Paseo del Prado 32 Ⓜ Atocha ☎ 914 201 569, Ⓦ www .hotelmora.com. MAP P.68–69, POCKET MAP H7. A slightly old-fashioned 62-room hotel perfectly positioned for the galleries on the Paseo del Prado. All of the refurbished rooms have a/c and some have pleasant views across the street (double glazing blocks out the worst of the traffic noise). **Doubles from €84.**

HOTEL PALACE > Plaza de las Cortes 7 Ⓜ Sol ☎ 913 608 000, Ⓦ www.westinpalacemadrid.com. MAP P.68–69, POCKET MAP H12–13. Colossal, sumptuous hotel with every imaginable facility but none of the snootiness of you might expect from its aristocratic appearance. A spectacular, glass-covered central patio and luxurious rooms are part of its charm. **Doubles from €275.**

HOTEL VILLA REAL > Plaza de las Cortes 10 Ⓜ Sol ☎ 914 203 767, Ⓦ www.derbyhotels.es. MAP P.68–69, POCKET MAP G12. Aristocratic and highly original, the *Villa Real* comes complete with its own art collection owned by Catalan entrepreneur Jordi Clos. Each of the 96 elegant double rooms has a spacious sitting area (there are several suites too) and many have a balcony overlooking the plaza. The rooftop restaurant, which has some Andy Warhol originals on the wall, affords splendid views down towards the Paseo del Prado. Discount rates start at around €150, although **doubles normally start from €200.**

HOTEL VINCCI SOMA > C/Goya 79 Ⓜ Goya ☎ 914 357 545, Ⓦ www .vinccihoteles.com. MAP P.68–69, POCKET MAP K3. This modern hotel, which is close to the Salamanca shops and Plaza Colón, has a sophisticated feel to it with its tasteful rooms and good service. Internet offers can bring the price down to around €99. **Doubles from €120.**

NH ALCALÁ > C/Alcalá 66 Ⓜ Príncipe de Vergara ☎ 914 351 060, Ⓦ www .nh-hotels.com. MAP P.68–69, POCKET MAP K4. Large, classy hotel belonging to the efficient *NH* chain, just to the north of the Retiro, with smart rooms, professional staff, laundry facilities and a car park. Expensive, but good deals available during the summer and at weekends. Special weekend offers can bring the price down to €70. **Doubles from €130.**

NH PASEO DEL PRADO > Plaza Cánovas del Castillo 4 Ⓜ Banco de España ☎ 914 292 887, Ⓦ www .nh-hotels.com. MAP P.68–69, POCKET MAP H13. A new addition to the hotels in the area, this large, plush member of the *NH Collection* chain is attractively situated in front of the Neptune fountain on the Paseo del Prado. It's not that pricey either, given the excellent facilities and luxurious surroundings. Website offers can bring prices down. There is a slightly cheaper sister hotel, the *NH Nacional*, just up the road at Paseo del Prado 48. **Doubles from €140.**

RADISSON BLU, MADRID PRADO > C/Moratín 52, Plaza de Platería Martínez Ⓜ Atocha ☎ 915 242 626, Ⓦ www.radissonblu.com/pradohotel -madrid. MAP 68–69, POCKET MAP J14. Designer hotel located along the Paseo del Prado featuring sleek rooms in black, brown and white, photos of the Madrid skyline adorning the walls, black slate bathrooms and coffee machines. There is a spa and indoor pool, a whisky bar and a restaurant too. **Doubles from €130.**

Gran Vía, Chueca and Malasaña

HOSTAL SIL/SERRANOS > C/Fuencarral 95, 2º & 3º Ⓜ Tribunal ☎ 914 488 972, Ⓦ www.silserranos .com. MAP P.82–83, POCKET MAP F2. Two friendly *hostales* located at the quieter end of C/Fuencarral in Malasaña. A variety of simple but comfortable rooms all with a/c, modern bathrooms and TV. Triples and quadruples available. **Doubles from €59.**

HOSTAL ZAMORA > Plaza Vázquez de Mella 1, 4º izqda Ⓜ Gran Vía ☎ 915 217 031, Ⓦ www.hostalzamora .com. MAP P.82–83, POCKET MAP F4. Seventeen simple rooms in an agreeable family-run place, most of which overlook the plaza. All rooms have a/c, modern bathrooms and TV. There are good-value family rooms too. **Doubles from €45.**

HOTEL ABALÚ > C/Pez 19, 1º Ⓜ Noviciado ☎ 915 314 744, Ⓦ www.hotelabalu.com. MAP P.82–83, POCKET MAP E3. This boutique hotel, which is just north of Gran Vía, has vibrant Luis Delgado-designed rooms, each one brimming with individual touches such as mini-chandeliers, butterfly prints and patterned mirrors. Personal service guaranteed. **Doubles from €119.**

HOTEL AROSA > C/Salud 21 Ⓜ Gran Vía ☎ 915 321 600, Ⓦ www .hotelarosa.es. MAP P.82–83, POCKET MAP F4. Right in the heart of town, the *Arosa* has 126 spacious, a/c rooms with modern furnishings and bathrooms. There are sixteen more expensive oriental-style ˝zen˝ rooms with extras such as a plasma TV, free mini-bar, bathrobe and slippers. Some of the surrounding streets are a little down-at-heel, but don't let this put you off. **Doubles from €90.**

HOTEL DE LAS LETRAS > Gran Vía 11 Ⓜ Gran Vía ☎ 915 237 980, Ⓦ www .hoteldelasletras.com. MAP P.82–83, POCKET MAP F10. An elegant design-conscious hotel housed in a lovely early nineteenth-century building at the smarter end of Gran Vía. The stylish, high-ceilinged rooms decorated with literary quotations come complete with plasma TVs. Downstairs there's a smooth bar and lounge area and a high-quality restaurant with reasonably priced dishes. **Doubles from €120.**

HOTEL SAN LORENZO > C/Clavel 8 Ⓜ Gran Vía ☎ 915 213 057, Ⓦ www .hotel-sanlorenzo.com. MAP P.82–83, POCKET MAP F4. A former *hostal* that has been upgraded to a neat and tidy three-star hotel offering clean and comfortable rooms with a/c and

bathrooms. Family rooms also available. **Doubles from €50.**

PETIT PALACE DUCAL > C/Hortaleza 3 Ⓜ Gran Vía ☎ 915 211 043, Ⓦ www .hthoteles.com. MAP P.82–83, POCKET MAP F4. Upgraded from an old *hostal* a few years back, this is now a member of the self-styled *High Tech* chain. Situated in the heart of Chueca, it has 58 sleek rooms with all manner of mod cons. Stylish **doubles cost around €90**, family rooms around **€130.**

ROOM MATE OSCAR > Plaza Vázquez de Mella 12 Ⓜ Gran Vía ☎ 917 011 173, Ⓦ www.room-matehotels.com. MAP P.82–83, POCKET MAP F4. Part of the hip *Room Mate* chain, this hotel is in the heart of Chueca and popular with the gay community. It has a garish psychedelic lobby, super cool sparkling white bar area, as well as space age, design-conscious rooms and a rooftop splash pool popular for evening cocktails. The restaurant serves up a good €12 *menú del día* and some creative tapas. **Doubles from €94.**

Salamanca

HOSTAL RESIDENCIA DON DIEGO > C/Velázquez 45, 5° Ⓜ Velázquez ☎ 914 350 760, Ⓦ www.hostal dondiego.com. MAP P.92, POCKET MAP K2. Although officially a *hostal*, this comfortable, friendly place situated in an upmarket area of town is more like a hotel. The quiet rooms, with full facilities, a/c and satellite TV, are reasonably priced for the area. Some English-speaking staff. **Doubles from €70.**

HOTEL GALIANO > C/Alcalá Galiano 6 Ⓜ Colón ☎ 913 192 000, Ⓦ www .hotelgaliano.com. MAP P.92, POCKET MAP H2. Hidden away in a quiet street by Plaza Colón, this small hotel has a sophisticated air about it. There's a pleasant, well-furnished salon off the entrance lobby, staff are polite and the 29 classic rooms have a/c. Breakfast costs €9.50 but better to go to a local café. Car parking available. **Doubles from €130.**

HOTEL ORFILA > C/Orfila 6 Ⓜ Alonso Martínez ☎ 917 027 770, Ⓦ www.hotelorfila.com. MAP P.92, POCKET MAP H2. Transport yourself back in time at this exclusive boutique hotel housed in a beautiful nineteenth-century mansion on a quiet street north of Alonso Martínez. Twelve of the exquisite rooms are suites, there is an elegant terrace for tea and drinks and an upmarket restaurant, too. Doubles from €275.

HOTEL SANTO MAURO > C/Zurbano 36 Ⓜ Rubén Darío ☎ 913 196 900, Ⓦ www.hotelacsantomauro.com. MAP P.92, POCKET MAP H1. This is where the Beckhams first installed themselves when David signed for Real Madrid in 2003 and this former aristocrat's residence has all the luxury and exclusivity you'd expect. Palatial rooms, a restaurant that looks like a gentleman's club, a delightful outdoor terrace and an indoor pool are all part of the package. Doubles from €250.

HOTEL SELENZA > C/Claudio Cuello 67 Ⓜ Serrano ☎ 917 810 173, Ⓦ www .selenzahoteles.es. MAP P.92, POCKET MAP J2. Luxury 44-room boutique-style hotel in a renovated nineteenth-century mansion. Large rooms, bathrooms with power showers, elegant communal areas and a garden terrace. The restaurant (see p.96) is run by distinguished Catalan chef Ramon Frexia. Website deals can bring prices down to around €165. Doubles from €250.

PETIT PALACE EMBASSY > C/Serrano 46 Ⓜ Serrano ☎ 914 313 060, Ⓦ www.hthotels.com. MAP P.92, POCKET MAP J2. A four-star member of the sleek *High Tech* chain of hotels, close to Plaza Colón and in the middle of the upmarket Salamanca shopping district. The *Embassy* has 75 rooms, including ten family ones for up to four people. Free internet access and flat-screen TVs. Doubles from €110.

Plaza de España

CASÓN DEL TORMES > C/Río 7 Ⓜ Plaza de España ☎ 915 419 746, Ⓦ www.hotelcasondeltormes.com. MAP P.100, POCKET MAP C4. Welcoming three-star place in a quiet street next to Plaza de España. The 63 a/c, en-suite rooms are very comfortable and hotel facilities include a bar and breakfast room, and helpful, English-speaking staff. €84 in July & Aug, though normally doubles from €104.

HOSTAL BUENOS AIRES > Gran Vía 61, 2º Ⓜ Plaza de España ☎ 915 420 102, Ⓦ www.hoteleshn .com. MAP P.100, POCKET MAP D4. Twenty-five pleasantly decorated rooms with a/c, satellite TV, free wi-fi, modern bathrooms, plus double glazing to keep out much of the noise. Doubles from €65.

HOTEL EMPERADOR > Gran Vía 53 Ⓜ Santo Domingo ☎ 915 472 800, Ⓦ www.emperadorhotel.com. MAP P.100, POCKET MAP D4. The main reason to come here is the stunning rooftop swimming pool with its magnificent views. The hotel itself is geared up for the organized tour market and is rather impersonal, but the rooms are large and well decorated. Doubles from €110.

HOTEL SANTO DOMINGO > C/San Bernardo 1 Ⓜ Santo Domingo ☎ 915 479 800, Ⓦ www.hotelsanto domingo.es. MAP P.100, POCKET MAP D4. What with the jungle paintings adorning the car park, the private art collection and the rooftop swimming pool with views over the city, this *Mercure* chain hotel is full of surprises. Rooms have tasteful individual decor, large beds and walk-in shower rooms. Doubles from €133.

HOTEL TIROL > C/Marqués de Urquiqo 4 Ⓜ Argüelles ☎ 915 481 900, Ⓦ www.t3tirol.com. MAP P.100, POCKET MAP B1. A good option if you are travelling with young children, the *Tirol* provides family rooms with a double bed and bunks or an adjoining kids' room. There is a play area too and the hotel is close to the Parque del Oeste and the teleférico into Casa de Campo. €140–165 for a family of four. Doubles from €75.

Arrival

Whatever your point of arrival, it's an easy business getting into the centre of Madrid. The airport is connected by metro, shuttle buses and taxis, while the city's main train and bus stations are all linked to the metro system.

By air

The **Aeropuerto de Barajas** (☎902 404 704, ⊛www.aena.es) is 16km east of the city. It has four terminals, including the vast T4 building designed by Richard Rogers and Carlos Lamela. All Iberia's domestic and international flights, as well as airlines that belong to the Oneworld group, such as British Airways and American Airlines, use T4 (a 10min shuttle bus ride from the other terminals); other international flights and budget airlines, including Aer Lingus, Easyjet and Ryanair, go from T1, while Air France, KLM and SAS use T2.

From the airport, the **metro link** (Line 8) takes you from T4 and T2 to the city's Nuevos Ministerios station in just twelve minutes (daily 6am–2am; €2.50). From there, connecting metro lines take you to city-centre locations in about fifteen minutes.

The route by road to central Madrid is more variable, depending on rush-hour traffic, and can take anything from twenty minutes to an hour. Airport express buses run round the clock from each terminal to Cibeles and Atocha (stops only at Cibeles 11.30pm–6am; €2) with a journey time of around forty minutes. Taxis are always available outside, too, and cost around €25 to the centre (including a €5.50 airport supplement), depending on the traffic. A new Cercanías train line is being built from the airport and once

completed it will take you from T4 to Chamartín in the north of the city in around ten minutes.

By train

Trains from France and northern Spain (including the high-speed links to Segovia and Valladolid) arrive at the **Estación de Chamartín**, in the north of the city, connected by metro with the centre, and by regular commuter trains (*trenes de cercanías*) to the more central **Estación de Atocha**. Atocha has two interconnected terminals: one for local services; the other for all points in southern and eastern Spain, including the high-speed services to Barcelona, Sevilla, Toledo, Malaga, Valencia and Zaragoza. For train information and **reservations** call ☎902 320 320 or go to ⊛www.renfe.com.

By bus

Bus terminals are scattered throughout the city, but the largest – used by all of the international bus services – is the **Estación Sur de Autobuses** at c/Méndez Álvaro 83, 1.5km south of Atocha train station (☎914 684 200, ⊛www.estacionde autobuses.com; Ⓜ Méndez Álvaro).

By car

All main roads into Madrid bring you right into the city centre, although eccentric signposting and even more eccentric driving can be unnerving. Both ring roads – the M40 and the M30 – and the Paseo de la Castellana, the main north–south artery, are all notorious bottlenecks, although virtually the whole city centre can be close to gridlock during **rush-hour periods** (Mon–Fri 7.30–9.30am & 6–8.30pm). Be prepared for a long trawl around the streets to find **parking** and even when you find somewhere, in most central areas you'll have to buy a ticket at one of the roadside meters (€2.55 for a maximum stay of two hours in the blue-coloured bays; €1.80 for a maximum stay of one hour in the green-coloured bays; charges apply Mon–Fri 9am–8pm, Sat & Aug 9am–3pm). Another option is to put your car in one of the many signposted parkings (up to €2 for an hour and around €29 for a day). Once in the city, and with public transport being both efficient and good value, your own vehicle is really only of use for out-of-town excursions.

Getting around

Madrid is an easy city to get around. The central areas are walkable and going on foot is certainly the best way to appreciate and get to know the city. The metro is clean, modern and efficient, buses are also very good and serve some of the more out-of-the-way districts, while taxis are always available.

The metro

The **metro** (ⓦ www.metromadrid.es) is by far the quickest way of getting around Madrid, serving most places you're likely to want to get to. It runs from 6am until 2am and the flat fare is €1.50 for the central zone stations or €9.30 for a ten-trip ticket (*bono de diez viajes*) which can be used on buses too. The network has undergone massive expansion in recent years and some of the outlying commuter districts are now connected by light railways which link with the existing metro stations (supplement fares for some of these). Lines are numbered and colour-coded, and the direction of travel is indicated by the name of the terminus station. You can pick up a free colour map of the system (*plano del metro*) at any station.

Local trains

The **local train** network, or Cercanías, is the most efficient way of connecting between the main train stations and also provides the best route out to many of the suburbs and nearby towns. Most trains are air-conditioned, fares are cheap and there are good connections with the metro. Services generally run every fifteen to thirty minutes from 6am to around midnight. For more information go to the RENFE website (ⓦ www.renfe.com) and click on the Cercanías section for Madrid.

The tourist travel pass

If you're using public transport extensively it's worth thinking about getting a **tourist pass** (*abono turístico*) covering the metro, train and bus. These are non-transferable and you'll need to show your passport or identity card at the time of purchase. Zone A cards cover the city of Madrid, Zone T cards cover the whole region including Toledo and Guadalajara but not the airport buses. They are available for a duration of one to seven days and range in cost from €6 for a Zone A daily card to €50 for a weekly one for Zone T (under-11s are half price, under-4s are free) and can be purchased at all metro stations, the airport and tourist offices. If you are staying longer, passes (*abonos*) covering the metro, train and bus are available for a calendar month.

Buses

The comprehensive **bus network** (ⓦ www.emtmadrid.es) is a good way to get around and see the sights. There are information booths at Plaza de la Cibeles and Puerta del Sol, which dispense a huge route map (*plano de los transportes de Madrid*) and also sell bus passes. Fares are the same as the metro, at €1.50 a journey, or €9.30 for a ten-trip ticket (*bono de diez viajes*) which can be used on both forms of transport. When you get on the bus, punch your ticket in a machine by the driver. You can also buy tickets from the driver, but try and have the right money.

Services run from 6am to midnight, with *búho* (owl) buses operating through the night on twenty routes around the central area and out to the suburbs: departures are half-hourly midnight–5.30am from Plaza de la Cibeles.

Taxis

Madrid has thousands of reasonably priced taxis that you can wave down on the street – look for white cars with a diagonal red stripe on the side. Seven or eight euros will get you to most places within the centre and, although it's common to round up the fare, you're not expected to tip. The minimum fare is €2.10 (€2.20 on Sun and hols) and supplements (€2.95–5.50) are charged for baggage, going to the airport, train and bus stations or outside the city limits. To phone for a taxi, call ⓣ 915 478 600 (also for wheelchair-friendly cabs), 914 051 213, 913 712 131 or 914 473 232.

Bicycles

Madrid is a bike-unfriendly city, but determined cyclists should try Calmera, C/Atocha 98 (Mon–Sat 9.30am–1.30pm & 4.30–8pm; ⓣ 915 277 574; Ⓜ Antón Martín), and Karacol at C/Tortosa 8 (Mon–Fri 10.30am–2pm & 5.30–8pm, Sat 10.30am–2pm; ⓣ 915 399 633; Ⓜ Atocha). For bike tours outside Madrid get in touch with ⓦ www .bravobike.com at Juan Alvarez Mendizábal 19 (ⓣ 915 582 945/ 607 448 440; Ⓜ Ventura Rodríguez) or ⓦ www.bikespain.info at Plaza de la Villa 1 (ⓣ 917 590 653/677 356 586; Ⓜ Ópera).

Useful bus routes

#2 From west to east: from Argüelles metro station running along C/Princesa, past Plaza de España, along Gran Vía, past Cibeles and out past the Retiro.

#3 From south to north: Puerta de Toledo, through Sol, up towards Gran Vía and then Alonso Martínez and northwards.

#5 From Sol via Cibeles, Colón and the Paseo de la Castellana to Chamartín.

#27 From Embajadores, via Atocha, up the length of the Castellana to Plaza de Castilla.

#33 From Príncipe Pío out via the Puente de Segovia to the Parque de Atracciones and Zoo in Casa de Campo.

#C1 and C2 The Circular bus route takes a broad circuit round the city from Atocha, via Puerta de Toledo, Príncipe Pío, Plaza de España, Moncloa, Cuatro Caminos, Avenida de América and Goya.

City tours

The *turismo* in Plaza Mayor (see p.28) can supply details of guided **English-language walking tours** around the city on the "Descubre Madrid" programme; these cost from €3.90 (info at ⓦ www.esmadrid.com/descubremadrid; tickets ☎ 902 221 424). For a **bus tour** of all the major sights, hop on at the stop between the Prado and the *Ritz* hotel; tickets cost €17.50 (children €9, under-6s free) and allow you to jump on and off at various points throughout the city. Pick-up points include Puerta del Sol, Plaza de Colón, Plaza de España and the Palacio Real. For the more adventurous, Madsegs offers a three-hour **segway tour** of the city (March–Oct 10am, Nov–Feb noon; meeting point in Plaza de España; €65 plus €15 deposit; ☎ 659 824 499, ⓦ www.madsegs.com), while GoCar (C/Santiago 20, near Ópera; ☎ 915 594 535, ⓦ www.gocartours.es/madrid; prices start at €29/hr for a two-person car, all day €99) offers tours in little yellow computer-guided storytelling vehicles.

Car rental

See p.132 for more information on driving in Madrid. Major operators have branches at the airport and train stations. Central offices include: Atesa, Atocha ☎ 915 061 846, ⓦ www.atesa.com; Avis, Gran Vía 60 (ⓜ Santo Domingo) ☎ 915 484 204, reservations ☎ 902 180 854, ⓦ www.avisworld.com; Europcar, C/San Leonardo 8 (ⓜ Plaza España) ☎ 915 418 892, ⓦ www.europcar.com; Hertz, Atocha station ☎ 902 023 932, ⓦ www.hertz.com; EasyCar, ⓦ www.easycar.com; Pepecar, near to Atocha and Chamartín stations ☎ 807 414 243, ⓦ www.pepecar.com.

Directory A-Z

Addresses

Calle (street) is abbreviated to C/ in addresses, followed by the number on the street, then another number that indicates the floor, eg c/Arenal 23, 5° means fifth floor of no. 23 Arenal Street. You may also see *izquierda* and *derecha*, meaning (apartment or office) left or right of the staircase.

Cinema

Madrileños love going to the cinema (*cine*) and, though most foreign films are dubbed into Spanish, a number of cinemas have original-language screenings, listed in a separate *versión original* (v.o.)/*subtitulada* section in the newspapers. Tickets cost €7–8 but most cinemas have a *día del espectador* (usually Mon or Wed) with a reduced admission charge. Be warned that on Sunday night what seems like half of Madrid goes to the movies and queues can be long. The most central cinemas showing v.o. films include the two Renoirs at C/Martín de los Heros 12 and C/Princesa 5, Golem at C/Martín de los Heros 14 and the Princesa on C/Princesa 3, all next to Plaza de España, and the nine-screen Ideal Yelmo Complex, C/Doctor Cortezo 6, south off C/Atocha and near Plaza Santa Ana (ⓜ Sol).

> For the police, medical services and the fire brigade, call ☎ 112.

Crime

Central Madrid is so densely populated – and so busy at just about every hour of the day and night – that it seems to carry very little "big city" threat. However, that's not to say that crime is not a problem, nor that there aren't any sleazy areas to be avoided. Tourists in Madrid, as everywhere, are prime targets for pickpockets and petty thieves so take care of belongings in crowded areas, on buses, in the metro, burger bars and in the Rastro. Be aware also that although the city council has taken some measures to combat the problem, the main routes through Casa de Campo and the Parque del Oeste are still frequented by prostitutes and are best steered clear of at night. Calle Montera, near Sol, and some of the streets just to the north of Gran Vía are also affected.

Electricity

220 volts. Plugs are two round pins.

Embassies and consulates

Australia, Torre Espacio, Paseo de la Castellana 259D (☎ 913 536 600, ⓦ www.embaustralia.es; Ⓜ Begoña); Britain, Torre Espacio, Paseo de la Castellana 259D (☎ 917 146 300, out of hours emergency ☎ 917 146 400, ⓦ www.ukinspain.com; Ⓜ Begoña); Canada, Torre Espacio, Paseo de la Castellana 259D (☎ 913 828 400, ⓦ www.canadainternational.gc.ca); Ⓜ Begoña); Ireland, Paseo de la Castellana 46 (☎ 914 364 093, ⓦ www.dfa.ie; Ⓜ Rubén Darío); New Zealand, C/Pinar 7, 3º (☎ 915 230 226, ⓦ www.nzembassy.com/spain; Ⓜ Gregorio Marañón); US, C/Serrano 75 (☎ 915 872 200, ⓦ www.embusa.es; Ⓜ Rubén Darío); South Africa, C/Claudio Coello 91 (☎ 914 363 780, ⓦ www.sudafrica.com; Ⓜ Rubén Darío).

Gay and lesbian travellers

The main gay organization in Madrid is Coordinadora Gay de Madrid, C/Puebla 9 (Mon–Fri 10am–2pm & 5–8pm; ☎ 915 230 070, ⓦ www.cogam.org), which can give information on health, leisure and gay rights. Feminist and lesbian groups are based at the Centro de la Mujer, C/Barquillo 44, 1º izda (☎ 913 193 689; Ⓜ Chueca). For a good one-stop shop with lots of info on the gay scene, try Berkana Bookshop, C/Hortaleza 64 (Mon–Sat 10.30am–9pm; Sun noon–2pm & 5–9pm; ⓦ www.libreriaberkana.com; Ⓜ Chueca).

Health

First-aid stations are scattered throughout the city and open 24 hours: one of the most central is at C/Navas de Tolosa 10, just south of Plaza Callao (☎ 915 210 025; Ⓜ Callao). Central hospitals include El Clínico San Carlos, C/Profesor Martín Lagos s/n (☎ 913 303 747; Ⓜ Islas Filipinas); Hospital Gregorio Marañón, C/Dr Esquerdo 46 (☎ 915 868 000; Ⓜ O'Donnell); Ciudad Sanitaria La Paz, Paseo de la Castellana 261 (☎ 917 277 000, Ⓜ Begoña). English-speaking doctors are available at the Anglo-American Medical Unit, C/Conde de Aranda 1 (☎ 914 351 823; Mon–Fri 9am–8pm, Sat 10am–3pm; Ⓜ Retiro). The Clínica Dental Plaza Prosperidad at Plaza Prosperidad 3, 2ºB (☎ 914 158 197; Ⓜ Prosperidad) has some English-speaking dentists as does the Clínica Dental Cisne at C/Magallanes 18 (☎ 914 463 221; Ⓜ Quevedo). The following **pharmacies** (distinguished by a green cross) are open 24 hours: C/Mayor 59 (☎ 915 480 014; Ⓜ Sol); C/Toledo 46 (☎ 913 653 458; Ⓜ La Latina); C/Atocha 46 (☎ 913 692 000; Ⓜ Antón Martín); C/Goya 12 (☎ 915 754 924; Ⓜ Serrano).

Internet

There are free wi-fi hotspots at many newspaper stands in the city and on buses, while the city centre is peppered with *locutorios* that provide internet. *Workcenter* on Plaza Canalejas (Mon–Fri 8am–10pm, Sat & Sun 10am–2.30pm & 5–8.30pm; ☎ 913 601 395; Ⓜ Sevilla), *La Casa de Internet* at C/Luchana 20 (Ⓜ Bilbao) are well-equipped, central internet cafés. *Café Comercial* on the Glorieta de Bilbao has an internet café upstairs. Prices range from €1 to €3.50 per hour.

Left luggage

There are left-luggage facilties (*consignas*) at Barajas Airport in terminals 1, 2 and 4 (open 24hr; €4.22–5.42/day); the Estación Sur bus station; and lockers at Atocha (open 5.45am–10.15pm; €2.40–4.50/day) and Chamartín (open 7am–11pm; €2.40–4.50/day) train stations.

Lost property

For lost property ring the municipal depot on ☎ 915 279 590 at Paseo del Molino 7 (open Mon–Fri 9am–2pm; Ⓜ Legazpi); bring ID. For property left in a taxi call ☎ 914 804 613; on a bus call ☎ 902 507 850; on the metro call ☎ 917 212 957.

Money

Banks are plentiful throughout the city and are the best places to change money. Opening hours are normally Mon–Fri 9am–2pm. Branches of El Corte Inglés have exchange offices with long hours and reasonably competitive rates; the most central is on C/Preciados, close to Puerta del Sol. Barajas Airport also has a 24 hour currency exchange office. The rates at the exchange bureaux scattered around the city are often very poor, though they don't usually charge commission. ATM cash machines (*cajeros automáticos*) are widespread and accept most credit and debit cards. Credit cards are widely accepted in hotels, restaurants and shops.

Opening hours

Smaller shops generally open 10am–2pm and 5–8pm Mon–Fri, but only open in the mornings on Sat. Department stores and chains tend not to close for lunch and open all day Sat; larger ones open on the first Sun of the month too (except in Aug). Stores in the tourist zones in the centre also open on Sun. Restaurants generally serve from 1.30–4pm and 8.30pm–midnight, with many closing for a rest day on Mon. Bars stay open till the early hours – usually around 2am – while clubs close around 5am, depending on the licence they hold. Museums close on Jan 1, Jan 6, May 1, Dec 24 and 31.

Phones

International calls can be made from any phone box or *locutorio* (call centre). The main Telefónica office at Gran Vía 30 (Ⓜ Gran Vía) has ranks of phones and is open until midnight. Phones accept either coins or phonecards that cost €5, €10, €15 and €20, available from post offices or *estancos* (see p.138). Calling Madrid from abroad, dial your international access code, then 34, followed by the subscriber's number which will nearly always start with 91. Mobile phone users from the UK should be able to use their phones in Spain – check with your service provider before leaving about costs. Most American cellphones do not work with the Spanish mobile network. For national directory enquiries ring ☎ 11818; for international enquiries call ☎ 11825.

Post offices

Centrally located post offices are at Paseo del Prado 1 and in El Corte Inglés, C/Preciados 3 (ⓜ Sol) and there's another with extended hours at C/Mejía Lequerica 7 (ⓜ Alonso Martínez). Buy stamps (*sellos*) at *estancos*.

Public holidays

The main national holidays are: Jan 1 (Año Nuevo); Jan 6 (Reyes); Easter Thursday (Jueves Santo); Good Friday (Viernes Santo); May 1 (Fiesta del Trabajo); May 2 (Día de la Comunidad); May 15 (San Isidro); Aug 15 (Virgen de la Paloma); Oct 12 (Día de la Hispanidad); Nov 1 (Todos Los Santos); Nov 9 (Virgen de la Almudena); Dec 6 (Día de la Constitución); Dec 8 (La Inmaculada); Dec 25 (Navidad).

Smoking

The Spanish government has recently introduced tougher legislation and banned smoking in all bars, restaurants and clubs.

Swimming pools and aquaparks

The Piscina Canal Isabel II, Avda de Filipinas 54 (daily 10am–8.30pm; ⓜ Ríos Rosas), is a large outdoor swimming pool, and the best central option. Alternatively, try the open-air *piscina* in the Casa de Campo (daily 10am–8.30pm; ⓜ Lago). There are also a number of aquaparks around the city, the closest being Aquópolis de San Fernando (ⓦ www.san-fernando .aquopolis.es), 16km out on the N-II Barcelona road (buses #221, #224A and #226 from the intercambiador at Arda de América). Outside May–Sept most outdoor pools are closed.

Ticket agencies

For theatre and concert tickets try: Atrapalo ☎ 902 200 808, ⓦ www .atrapalo.com; ⓦ www.entradas.com; Caixa de Catalunya/Tele Entrada ☎ 902 101 212, ⓦ www.telentrada .com; Caja de Madrid ☎ 902 488 488; El Corte Inglés ☎ 902 400 222, ⓦ www.elcorteingles.es; FNAC ☎ 915 956 100; Ticketmaster ⓦ www .ticketmaster.es; and Servi-Caixa ☎ 902 332 211, ⓦ www.servicaixa .com. The booth at Plaza del Carmen 1 near Sol (*taquilla último minuto*) sells last-minute tickets to a variety of events (Wed, Thurs, Sun 5–8pm, Fri & Sat 5–10pm; ⓦ www .taquillaultimominuto.com).

Time

Madrid is one hour ahead of Greenwich Mean Time during winter and two hours ahead from March–Oct. Clocks go forward in late March and back an hour in late Oct.

Tipping

When tipping, adding around five to ten percent to a restaurant bill is acceptable but rarely more than €5, while in bars and taxis, rounding up to the nearest euro is the norm.

Tourist information and passes

The chief tourist offices are at the following locations: Barajas International Airport T1 & T4; T1 (Mon–Sat 8am–8pm, Sun 9am–2pm; ☎ 913 058 656); T4 (daily 9.30am–8.30pm; ☎ 913 338 248); Colón (daily 9.30am–8.30pm; ☎ 915 881 636; ⓜ Colón); C/Duque de Medinaceli 2 (Mon–Fri 9am–7pm, Sat 9am–3pm; ☎ 914 294 951; ⓜ Banco de España); Estación de Atocha (Mon–Fri 9am–8pm, Sat & Sun 9am–1pm; ☎ 913 159 976; ⓜ Atocha Renfe); Estación de Chamartín (Mon–Fri 8am–8pm, Sat 9am–2pm; ☎ 913 159 976; ⓜ Chamartín); Plaza Mayor 27 (daily 9.30am–8.30pm; ☎ 915 881 636; ⓜ Sol). These are supplemented by booths near Cibeles, next to the

Reina Sofía and in Plaza del Callao off Gran Vía (daily 9.30am–8.30pm). The Madrid tourist board has a comprehensive website at ⓦ www.esmadrid .com, while the regional one has one covering the whole of the province at ⓦ www.turismomadrid.es. You can phone for tourist information in English on ☎ 902 100 007, a premium-rate number that links all the regional tourist offices mentioned below, and on ☎ 915 881 636.

Listings information is in plentiful supply in Madrid. The newspapers *El País* (ⓦ www.elpais.es) and *El Mundo* (ⓦ www.metropoli.com) have excellent daily listings (in Spanish), and on Friday both publish sections devoted to events, bars and restaurants. If your time in Madrid doesn't coincide with the Friday supplements, or you want a full rundown, pick up the weekly **listings magazine** *La Guía del Ocio* (ⓦ www.guiadelocio.com; €1) at any newsagent's stand. The *ayuntamiento* (city council) also publishes a monthly what's-on magazine, *esMadrid* (in English and Spanish), free from any of the tourist offices. Finally, *In Madrid* (ⓦ www.in-madrid.com) is a free monthly English-language paper, available in bars, that features useful reviews of nightlife.

The Madrid **tourist card** (☎ 902 877 996, ⓦ www.madridcard .com and www.neotourism.com) gives the holder admission to over fifty museums and sights, a tour of the Bernabéu, the teleférico, a guided walk of the old city, plus discounts at some shops and restaurants. It costs €32 for one day (€42 for two, €52 for three) and is on sale online and at the Plaza Mayor tourist office (see opposite). Do your sums before you splash out though, as you need to cram a lot into a day's sightseeing

to get your money's worth and if you want to concentrate on the big three art galleries, the Paseo del Arte ticket (see p.70) is better value.

Theatre

Madrid has a vibrant theatre scene which, if you speak the language, is worth sampling. You can catch anything from Lope de Vega to contemporary productions, and there's a good range on offer during the annual Festival de Otoño (Sept–Nov). For current productions, check the listings sources above.

Travelling with children

Although many of Madrid's main sights may lack children-specific activities, there's still plenty to keep kids occupied during a short stay, from various parks – including the Retiro (see p.72) – to swimming pools (see opposite) and the zoo (see p.104). There is also an ecological theme park/zoo on the outskirts of the city (ⓦ www.faunia.es). Children are doted on in Spain and welcome in nearly all cafés and restaurants.

Travellers with disabilities

Madrid is not particularly well geared up for disabled visitors (*minus-válidos*), although the situation is improving. The Organización Nacional de Ciegos de España (ONCE; National Organization for the Blind, C/Prim 3 (☎ 915 325 000, ⓦ www.once.es; ⓜ Chueca) provides specialist advice, as does the Federación de Asociaciones de Minusválidos Físicos de la Comunidad de Madrid (FAMMA) at C/Galileo 69 (☎ 915 933 550, ⓦ www .famma.org; ⓜ Islas Filipinas). ⓦ www.discapnet.es is a useful source of information (Spanish only). Wheelchair-accessible taxis can be ordered from Eurotaxi (☎ 630 026 478 or 687 924 027) and Radio Taxi (☎ 915 478 200 or 915 478 600).

Festivals and events

As well as these festivals, check out the **cultural events** organized by the city council, in particular the Veranos de la Villa (July–Sept) and Festival de Otoño (Sept–Nov), which include music concerts, theatre and cinema. There are annual festivals for alternative theatre (Feb), flamenco (Feb), books (end of May), dance (April–May), photography (mid-June to mid-July) and jazz (Nov). See ⓦwww.esmadrid.com.

CABALGATA DE LOS REYES

January 5
A celebration of the arrival of the gift-bearing Three Kings, the evening of January 5 sees a procession through the centre of Madrid in which children are showered with sweets.

CARNAVAL

The week before Lent
Partying and fancy-dress parades, especially in the gay zone around Chueca. The end of Carnaval is marked by the bizarre parade, El Entierro de la Sardina (The Burial of the Sardine), on Paseo de la Florida.

SEMANA SANTA

Easter week is celebrated with a series of solemn processions around Madrid, with Jueves Santo (Maundy Thursday) and Viernes Santo (Good Friday) both public holidays in the city.

FIESTA DEL DOS DE MAYO

May 2
Celebrations around Madrid, but particularly in Malasaña, are held to commemorate the city's uprising against the French in 1808. The main festive focus is Plaza Dos de Mayo.

FIESTAS DE SAN ISIDRO

May 15, for a week.
Evenings start out with traditional chotis, music and dancing, and bands play each night in the Jardines de las Vistillas (south of the Palacio Real). The fiestas mark the start of the bullfighting season.

LA FERIA DEL LIBRO

End of May
Madrid's great book fair takes place with stands set up in the Retiro Park.

GAY PRIDE WEEK

End of June or beginning of July
Gay Pride is a week-long party in Chueca culminating in a parade that brings the city centre to a standstill.

CASTIZO FIESTAS

August 6 to 15
Madrileños put on traditional fiestas to celebrate the saints' days of San Cayetano, San Lorenzo and La Virgen de la Paloma. Much of the activity centres around C/Toledo, Plaza de la Paja and the Jardines de las Vistillas.

NAVIDAD

The Christmas period in Madrid sees Plaza Mayor taken over by a model of a Nativity crib and a large seasonal market with stalls selling all manner of festive decorations.

NOCHE VIEJA

Dec 31
Puerta del Sol is the customary place to gather for midnight, waiting for the strokes of the clock and then attempting to swallow a grape on each strike to bring good luck in the coming year.

Chronology

800s > Muslims establish a defensive outpost on the escarpment above the Manzanares river. It becomes known as "mayrit" – the place of many springs – successively modified to Magerit and then Madrid.

1086 > Madrid taken by the Christians under Alfonso VI, but it remains a relatively insignificant backwater.

1561 > Felipe II chooses Madrid as a permanent home for the court because of its position in the centre of the recently unified Spain. The population surges with the arrival of the royal entourage, and there is a boom in the building industry.

1700–1746 > With the emergence of the Bourbon dynasty under Felipe V, a touch of French style, including the sumptuous Palacio Real, is introduced into the capital.

1759–88 > Carlos III tries to make the city into a home worthy of the monarchy. Streets are cleaned up, sewers and street lighting installed, and work begins on the Museo del Prado.

1795–1808 > Spain falls under the influence of Napoleonic France, with their troops entering the capital in 1808. The heavily out-gunned Madrileños are defeated in a rising on May 2 and Napoleon installs his brother Joseph on the throne.

1812–14 > The French are removed by a combined Spanish and British army and the monarchy makes a return under the reactionary Fernando VII.

1833–1875 > Spanish society is riven with divisions which explode into a series of conflicts known as the Carlist Wars and lead to chronic political instability, including a brief period as a republic.

1875–1900 > Madrid undergoes significant social changes prompted by a rapid growth in population and the emergence of a working class. The socialist party, the PSOE, is founded in the city in 1879.

1923–1931 > A hard-line military regime under Miguel Primo de Rivera takes control, with King Alfonso XIII relegated to the background. The king eventually decides to abdicate in 1931, and the Second Republic is ushered in.

1936–39 > The Right grows increasingly restless and a group of army generals organize an uprising in July 1936 which ignites the Spanish Civil War. Madrid resists and becomes a Republican stronghold.

1939 > Franco and his victorious Nationalists enter the city. Mass reprisals take place and Franco installs himself in the country residence of El Pardo.

1939–1953 > Spain endures yet more suffering during the post-war years until a turnaround in American policy rehabilitates Franco, as the US searches for anti-Communist Cold War allies.

1970s > Franco eventually dies in November 1975. He is succeeded by King Juan Carlos who presides over the transition to democracy.

1981 > In a last-gasp attempt to re-establish itself, the military under Colonel Tejero storms the parliament in Madrid, but a lack of support from the king and army cause its collapse. The Socialists led by Felipe González win the 1982 elections.

1980s > Freedom from the shackles of dictatorship and the release of long-pent-up creative forces help create La Movida, with Madrid becoming the epicentre of the movement.

1990s > The Socialists become increasingly discredited as they are entangled in a web of scandal and corruption, losing control of Madrid in 1991 and the country in 1996 to the conservative Partido Popular (PP).

1992 > Madrid was named European Capital of Culture.

2004 > The March 11 bombings carried out by Muslim extremists at Atocha train station kill 191 and injure close to 2000. The Socialists return to power in the general elections which follow, although the PP remain firmly in control of the local government.

2004–present > Madrid fails in its bids for the 2012 and 2016 Olympics, losing out to London and then Rio de Janeiro. High-profile building projects such as the Richard Rogers airport terminal, Norman Foster's Torre Caja Madrid skyscraper, Rafael Moneo's Prado extension and the M30 ring road 6-km long mega-tunnel are all completed before the onset of the recession and the end of the property boom.

Spanish

Once you get into it, Spanish is one of the easiest languages around, and people are eager to try and understand even the most faltering attempt. English is spoken at the main tourist attractions, but you'll get a far better reception if you try communicating with Madrileños in their own tongue.

Pronunciation

The rules of pronunciation are pretty straightforward and strictly observed.

A somewhere between the A sound of back and that of father.

E as in get.

I as in police.

O as in hot.

U as in rule.

C is spoken like a TH before E and I, hard otherwise: *cerca* is pronounced "thairka".

G is a guttural H sound (like the ch in loch) before E or I, a hard G elsewhere – *gigante* becomes "higante".

H is always silent.

J is the same as a guttural G: *jamón* is "hamon".

LL sounds like an English Y: *tortilla* is pronounced "torteeya".

N is as in English unless it has a tilde (accent) over it, when it becomes NY: *mañana* sounds like "manyana".

QU is pronounced like an English K.

R is rolled when it is at the start of a word, RR doubly so.

V sounds more like B, *vino* becoming "beano".

X has an S sound before consonants, normal X before vowels.

Z is the same as a soft C, so *cerveza* becomes "thairbaytha".

Words and phrases

BASICS

yes, no, ok	sí, no, vale
please, thank you	por favor, gracias
where?, when?	¿dónde?, ¿cuándo?
what?, how much?	¿qué?, ¿cuánto?
here, there	aquí, allí
this, that	esto, eso
now, later	ahora, más tarde
open, closed	abierto/a, cerrado/a
with, without	con, sin
good, bad	buen(o)/a, mal(o)/a
big, small	gran(de), pequeño/a
cheap, expensive	barato, caro
hot, cold	caliente, frío
more, less	más, menos
today, tomorrow	hoy, mañana
yesterday	ayer
the bill	la cuenta
price	precio
free	gratis

GREETINGS AND RESPONSES

hello, goodbye	hola, adiós
good morning	buenos días
good afternoon/ night	buenas tardes/ noches
see you later	hasta luego
sorry	lo siento/disculpe
excuse me	con permiso/perdón
How are you?	¿Cómo está (usted)?
I (don't) understand	(no) entiendo de
not at all/you're welcome	nada
Do you speak english?	¿Habla (usted) inglés?
I (don't) speak Spanish	(no) hablo español
My name is...	Me llamo...
What's your name?	¿Cómo se llama usted?
I am English/ Scottish/ Welsh/ Australian/ Canadian/ American/ Irish/ New Zealander	Soy inglés(a)/ escocés(a)/ galés(a)/ australiano(a)/ canadiense/ americano(a)/ irlandés(a)/ neocelandés(a)

HOTELS, TRANSPORT AND DIRECTIONS

I want	Quiero
I'd like	Quisiera
Do you know...?	¿Sabe....?

I don't know	No sé
Give me (one like that)	Deme (uno así)
Do you have...?	¿Tiene...?
the time	la hora
two beds/double bed	dos camas/cama matrimonial
with shower/bath	con ducha/baño
it's for one person	es para una persona
for one night	para una noche
for one week	para una semana
how do I get to...?	¿por dónde se va a....?
left, right, straight on	izquierda, derecha, todo recto
Where is the bus station/post office/toilet?	¿Dónde está la estación de autobuses/la oficina de correos/el baño?
What´s this in Spanish?	¿Cómo se llama ésto en español?
Where does the bus to... leave from?	¿De dónde sale el autobús para...?
I'd like a (return) ticket to...	quisiera un billete (de ida y vuelta) para...
What time does it leave?	¿a qué hora sale?

MONEY

How much?	¿Cuánto es?
I would like to change some money	Me gustaría cambiar dinero
ATM cash machine	cajero automático
foreign exchange bureau	la oficina de cambio
credit card	tarjeta de crédito
travellers' cheques	cheques de viaje

NUMBERS/DAYS/MONTHS/SEASONS

1	un/uno/una
2	dos
3	tres
4	cuatro
5	cinco
6	seis
7	siete
8	ocho
9	nueve
10	diez
11	once
12	doce
13	trece
14	catorce
15	quince
16	dieciséis
17	diecisiete
18	dieciocho
19	diecinueve
20	veinte
21	veintiuno
30	treinta
40	cuarenta
50	cincuenta
60	sesenta
70	setenta
80	ochenta
90	noventa
100	cien(to)
101	ciento uno
200	doscientos
500	quinientos
1000	mil
Monday	lunes
Tuesday	martes
Wednesday	miércoles
Thursday	jueves
Friday	viernes
Saturday	sábado
Sunday	domingo
today	hoy
yesterday	ayer
tomorrow	mañana
January	enero
February	febrero
March	marzo
April	abril
May	mayo
June	junio
July	julio
August	agosto
September	septiembre
October	octubre
November	noviembre
December	diciembres
spring	primavera
summer	verano
autumn	otoño
winter	invierno

Food and drink

BASICS

aceite	oil
agua	water
ajo	garlic
arroz	rice
azucar	sugar
huevos	eggs
mantequilla	butter
miel	honey
pan	bread
pimienta	pepper
pinchos/pintxos	a small bite-sized tapa
queso	cheese
sal	salt
sopa	soup
tapa	small serving of food
vinagre	vinegar

MEALS

almuerzo/comida	lunch
botella	bottle
carta	menu
cena	dinner
comedor	dining room
cuchara	spoon
cuchillo	knife
desayuno	breakfast
menú (del día)	daily set-lunch
menú de degustación	set menu offering a taste of several house specialities
mesa	table
platos combinados	mixed plate
ración	a plateful of food
tenedor	fork
vaso	glass

MEAT

albóndigas	meatballs
callos	tripe
caracoles	snails
chorizo	spicy sausage
conejo	rabbit
cochinillo	roast suckling pig
hígado	liver
jamón serrano	cured ham
jamón de york	regular ham
morcilla	black pudding
pollo	chicken
salchicha	sausage

SEAFOOD

ahumados	smoked fish
almejas	clams
anchoas	anchovies
atun	tuna
a la marinera	seafood cooked with garlic, onions and white wine
bacalao	cod
bonito	tuna
boquerones	small, anchovy-like fish, usually served in vinegar
calamares	squid
cangrejo	crab
champiñones	mushrooms
gambas	prawns
langostinos	langoustines
mejillones	mussels
ostras	oysters
pulpo	octopus

FRUIT AND VEGETABLES

aceitunas	olives
alcachofas	artichokes
berenjena	aubergine/ eggplant
cebolla	onion
cerezas	cherries
coliflor	cauliflower
ensalada	salad
fresa	strawberry
granada	pomegranate
habas	broad/fava beans
higos	figs
lechuga	lettuce
lentejas	lentils
limón	lemon
manzana	apple
melocotones	peaches
nabos	turnips
naranja	orange
pepino	cucumber
pimientos	peppers

pimientos de padrón	small peppers, with the odd hot one thrown in
piña	pineapple
pisto	assortment of cooked vegetables (like ratatouille)
plátano	banana
puerros	leeks
pure	mashed potato
repollo	cabbage
sandía	watermelon
setas	oyster mushrooms
tomate	tomato
toronja	grapefruit
uvas	grapes
zanahoria	carrot

SPECIALITIES

bocadillo	French-loaf sandwich
cocido	meat and chickpea stew
croquetas	croquettes, with bits of ham in
empanada	slices of fish/ meat pie
ensaladilla	Russian salad (diced vegetables in mayonnaise, often with tuna)
patatas alioli	potatoes in garlic mayonnaise
patatas bravas	fried potatoes in spicy tomato sauce
tortilla (española)	potato omelette
tortilla francesa	plain omelette

tostas	toasted bread with a topping

COOKING METHODS

al ajillo	with olive oil and garlic
a la parilla	charcoal-grilled
a la plancha	grilled on a hot plate
a la romana	fried in batter
al horno	baked in the oven
asado	roast
frito	fried

DESSERTS

arroz con leche	rice pudding
crema catalana	Catalan crème brûlée
cuajada	cream-based dessert often served with honey
flan	crème caramel
helado	ice cream
melocotón en almíbar	peaches in syrup
membrillo	quince paste
nata	whipped cream
natillas	custard
yogur	yoghurt

DRINKS

anís	aniseed liqueur
café (con leche)	(white) coffee
cerveza	beer
té	tea
vino (blanco/rosado/ tinto)	(white/rosé/red) wine
zumo	juice

Glossary

alameda park or grassy promenade

alcázar Moorish fortified palace

avenida avenue (usually abbreviated to avda)

ayuntamiento town hall or council

azulejo glazed ceramic tilework

barrio suburb or neighbourhood

bodega cellar or wine bar

calle (usually abbreviated to C/) street or road

capilla mayor chapel containing the high altar

capilla real royal chapel

castillo castle

cervecería bar specializing in beers

correos post office

corrida bullfight

cuadrilla a bullfighter's team of assistants

edificio building

ermita hermitage

estanco small shop selling stamps and tobacco, recognizable by the brown and yellow signs bearing the word *tabacos*

iglesia church

lonja stock exchange building

marisquería seafood restaurant

mercado market

mesón an old-style restaurant

mirador viewing point

Movida late Seventies/early Eighties creative explosion in Madrid, viewed as Spain's Swinging Sixties

Mudéjar Muslim Spaniard subject to medieval Christian rule, but retaining Islamic worship; most commonly a term applied to architecture which includes buildings built by Moorish craftsmen for the Christian rulers and later designs influenced by Moors. The 1890s to 1930s saw a Mudéjar revival, blended with Art Nouveau and Art Deco forms

museo museum

palacio aristocratic mansion

parador state-run hotel, usually housed in a building of historic interest

patio inner courtyard

Plateresque elaborately decorative Renaissance style, the sixteenth-century successor of Isabelline forms. Named for its resemblance to silversmiths' work (plateria)

plaza square

plaza de toros bullring

posada old name for an inn

puerta gateway

puerto port

sidreria bar specializing in cider

terraza summer outdoor bar

turismo tourist office

zarzuela light opera

PUBLISHING INFORMATION

This first edition published March 2012 by **Rough Guides Ltd**

80 Strand, London WC2R 0RL

11, Community Centre, Panchsheel Park, New Delhi 110017, India

Distributed by the Penguin Group

Penguin Books Ltd, 80 Strand, London WC2R 0RL

Penguin Group (USA) 375 Hudson Street, NY 10014, USA

Penguin Group (Australia) 250 Camberwell Road, Camberwell, Victoria 3124, Australia

Penguin Group (NZ) 67 Apollo Drive, Mairangi Bay, Auckland 1310, New Zealand

Rough Guides is represented in Canada by

Tourmaline Editions Inc., 662 King Street West, Suite 304, Toronto, Ontario, M5V 1M7

Typeset in Minion and Din to an original design by Henry Iles and Dan May.

Printed and bound in China

© Simon Baskett 2012

Maps © Rough Guides except Madrid Metro map © Diseño Raro S.L. 2011

No part of this book may be reproduced in any form without permission from the publisher except for the quotation of brief passages in reviews.

160pp includes index

A catalogue record for this book is available from the British Library

ISBN 978-1-40538-533-6

The publishers and authors have done their best to ensure the accuracy and currency of all the information in **Pocket Rough Guide Madrid**, however, they can accept no responsibility for any loss, injury, or inconvenience sustained by any traveller as a result of information or advice contained in the guide.

1 3 5 7 9 8 6 4 2

MIX
Paper from responsible sources
FSC www.fsc.org FSC™ C018179

ROUGH GUIDES CREDITS

Text editor: Lucy White

Layout: Nikhil Agarwal

Cartography: Ed Wright

Picture editor: Nicole Newman

Photographers: Lydia Evans and Tim Draper

Production: Emma Sparks

Proofreader: Jennifer Speake

Cover design: Nicole Newman and Dan May

THE AUTHOR

Simon Baskett lives and works in Madrid with his wife, Trini, and two young children Patrick and Laura. He is a long-suffering Atlético Madrid fan, and has not yet given up hope that he might live long enough to see them do "the double" once more. His ambition is to win El Gordo (the huge Christmas lottery) and retire to a local bar.

ACKNOWLEDGEMENTS

Special thanks to Trini once again for all her hard work and patience. Thanks, too, go to Antonio and Javier of the *Hostal Gonzalo*, Jorge Barrero Manzano of the Metro de Madrid and to Lucy at Rough Guides.

HELP US UPDATE

We've gone to a lot of effort to ensure that the first edition of the **Pocket Rough Guide Madrid** is accurate and up-to-date. However, things change – places get "discovered", opening hours are notoriously fickle, restaurants and rooms raise prices or lower standards. If you feel we've got it wrong or left something out, we'd like to know, and if you can remember the address, the price, the hours, the phone number, so much the better.

Please send your comments with the subject line "**Pocket Rough Guide Madrid Update**" to ✉ mail@roughguides.com. We'll credit all contributions and send a copy of the next edition (or any other Rough Guide if you prefer) for the very best emails.

Find more travel information, connect with fellow travellers and book your trip on ⓦ www .roughguides.com

PHOTO CREDITS

All images © Rough Guides except the following:

Front cover Puerta del Sol © Peter M Wilson/ Axiom
Back cover Monument to King Alfonso XII in El Retiro Park © Fuste Raga/Robert Harding
p.2 Calle del Carmen © Fabian von Poser/ SuperStock
p.11 Plaza de Comendadoras © PjrTravel/ Alamy
p.12 Plaza de Cibeles © Jean-Pierre Lescourret/Superstock
p.17 and **p.97** *Ramón Freixa* © *Ramón Freixa* PR
p.21 Museo Sorolla © Upperhall Ltd/Superstock
p.66 *The Garden of Earthly Delights* in the Prado © Superstock

p.90 Museo Arqueológico Nacional © Alfredo Dagli Orti/Corbis
p.99 Centro Cultural Conde Duque © Michael Zegers/Superstock
p.116 Gardens of El Escorial © Juan Silva/Getty
p.108 Segovia castle and cathedral © Travelpix/Getty
p.110 Alcázar, Toledo © Peter Adams/Getty
p.113 Town Hall, Toledo © Juan Pascual/ Photolibrary
p.115 Segovia aqueduct © John W Banagan/ Getty
p.118 Smoking room at Palacio Real, Aranjuez © Francisco Ruiz/Superstock

Index

Maps are marked in **bold**.

ROUGH GUIDES

MAKE THE MOST OF YOUR CITY BREAK

BARCELONA · **LONDON** · **NEW YORK CITY** · **PARIS** · **ROME**

FREE PULL OUT MAP WITH EVERY SIGHT AND LISTING FROM THE GUIDE

ESSENTIAL ITINERARIES AND RELIABLE RECOMMENDATIONS

BOOKS | EBOOKS | APPS

Start your journey at **roughguides.com**
MAKE THE MOST OF YOUR TIME ON EARTH™

ROUGH GUIDES

MAKE THE MOST OF YOUR GADGETS

roughguides.com/downloads

FROM **ANDROID** TO **iPADS** TO **WINDOWS 7**

BOOKS | EBOOKS | APPS

MAKE THE MOST OF YOUR TIME ON EARTH™

ROUGH GUIDES

QUÉ?

When you need some help with the lingo

DUTCH   FRENCH   GERMAN   GREEK

ITALIAN   JAPANESE   LATIN AMERICAN SPANISH   MANDARIN CHINESE

PORTUGUESE   SPANISH   THAI   TURKISH

OVER 5000 WORDS AND PHRASES
FREE AUDIO DOWNLOAD

BOOKS | EBOOKS | APPS

Start your journey at **roughguides.com**
MAKE THE MOST OF YOUR TIME ON EARTH™

ROUGH GUIDES

OVER 300 DESTINATIONS

ANDORRA Spain
ANTIGUA The Caribbean
ARGENTINA Argentina, Buenos Aires, South America on a Budget
AUSTRALIA Australia, Australia Map, East Coast Australia, Melbourne, Sydney, Tasmania
AUSTRIA Austria, Europe on a Budget, Vienna
BAHAMAS The Bahamas, The Caribbean
BARBADOS The Caribbean
BELGIUM Belgium & Luxembourg, Brussels
BELIZE Belize, Central America On a Budget, Guetemala & Belize Map
BENIN West Africa
BOLIVIA Bolivia, South America on a Budget
BRAZIL Brazil, Rio, South America on a Budget
BRUNEI Malaysia, Singapore & Brunei [1 title], South East Asia on a Budget
BULGARIA Bulgaria, Europe on a Budget
BURKINA FASO West Africa
CAMBODIA Cambodia, South East Asia on a Budget, Vietnam
CAMEROON West Africa
CANADA Canada, Toronto, Toronto Map, Vancouver
CAPE VERDE West Africa
CARIBBEAN The Caribbean
CHILE Chile, South America on a Budget
CHINA Beijing, China, Hong Kong & Macau, Shanghai
COLOMBIA South America on a Budget
COSTA RICA Central America on a Budget, Costa Rica
CROATIA Croatia, Croatia Map, Europe on a Budget
CUBA Cuba, Cuba Map, Havana, The Caribbean
CYPRUS Cyprus
CZECH REPUBLIC The Czech Republic, Czech Republic Map, Europe on a Budget, Prague, Prague Map, Prague Pocket
DENMARK Copenhagen, Denmark, Europe on a Budget, Scandinavia
DOMINICAN REPUBLIC Dominican Republic, Dominican Republic Map, The Caribbean
ECUADOR Ecuador, South America on a Budget
EGYPT Egypt, Cairo & The Pyramids
EL SALVADOR Central America on a Budget

ENGLAND Britain, Camping, Devon & Cornwall, The Cotswolds, Dorset, Hampshire & The Isle of Wight [1 title], England, Europe on a Budget, The Lake District, London, London Pocket, London Map, London Mini Guide, Walks in London & Southeast England, Yorkshire
ESTONIA Europe on a Budget, Estonia, Latvia & Lithuania [1 title]
FIJI Fiji
FINLAND Europe on a Budget, Finland, Scandinavia
FRANCE Brittany & Normandy, Brittany Map, Corsica, Corsica Map, The Dordogne & the Lot, Europe on a Budget, France, Languedoc & Roussillon, The Loire Valley, Paris, Paris Mini Guide, Paris Pocket, Provence & the Cote d'Azur
FRENCH GUIANA South America on a Budget
GAMBIA West Africa
GERMANY Berlin, Europe on a Budget, Germany
GHANA West Africa
GIBRALTAR Spain
GREECE Athens Map, Athens Pocket, Crete, Crete Map, Europe on a Budget, Greece, Greek Islands
GUATEMALA Central America on a Budget, Guatemala, Guatemala & Belize Map
GUINEA West Africa
GUINEA-BISSAU West Africa
GUYANA South America on a Budget
HOLLAND see Netherlands
HONDURAS Central America on a Budget
HUNGARY Budapest, Europe on a Budget, Hungary
ICELAND Iceland, Iceland Map
INDIA Goa, India, Kerala, Rajasthan, Delhi & Agra [1 title]
INDONESIA Bali & Lombok, South East Asia on a Budget
IRELAND Dublin Map, Europe on a Budget, Ireland, Ireland Map
ISRAEL Jerusalem
ITALY Europe on a Budget, Florence & Siena Map, Florence & the best of Tuscany, Italy, Italy Map, The Italian Lakes, Naples & the Amalfi Coast, Rome, Rome Pocket, Sardinia, Sicily, Sicily Map, Tuscany & Umbria, Venice, Venice Pocket
JAMAICA Jamaica, The Caribbean
JAPAN Japan, Tokyo
JORDAN Jordan
KENYA Kenya, Kenya Map

Download or buy Rough Guide **books, ebooks,** & **apps** online and instore

Start your journey at **roughguides.com**
MAKE THE MOST OF YOUR TIME ON EARTH™

ROUGH GUIDES

WE GET AROUND

ONLINE start your journey at roughguides.com

EBOOKS & MOBILE APPS

GUIDEBOOKS from Amsterdam to Zanzibar

PHRASEBOOKS learn the lingo

MAPS so you don't get lost

GIFTBOOKS inspiration is our middle name

LIFESTYLE from iPads to climate change

...SO YOU CAN TOO

BOOKS | EBOOKS | APPS

Start your journey at **roughguides.com**

MAKE THE MOST OF YOUR TIME ON EARTH™